GOD'S PHALLUS

GOD'S
PHALLUS

AND OTHER

PROBLEMS

FOR MEN

AND

MONOTHEISM

HOWARD EILBERG-SCHWARTZ

BEACON PRESS
BOSTON

BEACON PRESS
25 Beacon Street
Boston, Massachusetts 02108-2892

Beacon Press books are published under the auspices of
the Unitarian Universalist Association of
Congregations.

LIBRARY OF CONGRESS CATALOGING-IN-
PUBLICATION DATA
Eilberg-Schwartz, Howard, 1956–
God's Phallus and other problems for men and
monotheism / Howard Eilberg-Schwartz.
p.   cm.
Includes bibliographical references and index.
ISBN 0-8070-1224-6
1. God (Judaism)—History of doctrines.
2. Masculinity of God—History of doctrines.   3. Sex
role—Religious aspects—Judaism.   4. Phallicism.
I. Title.
BM610.E44 1994   93-39952
296.3'11—dc20

99 98 97 96 95 94   8 7 6 5 4 3 2 1

Text design by David Bullen
Composition by Wilsted & Taylor

FOR LEON SCHWARTZ,

MY FATHER,

WITH MUCH LOVE

Contents

Acknowledgments

As WITH ALL MY work, I owe an enormous debt to friends, colleagues, and family. As always, Louis Newman, Riv-Ellen Prell, Martin Jaffee, and Paul Lauritzen were constant sources of loving encouragement and gentle but pointed criticism as I struggled to figure out what this project was about. They did not dismiss my ideas when I was groping to formulate a question that I could not yet conceive. Without them, I would never have found my way. During the period I was writing this book, David Biale and Daniel Boyarin were working on intersecting issues. The shape of this book in many ways came about through conversations with them, and their work pushed me to think more deeply about the issues on which I was working. Each made numerous important suggestions. Many other people read and responded to significant portions of the manuscript or ideas related to the project: Rebecca Alpert, Alice Bach, Kathy Bell, Shaye Cohen, Muriel Dimen, Wendy Doniger, Tikva Frymer-Kensky, Naomi Goldenberg, Art Green, Yitz Greenberg, Ron Hendel, Larry Hoffman, Paula Hyman, Diane Jonte-Pace, Karen King, Lori Lefkowitz, Herb Levine, Harriet Lutzsky, Shulamith Magnus, Saul Olyan, Judith Plaskow, Lou Roberts, Stan Stowers, Ruth Tonner, Phyllis Trible, Ellen Umansky, Elliot Wolfson, and Lee Yearley. The feedback of all of these people helped refine my thinking in critical ways. Thanks in particular to Jay Geller, Diane Jonte-Pace, and Judith van Herik for reading my chapter on Freud and to the anonymous readers of my book. Special thanks, too, to Lauren Bryant, my editor at Beacon Press, who has nurtured me through two books. I have incorporated a countless number of her stylistic and conceptual improvements. She has been exceptionally supportive throughout the process. And to Carlisle Knowlton Rex-Waller for her wonderful and careful copyediting.

I also received helpful feedback from the participants in the Seminar on Psychoanalysis and Sexual Difference at the New York Institute for the Humanities at NYU. Throughout this period, I profited as well from the many discussions I had with my own students, as well as those I met when speaking at both the American Academy of Religion and the American Anthropological Association, at Brown University, the University of Minnesota, the Graduate Theological Union, Hebrew Union College, Arizona State University, Occidental College, UCLA, and elsewhere. This book might never have been completed without a fellowship from the John Simon Guggenheim Foundation, which made sustained work possible at a critical juncture. Special thanks to Froma Zeitlin, Susan Niditch, Daniel Boyarin, and Wendy Doniger for their help. And Stanford University made the fellowship workable with support for a sabbatical leave. My colleagues in religious studies generously made an additional period of writing possible. I especially want to thank the CLAL faculty for helping me to realize that my work makes contact with real people. Thanks to A. J. Levine and Jay Geller for the initial conversations while walking near Penn.

Various research assistants helped me over the years: Tammy Watts, Hank Seaman, Kirsten Sword, and Max Moerman. Special thanks to Alice Bach and Lou Roberts, colleagues who were there at very bleak moments and who believed in me and this project, to Ann Sulivan for helping me to reclaim myself, to Mona and Sage for unconditional love. And to Kat for love I didn't believe possible and deliciousness only the soul can know. So too my gem, Penina, for constantly providing me with the opportunity to reap the joys of fatherhood. And finally, to the man to whom this book is dedicated, my father. I love you.

ACKNOWLEDGMENTS

ARNA	Avot de Rabbi Nathan (version A)
A.Z.	Avodah Zarah
B.B.	Baba Batra
Bekh	Bekhorot (Bekh.)
Ber.	Berakhot
Bik.	Bikkurim
B.Q.	Baba Qama
BT	Babylonian Talmud
Eduy.	Eduyot
ExodRab	Exodus Rabbah
GenRab	Genesis Rabbah
GenRabbati	Genesis Rabbati
Hag.	Hagigah
Hor.	Horayot
Hul.	Hullin
Jub.	Jubilees
Jos. Anti.	Josephus' Antiquities
Kel.	Kelim
Ker.	Keritot
Ket.	Ketubot
M.	Mishnah
Meg.	Megillah
Mek.	Mekilta
Men.	Menahot
Nid.	Niddah
Num Rab	Numbers Rabbah

PT	Palestinian Talmud
Qoh.	Qohelet (Ecclesiastes)
R.	Rabbi
San.	Sanhedrin
Shab.	Shabbat
SifreDeut	Sifre Deuteronomy
SifreNum	Sifre Numbers
SongRab	Song of Songs Rabbah
Sot.	Sotah
Suk.	Sukkot
Tanh.	Tanhuma
TanhBub	Tanhuma Buber
Ter.	Terumot
Tos.	Tosefta
Yeb.	Yebamot

GOD'S PHALLUS

The Divine Phallus
and the Dilemmas
of Masculinity

THE TITLE OF THIS book is shocking, because the thought of God having a penis is shocking. Most Jews and Christians think of God the father as lacking a body and hence as beyond sexuality. Without a body, God obviously can have no sexual organ.

But from where does the idea of a disembodied God come? What if, historically speaking, it is discomfort with the idea of God's penis that has generated the idea of an incorporeal God? What if this uneasiness flows from the contradictions inherent in men's relationship with a God who is explicitly male? This in a nutshell is the argument of this book. This is why the title "God's Phallus" is a serious one that points to interesting questions about the nature of religious symbols and the way in which issues of gender, sexuality, and desire are inseparable from them.[1] More specifically, this is a book about divine fatherhood and the ways in which the sexual body of a father God is troubling for the conception of masculinity.

It may, of course, seem counterintuitive to think of a male God as being problematic for the conception of masculinity. After all, dozens of feminist studies over the past twenty years have explored the way in which images of male deities authorize male domination in the social

1

order.[2] As these studies have well demonstrated, a divine male both legitimates male authority and deifies masculinity. It thus may seem paradoxical to consider that the symbol of a male God generates dilemmas for the conception of masculinity. Nevertheless, I would argue that at the same time that such a symbol works to legitimate masculinity, which may in fact be its primary and even original function, it also renders the meaning of masculinity unstable. This book explores how tensions arising from the idea of the sexual body of the father God are expressed in the myth and ritual of one religious tradition, namely, that of ancient Judaism.

Ancient Judaism is a particularly appropriate context in which to explore these tensions, for Jewish monotheism has in many ways exemplified how an image of a male deity supports a patriarchal order. I use the term "ancient Judaism" to refer to the various religious cultures of ancient Jews, from the period of Israelite religion under the monarchy (ninth century B.C.E.) through the rabbinic period (200–600 C.E.). This is a long and complex tradition in which many different religious forms emerge and pass away. In fact, it is customary for scholars to designate these forms by different names (Israelite religion, Second Temple Judaism, early Judaism, late antique Judaism, rabbinic Judaism). By moving in and out of these various religious configurations, however, I hope to show that certain ambiguities in the representation of masculinity recur, albeit in different and unexpected forms, and that at different moments they are handled in different ways. This is obviously not a traditional historical exercise focusing on a limited time frame and exploring religious meanings in their broadest possible context. My intention is to explore the ongoing problems generated by a certain kind of religious symbol and to show that part of what has defined Judaism as a religious tradition is its taking up, time and time again, the relationship of men to the father God. By exposing the conflicted image of masculinity in monotheism, I want to offer an alternative way of thinking about the nature of religious symbols and how gendered symbols work in religious systems.

So what are the dilemmas evoked by the maleness of God in ancient Judaism? The first is homoeroticism: the love of a male human for a male God. The issue of homoeroticism arises in ancient Israel because the divine-human relationship is often described in erotic and sexual terms. Marriage and sexuality are frequent biblical metaphors for describing God's relationship with Israel. God is imagined as the husband to Israel the wife; espousal and even sexual intercourse are metaphors for the covenant. Thus when Israel follows other gods, "she" is seen to be whoring. Israel's relationship with God is thus conceptualized as a monogamous sexual relation, and idolatry as adultery. But the heterosexual metaphors in the ancient texts belie the nature of the relationship in question: it is human males, not females, who are imagined to have the primary intimate relations with the deity. The Israel that is collectively imagined as a woman is actually constituted by men—men like Moses and the patriarchs. And these men love, in ways that are imagined erotically and sensually, a male deity.

This would not have posed a problem if human masculinity was not so strongly associated with procreation in ancient Judaism. Being a man in ancient Israelite culture involved marrying, having children, and carrying forward the lineage of one's father or tribe. Thus ancient Judaism's concept of masculinity was deeply entangled in images of what is now called heterosexuality.[3] In the culture of ancient Israel, woman was imagined as the natural counterpart of man, and sexual acts between men were condemned. Thus, at the heart of this religious system was a deep tension in defining masculinity. Men were complementary to women; marriage was a return to a primordial unity. At the same time, a man's relationship to God was conceptualized as loving and sensual. It is for this reason, I propose, that various myths and rituals of ancient Judaism attempted to suppress the homoerotic impulse implicit in the male relationship with God. The denial of homoeroticism takes two significant forms: a prohibition against depicting God (veiling the body of God) and the feminization of men. By imagining men as wives of God, Israelite religion was partially able to preserve the heterosexual complementarity that helped to define the culture. But this also undermined accepted notions of masculinity, as we shall see in part 3. The feminization of men also disrupted what the tradition posits as a natural complementarity between a divine male and human women. When male-female complementarity is the structure of religious imagery, human women are the natural partners of a divine male, but this connection also renders human males superfluous in the divine-human relationship. As we'll see in later chapters, the potential superfluousness of human masculinity may offer additional insights into the misogynist tendencies of ancient Judaism: women were deemed impure and men were feminized in contradiction to what in this religious culture was a natural complementarity between the divine male and human females.

Still another set of dilemmas are generated by the monotheistic image of a sexless father God. As has been pointed out by many interpreters, the God of the Jews, unlike the gods of the ancient Near East and many other religious traditions, does not have sexual intercourse or father children, at least in the literature that made its way into the Hebrew Bible. The archaeological record suggests that many Israelites may have imagined the goddess Asherah to be a partner of Yahweh, but in the Hebrew Bible, and in the variety of Judaisms that flourished subsequently, Israel imagined God as having no sexual partners. Despite the fact that God metaphorically gets married (e.g., Hos. 1–2; Jer. 2:2), and even has sexual intercourse with the entity Israel (Ezek. 16:8), who is imagined as a woman, this metaphorical union differs from the couplings of male and female deities found in the mythology of many other religious traditions (chapter 5).

The sexlessness of the father God was problematic in a culture defined by patrilineal descent. A man was expected to reproduce, to carry on his line, yet he was also understood to be made in the image of a God who was essentially celibate. As we shall see, the decreasing importance of patrilineage in late antique Judaism would have an enormous impact on the religious conception of masculinity. The story of the virgin birth of Jesus makes explicit what had always been a latent tension in monotheism: God fathers a son and the human father becomes irrelevant. This was intolerable to ancient Judaism in which tracing the father's line remained important, but it was a perfect myth for certain forms of what would become Christianity, in which the father's line became less relevant. At the same time, one can trace an impulse toward asceticism within Judaism itself, which led to a masculinity increasingly at odds with the male body. The hiding of the penis in prayer, and analogies made between the transmission of oral Torah and the fathering of children are ways in which this refiguring of masculinity found its symbolic expression (chapter 8).

These points about the dilemmas of masculinity rest upon a reinterpretation of monotheism. In other words, the theoretical claims about the symbol of a male deity and its effects on masculinity in ancient Israel both inform the analysis of monotheism and at the same time depend upon it. I acknowledge the circularity of this process at the outset. But all interpretations—even the most stubbornly historical and inductive—rest upon theoretical assumptions, although such assumptions are often tacit and unexamined.[4]

Three different disciplinary traditions shape my own reinterpretation of monotheism: feminist and gender criticism, psychoanalysis, and anthropology. To put it more accurately, I have been led to see matters in the way I do because these disciplines have shaped my own conception of religion, culture, and gender. Feminist and gender criticism convinced me that gender is not just another subject that intersects with religion, but is central to the work that religion accomplishes and the ways in which it goes about it. I have learned to take very seriously the ways in which symbols are gendered and the ways such gendered images influence conceptions of men and women. At the same time, I have found that gendered images themselves are inextricably entangled in issues of sexuality, desire, and the body. More specifically, feminist criticism and gender theory impressed me with the importance of taking seriously the gender of God. God's imagined masculinity is critical to understanding many central rituals and myths of monotheism.

Feminist theorists have yet to explore fully the question of how a male God is problematical for men's conceptions of self. For obvious and important reasons, feminist criticism has tended to focus instead on the ways in which a masculine image of God undermines female experience. But this focus has tended to conflate human and divine masculinities into one undifferentiated symbol. However, I see divine masculinity and human masculinity as two separable and sometimes conflicting symbols. In this regard, I have found Freud useful, despite my reservations about psychoanalytic theory generally. Freud, of course, reflected on the tensions between fathers and sons. But it is less widely known that he explored the issue of son-father homoeroticism and its impact on religious conceptions (chapter 2). As I explored the problems posed to human men by a father God, I began to see that the issues had been anticipated in Freud's analysis of the erotic relationship of father and son and in his early writings on religion. Significantly, however, Freud was unable to see the relevance of his ideas when it came to analyzing his own father religion, Judaism. In part, this book represents an attempt to do what Freud did not: to rethink *Moses and Monotheism* in light of Freud's ideas about religion and homoeroticism found in his earlier writings.

Though influenced deeply by Freud's writings on religion and gender, I do not endorse his assumptions about the relationship between the psyche and culture, nor do I assume a priori that certain symbols have specific meanings. Historians and anthropologists have rightly criticized the universalizing tendencies of Freud's work on myth and ritual. Freud assumed that the processes of gender development were universal, embedded both in biology and in the structure of family relations. For this reason, he tended to assign to symbols particular psychoanalytic meanings without providing the historical or cultural context necessary to analyze those symbols. But one cannot decide a priori whether a cigar is just a cigar or a symbol of something else. The meaning of symbols must be established by a thorough analysis and interpretation of a given tradition.[5]

I also dissent from Freud's assumption that cultural and religious symbols reflect conflicts within individuals. I analyze here a cultural system of religious symbols that circulated among certain groups of ancient Jews, but I do not assume that the conflicts discovered at the level of culture were necessarily operative in the psyches of all ancient Israelites or Jews. Instead, my analysis of ancient Jewish myths and rituals derives from the discipline of anthropology, viewing culture as a complex and conflicting set of symbolic domains. By symbolic domains, I mean a set of representations or conceptions that deal with a particular matter, such as conceptions and statements about God. The symbolic domains of God, Israel, the covenant, marriage, and so on are constructed in relationship to and in terms of one another. For example, conceptions of marriage become metaphors for God's relationship with Israel. At the same time, the relationship with God helps to define what it is to be married. One of the central claims of this book is that symbolic domains interpenetrate and through their interpenetration spawn unintended and unpredictable consequences. In this way, the image of God loving a female Israel cannot be entirely divorced from the image of God in relationship with specific Israelite men. And these various images of the deity cannot be dismissed as "just metaphors." There is no idea that is not embodied in metaphors, and to be embodied in that way is to be caught up in a set of meanings and connotations that are woven into the very fabric of an idea.

In short, I view cultures not as harmonious unified systems, but as streams of circulating symbols that are often in collision with one another. One of the purposes of religious myth and ritual is to struggle with, partially hide, and overcome the various tensions that arise in a religious culture.[7] Religious symbols thus have lives of their own. Much of what this book explores are the unanticipated and often unconscious effects of religious symbols. These effects are not "unconscious" in the Freudian sense. There is sufficient evidence from anthropological writings that a culture's rituals and myths carry meanings that are not readily accessible to religious actors.[8] These meanings or effects may threaten the more stable uses for which symbols are primarily created and maintained.

While this study is indebted in obvious ways to gender theory, psychoanalysis, and anthropology, I regard theory as only a tool. Evidence does resist interpretation and require revisions in theory. Interpretation is thus a two-way street in which theory guides analysis but is in turn modified by it. For this reason, my analysis is also and in particular a challenge to certain assumptions in feminist and psychoanalytic theories of religion.

Indeed, Western theories of religion, of which feminist and psychoanalytic theories are important examples, have developed hand in hand with the understanding of monotheism. Most of these theories of religion, for example, uncritically take over the claim that the God of the Jews is incorporeal. But what happens if the body of God is hidden rather than nonexistent? I have brought these and other theoretical reflections together in chapter 1, where I contrast feminist and psychoanalytic theories of religions.

Undoubtedly some critics will greet my treatment of monotheism as reductionist. But what counts as reductionism is a matter of perspective. The now classic explanations of monotheism, which tend to view everything solely in terms of theological, intellectual, or moral problems, are themselves forms of "spiritual" or "theological" reductionism. Ideas about the body, sexuality, desire, and gender have largely been ignored in modern interpretations of ancient Judaism to prevent it from seeming primitive.[9] I attempt to move beyond this kind of reductionism to explore what dominant traditions of criticism have systematically excluded.

In a certain respect, in fact, this work is an attempt to resist the spiritualizing and Hellenistic models that continue to inform modern understandings of monotheism. This is particularly clear in regard to the issue of why God's body posed a problem to ancient Jews, a question which has preoccupied interpreters of Judaism since the first Greek contact with the Jews, at least as early as the second century B.C.E. The Greeks were intrigued by a people who prohibited divine images. The prohibition on making divine images testified, so the Greeks thought, to the Jewish belief that God did not have a human form.[10] Jews were admired for this abstract and philosophical conception of God and explicitly contrasted with Egyptians, who imagined their gods in animal form. It is not surprising that some Greek writers regarded Moses as a great philosopher for having instituted the prohibition on images. Nor is it surprising that Greek writers, and perhaps their Jewish informants, singled out this Jewish prohibition as one of the most distinctive qualities of Jewish monotheism, one that seemed to embody the most basic assumptions of Greek philosophy. After all, Greek philosophers had criticized their own culture's myths for imagining gods in human form and with human foibles. If God was perfect, God could not be embodied, since the body was full of imperfections. The Jews' prohibition on divine images suggested that they had come to similar conclusions. Whether it was Greek writers or Jews themselves who first proposed this interpretation is unclear. In any case, Jews found the argument persuasive, and interpreters such as Philo and Maimonides, to name only the most notable, explained the ancient tradition in the same way. [11] This view came to dominate the understanding of Judaism for well over a thousand years and continues to shape thinking about the tradition today.

There is, however, another way of understanding the prohibition on divine images. I suggest that the ambivalence was not about the idea of a divine body generally speaking, but about God's sexual body in particular. In other words, it is "male-morphism," rather than anthropomorphism, about which Jews felt ambivalent. To imagine God as male threatened to expose a number of tensions of the religious system. This interpretation represents a very different way of thinking about the development and nature of Jewish monotheism. The argument may strike many readers as initially implausible, but again, the plausibility of an interpretation must be judged against the evidence. And my analysis here tries to show that much of what we have accepted as true about Jewish monotheism has no more evidence to support it than the alternative I propose in the following pages.

Furthermore, there are reasons at the outset to assume that the classic treatment of monotheism serves very strong apologetic and theological interests. The fact that modern scholars have been repeating versions of an interpretation with a thousand-year history is grounds enough for suspicion. For example, the assertion that Jews found a notion of an embodied God problematic assumes that the Jews came to believe in a God who was superior to the gods of their neighbors. Not only did they abandon the primitive belief in many gods, but they realized the folly of thinking of God as a big person. This revolution in religious thinking becomes one of the hallmarks of monotheism that makes it supposedly superior to other religions. But there is in fact no statement anywhere in ancient Israelite literature that explicitly criticizes the notion of God having a body. This interpretation of ancient Judaism is just that: an interpretation.

Scholars have grown so accustomed to thinking of monotheism as a moral and intellectual breakthrough that it no longer requires explanation. Even interpreters who are not committed to the superiority of monotheism have often uncritically inherited biases from their predecessors and teachers. But I am asking that we temporarily bracket our familiar assumptions in order to encounter monotheism afresh, as if we never heard of it before. What might we say about it if it was just another religious tradition that had been discovered among some unheard-of people?

In conclusion, I want to acknowledge the relationship of this interpretation to the ongoing concerns of my life. This book was written at a time when I was struggling with my own masculinity, rediscovering intimacy with my father, learning to be a father of my own daughter, working through a painful divorce, and rediscovering love. The subject of this book reflects all of these experiences. In the conclusion to this book, I reflect on the possible implications of this study for contemporary men and women who struggle with images of gendered deities they inherit from ancient traditions. There will undoubtedly be those who will dismiss this book as a projection of my own struggles. But I would argue that these struggles have freed me to see the gaps in the dominant interpretation of monotheism, and thus to see what has been avoided or suppressed.

PART I

Divine
Fatherhood

Chapter One

Feminism, Freud, and the Father God

> *If God in "his" heaven is a father ruling "his" people, then it is in the "nature" of things and according to the divine plan and the order of the universe that society be male-dominated. Within this context a mystification of roles takes place: the husband dominating his wife represents God "himself."*
>
> MARY DALY, Beyond God the Father

> *The psychoanalysis of individual human beings, however, teaches us with quite special insistence that the god of each of them is formed in the likeness of his father, that his personal relation to god depends on his relation to his father in the flesh and oscillates and changes along with that relation, and that at bottom God is nothing other than an exalted father.* SIGMUND FREUD, Totem and Taboo

THE AGE OF REASON left many puzzles for those in the modern period to solve. Among the most difficult was the question of how and why humans created religion. This was a fundamentally new question in the eighteenth century. On the traditional understanding, God made humans in the divine image and gave them religion. But the Age of Reason overturned this view. The new view, which took a full century to work out, took for granted that humans created God or the gods in their own image and that religion is a projection of human experience.[1]

This understanding has provided the point of departure for some of the most powerful accounts of religion in the modern period, including those of Feuerbach, Marx, Tylor, Durkheim, Freud, Geertz, and Daly, to mention only a few. In many ways, modern discussions of religion simply refined this theory, exploring the various ways in which human beings project their own experiences, desires, fears, and hopes into religion. But one of the questions that has remained is whether religion represents human experience writ large or the experience and desires of specific categories of people. In other words, on the assumption that religion is a human projection, whose interests and experiences does it represent and legitimate? Does it answer and speak for deep human needs and desires in general or does it emerge from the desires of certain groups in particular? And if it speaks for and to specific interests, is it the projection of a dominant elite attempting to legitimate its position or an underprivileged group needing solace? These sorts of questions, which have always been at the heart of projection theory, took on a new importance in light of the feminist critique of religion, a critique which has shown how deeply male experiences and desires have shaped religious symbols and dominated religious practices.

Feminist criticism has not been alone in focusing on the connection between masculinity and religion. The nature of this relationship has also been central to psychoanalytic theories of religion. Despite important tensions and differences between feminist and psychoanalytic discourses, both regard masculinity and religion as deeply entangled symbolic domains. Both are interested in exploring how male experience and ideas about masculinity shape and are in turn shaped by religious symbols, particularly images of divinity.

The precise nature of male projection, however, is typically understood differently within psychoanalytic and feminist criticism. For Freud and his followers, religion reflects and repeats the experience of having a father.[2] Freud, of course, works this out in different ways in his writings. At times, it is every child's (the daughter's as well as the son's) experience of having a father that shapes religious symbols. At other times, it is the boy's oedipal struggles, his feelings of love, hate, and competition toward his father, that are projected onto the heavenly father. At still other times, the father figure satisfies the need for solace and consolation in a world that is intolerable and unpredictable (Freud 1927). And then, of course, there is Freud's claim that religion is a memory of an actual historical event in which the brothers killed and ate the father (Freud 1912–13). For now the complexity of Freud's theory need not detain us. The point is that for Freud the conception of the divinity arose from and is continually implicated in the experience of having a father.

In much feminist criticism of religion, by contrast, it is not the experience of having a father that is projected heavenward but the very idea of masculinity. This ideal of masculinity is itself embedded in a particular configuration of social relations in which the most valued social prerogatives and power are in the hands of men. What it means to be a man is expressed and symbolized in images of male deities, which thus reflect and authorize a social order in which male domination is the norm. The deification of masculinity justifies the social order even as it interprets and shapes the meaning of masculinity. And this shaping requires a representation of femininity against which masculinity is defined, as Mary Daly put it in the quote from her classic work that begins this chapter. Or as Judith Plaskow puts it, "When God is pictured as male in a community that understands 'man' to have been created in God's image, it only makes sense that maleness functions as the norm of Jewish humanity" (Plaskow 1990, 127).

Feminist writings on religion have thus tended to focus on either a correspondence or legitimation theory of male projection.[3] On the legitimation model, divine masculinity reflects and authorizes a social order in which men dominate. On a correspondence model, the domination of men is already made possible by a cultural order in which the masculine is deified.[4] In either case, however, conceptions of divine and human masculinity correspond to and reinforce one another. Feminist writings on religion have in this way conflated divine and human masculinities, treating them as part of one undifferentiated category.

The Freudian model, on the other hand, encompasses a conflictual model of male projection. It leaves room for and presupposes tensions between different kinds of masculinities. If the deity is the father writ large, then this divine masculinity is by no means simply a confirmation of human masculinity. It is at the same time a fundamental threat and challenge to it. To summarize for a moment, then, we might say that while Freudian theory tends to treat religion as a projection of a desirable and unattainable ideal, feminist theory treats it as a reflection of a problematic real.

These two effects of religious symbols are to some extent compatible. While religious symbols may reflect and promote the social order in some respects, they may also stand in tension with it.[5] To put it another way, images of male deities may authorize male domination while rendering masculinity an unstable representation. The uncertainty of masculinity, however, does not mean that the power relationship between men and women is altered; in fact, the feminizing of men in relationship to God reinforces the association of femininity and subordination. But attentiveness to the alienating effects of a male deity involves looking at how power flows, not just between images of men and women, but between images of masculinity. In this respect Freud was right. A divine masculine generates all kinds of tensions for men and masculinity. These are conflicts that have largely been ignored in recent feminist writings on religion.[6] Masculinity is a symbolic construction at odds with itself. And like the feminine, the human masculine is confronted by a divinity which is "other," although in different ways than it is for women.

Male projection, then, is by no means as straightforward and unproblematic as many interpreters think or wish. Masculinity is threatened by the very constructions that seem to make it possible in the first place, and human men are diminished and challenged by the projection that authorizes their power and social position. Images of deities, of which a divine father is one primary example, thus do more than simply reflect the social order; they challenge and subvert it as well.

And they exert their critical and alienating effects in several different ways that we need to distinguish.

First, images of gods provide ideals one is expected to admire and imitate, yet they are ideals that may in fact be unattainable. They are symbols not just of what is but of what has not yet come to be. I take it that this is what Clifford Geertz meant when he said that religion is both a "model of and model for" human beings (1973, 93). As a model *of* the social world, religious representations reflect social reality. But as a model *for* the social world, religious representations are an ideal toward which humans are to strive and against which human relations fall short. This discrepancy between what humans are and what the religious representations tell them they should be creates dilemmas for those the images serve. Feminist critics are well aware of the alienating effects symbols can have, such as the impact of beauty images for women.[7] A masculine god, I suggest, is a kind of male beauty image, an image of male perfection against which men measure themselves and in terms of which they fall short.

Second, in addition to serving as objects of emulation, divine representations can also be sources of competition and rivalry. Freud pointed out how identification and emulation go hand in hand with competition. To identify with someone is to share that person's qualities and desires, what Girard recently called "mimetic desire" (1977, 143–48). Part of what it can mean for a boy to identify with his father is to compete for the love and attention of his mother. Analogously, if it is the divine father who is responsible for opening a woman's womb, it is not clear at all what role the human father plays. The deity is sometimes regarded as competition for human males, since the human male's ability to reproduce is dependent upon the will or participation of the deity. To be sure, the human husband contributes the seed. But this alone does not guarantee pregnancy. In numerous instances in the Hebrew Bible, the pregnancy of a woman is a sign of God's favor. The human husband must wait until his wife is blessed by God.[8] In this sense, the virility of the human male is put at risk by representations of divine masculinity. The symbol of a divine father incorporates some of what it means to be a human father, and through that projection of the human, the divine masculine comes to compete with the human male.

Third, as objects of desire and desiring beings, divine images also generate important paradoxes. Again we can look to Freud's theory of gender development to illustrate this point. Freud argued that boys not only identify and compete with their fathers but also want to be objects of their fathers' desire. It is this desire that leads a boy to wish at some level to be castrated, that is, to become a woman. One need not embrace Freud's theory of the Oedipus complex or believe a boy has a real wish to be castrated to find an important insight here. If we take Freud's insight as being about symbol systems rather than the psyche, we see that he is in effect exposing the symbolic and cultural pressures that impose heterosexual images on male-male relationships. When a cultural system treats male-female relations as the norm and ideal, then the object of male desire should be a woman. If the object is another male, then there is pressure to feminize one of the males involved. Caroline Walker Bynum points to a similar tension in twelfth-century Cistercian images of Jesus as Mother: "Given the twelfth-century partiality for metaphors drawn from human relationships, religious males had a problem. For if the God with whom they wished to unite was spoken of in male language, it was hard to use the metaphor of sexual union unless they saw themselves as female" (1982, 161). A similar symbolic gender reversal occurs, for example, in some cultures where being male is associated with being higher in the hierarchy. Since being "on top" is male, the partner who is entered sexually is sometimes viewed as feminine and described in female imagery.[9] This can also be seen in the culture of ancient Judaism, where the feminine and the subordinate were equated. In the divine male–human male relationship it was God who was at the top and the human male at the bottom. When males wished to know or be known by God, a potentially homoerotic relationship was avoided by feminizing one of the parties involved.

These three effects of divine images, as objects of emulation, as sources of competition and rivalry, and as objects of desire and as desiring beings, are meant to be taken as rough guidelines for understanding how representations of divinities operate in religious cultures. The classification is necessarily schematic. Since religious cultures differ, it is impossible to predict a priori how images of divinity might support or undercut the social order, but these three functions provide a starting point for analysis.

In understanding the image of a male God as a symbol that generates conflicts for men, I follow certain impulses in contemporary feminist writings about gender. Specifically, recent poststructuralist theories of gender have begun to describe the ways in which the category of gender is itself always unstable and problematic. As theorists have tried to understand gender (what makes a woman a woman and a man a man), it has become increasingly apparent that we cannot define any of these categories too rigidly.[10] Pinning down the essence of being a woman or man has proven impossible. There is no identifiable experience that all women or all men share cross-culturally, no experience that emerges from the nature of anatomy, hormones, or culture. Being a woman or man means many different things, even within the same culture, let alone between cultures. What characterizes the category women, and men, too, for that matter, is a set of what Wittgenstein refers to as "family resemblances" that are potentially alterable and culturally specific.

The postessentialist view of gender is only beginning to make its impact on the study of masculinity. Judith Butler, for example, has noted how the concept of patriarchy threatens to become a universalizing concept when in fact male domination takes various historical forms. Making an analogous point, Sylvia J. Yanagisako and Jane F. Collier have noted that "despite this skepticism about the existence of a unitary woman's point of view in any society, anthropologists appear to have been less critical of the notion of a unitary 'man's point of view'" (1990, 138). Attending to the conflict between divine and human masculinities in the culture of ancient Israel is an attempt to begin taking apart the previously undifferentiated category of masculinity. To use the felicitous phrase of Luce Irigaray, masculinity is also "a sex which is not one" (1985a; 1985b).[11]

This refiguring of masculinity has important implications for understanding the constructions of femininity and female experience. The focus on conflicting and troubled masculinities will provide an alternative way of thinking about why women and female experience are denigrated within religious systems. Following Simone de Beauvoir, most feminist critics of religion have argued that in a culture and society which defines men as the norm, women's otherness results in the devaluing of women's bodies and experiences.[12] The symbol of a male God doubly reinforces women's otherness. As Rita Gross puts it, "If God is male and we are in God's image, how can maleness not be the norm of Jewish humanity? If maleness is normative, how can women not be Other? And if women are Other, how can we not speak of God in language drawn from the male norm?" (1983, 228). But as I am suggesting, men are also "other" with respect to a male God. Indeed, as I've said, in at least one respect men's relationship with God is even more problematic than women's, for on a heterosexual model of intimate relationships, women are more appropriate objects of divine desire than are men. One way of escaping this problem is by symbolically displacing male tensions and contradictions onto women. The otherness of women is exaggerated to minimize the ways men are made into others in a system which validates male authority.

This rethinking of masculinity challenges the claim that the feminine is the only gender. By this, theorists mean that masculinity is not thought of as a gender but is equated with a generalized or universal subject, Man (Butler 1990, 11). But in ancient Israel, masculine gender was also marked, albeit in different ways than the feminine, as it was set apart from the divine masculine.

Divinity, Masculinity, and Monotheism

Although the mutual entanglement of masculinity and religion is evident in diverse religious forms and traditions, the operations of male projection are often considered most obvious in montheism. Indeed, monotheism has often been taken as a kind of ideal of male projection. What distinguishes monotheism, of course, is the exclusive relationship with one God.[13] For both Freud and feminist theorists, the shift from polytheism to monotheism has important consequences. For Freud, "now that God was a single person, man's relation to him could recover the intimacy and intensity of the child's relation to his father" (1927, 19).[14] Before monotheism, Freud argues, the child's relation to the father was expressed less directly because it was diffused through multiple representations of the deity.

For somewhat different reasons, feminist critics also see the processes of male projection as being exhibited in their purest form in monotheism. In feminist interpretations, the experiences of men, the dominant figures in the social order, are projected onto the one and only God, and femininity, although sometimes influencing the representation of God, is more or less excluded from the divine realm.[15] Ancient Judaism, as the first instantiation of monotheism, illustrates most clearly the ways in which masculinity and divinity are bound up with each other. This is one of the reasons why much feminist criticism of religion has focused on analyses of ancient Judaism.[16] Interpretations of ancient Judaism are central to major feminist works, including those by Daly, Ruether, Collins, Sanday, Lerner, Kristeva, and Plaskow, among others.[17] Judaism was also critical for Freud, as evident by his designation of Judaism as the "Father" religion. Since in Freud's view all religions were Father religions in some fashion, the designation of Judaism as the Father religion pointed to its exemplary status. Indeed, Freud believed it was monotheism that disclosed once and for all the father who had all along hidden behind every divine figure (1927, 19).

I believe, however, that these theories of male projection rest on faulty analyses of monotheism. Theoreticians of gender and religion alike have been led astray by the entrenched assumption that the Jews believed in an invisible, disembodied deity. Freud, as we shall see in the next chapter, assumed that the Mosaic prohibition on divine images and the "dematerialization" of God raised the Jews to a higher level of spirituality. And feminist theorists argue that the representation of a disembodied masculine God ends up supporting the association of masculinity with spirituality and, by way of contrast, denigrating femininity as being associated with the body.[18] In this view, since

God creates by the word and not the body, masculinity is linked to intellectual and spiritual activity while femininity is bound to the passive functions of the body—the bearing and nurturing of children.[19]

There are, however, a number of myths in ancient Judaism that imagine God as having, or at least appearing in, human form. To cite but one example, Moses and other Israelite leaders are described in Exodus going up to the top of the mountain and seeing God: "Then Moses and Aaron, Nadab and Abihu, and seventy elders of Israel ascended; and they saw the God of Israel: under His feet there was the likeness of a pavement of sapphire, like the very sky for its purity. Yet He did not raise His hand against the leaders of the Israelites; they beheld God, and they ate and drank" (Exod. 24:9–11).[20]

This extraordinary statement raises many issues to be explored later. For the present purposes, it is enough to observe that it calls into question the widespread assumption that the Jews did not imagine their God in human form. The important point is that all sorts of other misunderstandings arise from the failure to take the image of a divine figure seriously. Or more important, *all sorts of questions fail to be imagined because a whole avenue of research has been closed off by thinking that the Jews did not imagine their God in human form.* The idea of God's body has enormous implications, not only for understanding how ancient Jews figured procreation, conception, masculinity, the male body, and the phallus, but also for feminist and analytic views of religion.

How must the terms of this discussion change if God's body is veiled rather than nonexistent? I suggest that both Freudian and feminist criticism need to confront more directly the question of God's male sex. By sex, I mean something different from gender. I mean the anatomical sex of the deity, that is, whether this deity has a penis and other anatomical markings that signify his maleness and not just his masculinity. The question of a divine penis (or a beard) seems absurd only in a tradition that imagines God to lack a human shape. But since, as we'll see, Jews sometimes did imagine God in human form, it is reasonable to ask about the imagined sexual features of that divine form.

First, it is critical to understand what I mean by sex as opposed to gender and why that analytical distinction is necessary in the first place. Initially, this distinction emerged in gender studies as a way to differentiate the purported biological (sex) versus cultural (gender) aspects of identity, nature versus nurture. But the distinction has recently proven problematic because, as many theorists have shown, the very notion of sex (biological substratum) is thoroughly informed by gender.[21] Nonetheless, I suggest that a distinction between sex and gender is still a useful heuristic device, if sex is defined as the anatomical markings (penis, vagina, womb, breasts, facial hair, for example) that are associated with being a man or woman. A distinction between sex and gender is necessary as a way to come to terms with the potential discrepancy between a person's anatomy (sex) and their qualities or characteristics (gender). As Freud aptly noted, when you meet a human being, "the first distinction you make is 'male or female?' and you are accustomed to making the distinction with unhesitating certainty" (1931, 113). But how does one determine this when the genitals are hidden from view? Freud never satisfactorily answers this question. But clearly a variety of factors go into the automatic and unreflective judgment of whether one is speaking to a man or woman: the type of clothes, the hairstyle, the appearance or lack of facial hair, the protrusion or absence of breasts, the nature of the voice, the mannerisms and other personal qualities. None of these alone is generally sufficient to make a determination. A woman may not have large breasts and a man might. But taken together, the medley of cultural signs and anatomical indications shape our assumptions about the kind of person with whom we are interacting. Usually, this sort of information is tacitly processed. We unreflectively assume we are dealing with either a man or woman and we modify our behavior accordingly. And generally the assumptions we make are correct. But there are cases in which a discrepancy could be discovered: a person seems to have all the markings of a man, for instance, facial hair and no noticeable breasts, but in fact has a vagina and womb. This occurs more frequently than we might imagine, as reported by people who experience being mistakenly identified.[22] A more extreme example of this phenomenon is transvestism, the intentional adoption of the appearance and mannerisms of the opposite sex, or transsexualism, living one's live as if one is the other sex. For example, there are at least a few cases reported of men who learn that women whom they have been dating have a penis. And in one case, the woman delayed telling her husband about her penis until after marriage.[23] In our culture, as is still the case in many others, genitals are a primary determiner of a person's identity. A person who dresses as a woman but who is discovered to have a penis we would call a man, not a woman.[24] It is this potential discrepancy between personal qualities and anatomy that necessitates a distinction between sex and gender. Although gender and sex generally tend to be coordinated, liminal cases show that this is not always so.

If we shift attention back to the divine, we find a great deal of information is available about the gender of the monotheistic God, but the sex of this God is carefully obscured. In accounts of God sightings, the gaze is averted from the face and front, parts of the anatomy that are critical to an identification of a body's sex. Not only is there no indication that this God has a penis, but we do not even know whether this being has secondary sexual characteristics such as facial hair. We have no information about the divine anatomy. From bodily characteristics alone, it is impossible to say anything definitive about the sex of God.

At issue, then, is the significance of the sexual veiling of God. God is primarily imagined in masculine gender images. Images abound of God as king, father, shepherd, and man of war. God is routinely described with masculine nouns, pronouns, and adjectives. To be sure, there are some feminine images of God, but they are few and far between.[25] Moreover, the feminine gendering of God as mother or nursemaid can be construed as acts of male appropriation: God the father usurping the positive roles of women.[26] Following the lead of Daly, Gross, Plaskow, and others, I assume that the maleness of God is implied by the predominantly masculine gender images of the deity, but that maleness is hidden.[27]

Because it is hidden, many writers mistakenly assume that God has no body and no sex, and even that God has no gender. Or to put it another way, interpreters assume that because the God of the Jews was not explicitly male, that God was also not masculine. Feminist interpreters have rightly challenged this view. Rita Gross, for example, writes that those who use masculine gender images

> contend that their automatic use of male pronouns and images as well as their out of hand rejection of female images and pronouns doesn't mean anything; certainly it does not mean, they contend, that they think of God as male. "That God is exalted above all sexuality is part of *His* transcendence," one commonly hears. However, if one insists that one must use the pronoun "His" in the preceding sentence and that the pronoun "Her" is improper, the claim that gender-specific images are not part of one's image of God becomes self-contradictory and a bit ridiculous. . . . I suspect that those who become entangled in such absolutizing of masculine pronouns and imagery genuinely do believe in and are trying to express the concept of a God who transcends sexuality. . . . However, the metaphor of a gender-free person is impossible. Persons are male or female. A person without gender defies the imagination; few people can imagine a concrete specific person without also imagining some female or male characteristics. (1983, 236)

Gross is absolutely right that the use of the pronoun "he" cannot be dismissed as meaningless. It indicates that people conceptualize God as masculine. But because Gross conflates gender and sex another kind of confusion enters: She assumes that if God is a he, God cannot transcend sexuality, that people necessarily think of God as male. But this is precisely what I am arguing against: that while God is thoroughly gendered as a he, God's anatomy is carefully cloaked. God is a masculine deity whose maleness is repressed and avoided. People do think of God as a he *without* a male body.

The conflation of masculinity and maleness makes the image of a masculine God appear to authorize male sexuality much more than it actually does. For example, it undergirds Mary Daly's argument that images of a masculine God support a "phallic morality" in which she includes various kinds of sexual abuse, such as rape and father-daughter incest. Israelite religion provides some of her prime examples of this phallic morality. For Daly, then, sexual abuse is legitimated by the imagination of a male God with a phallus: "The divine patriarch castrates women as long as he is allowed to live on in the human imagination. The process of cutting away the Supreme Phallus can hardly be a merely 'rational' affair" (1973, 19). Gross, too, sees the God of the Jews as legitimating male sexuality. People imagine, she writes, "that the traditional images of deity, God the Father, the God of our fathers, is a nonsexual symbol. We have already seen how possible it is to have a concept of a theistic Ultimate that is also exalted above all sexuality. In fact, God has been exalted above female sexuality only" (1983, 236).

But the apparent absence of a divine phallus exalts God above male sexuality, too, and renders it problematic in critical ways.[28] That is, it is around matters of sexuality and the need to procreate that men experience their otherness from God. To be like God the creator, they must procreate. But to be like God they should have no sex and no desire. It is a crucial question, then, to consider why divine masculinity is figured without desire and without its potent symbol, the phallus. In my view, male projection theory must come to terms with the veiling of the divine sex. In other words, in what ways does the veiling of a divine phallus affect the way in which the deity, as symbol of the male, serves as an object of male emulation, as a source of conflict and rivalry for men, and as an object of male desire?

The ambivalence about the divine phallus points to a whole set of tensions within masculinity as it is constructed in monotheism. To get at these tensions we must explore the meaning of the father's nakedness, the homoeroticism implicit in monotheism, the importance of procreation, ideas about conception and creativity, circumcision, and much more. To understand how the divine phallus figures in monotheism, I want to examine unnuanced constructions that assume some stable relationship between masculinity and the penis. The meaning of the penis and the experience of having a penis are not uniform cross-culturally and are historically variable. Furthermore, masculinity is about more than just having a penis. Masculinity is a symbol and identity that rests on the symbolization of other parts of the male body and other aspects of male experience. Attitudes toward the penis are bound up in competing and often conflicted ideas about desire, sex, procreation, genealogy, nakedness, divinity, and cultural reproduction that intersect and undergo revision over time.

A Note on the Phallus/Penis Controversy

"The Phallus must be veiled," wrote Jacques Lacan, one of Freud's most important twentieth-century interpreters (1985, 288). Although this book is not concerned centrally with Lacanian theory, thinkers familiar with Lacan will naturally wonder about the relationship between Lacan's understanding of the phallus and my analysis of monotheism. So I conclude this chapter with a brief consideration of the veiling of God's phallus in Lacanian terms. First, I should point out that the terms are by no means clear. What I call the "phallus" of God, Lacan would refer to as a "divine penis." What is the difference between a phallus and a penis? To answer that question involves entering into the complexity of Lacan's theory, an experience that is a lot like learning to speak a new language. By necessity, therefore, this discussion is but an overture.

From one perspective, Lacanian theory is in many ways an attempt to take the body out of Freudian theory (de Certeau 1986, 58–61). Lacan argues that the truly significant part of Freud's work was not his biological essentialism but his discovery of the nature of language and its relationship to the unconscious. Freud's great contribution in Lacan's view was to anticipate subsequent linguistic theory in his understanding of how the unconscious expresses itself through slips of the tongue, puns, and other word associations. In the language of linguistic theory, Freud discovered how the signifier is caught up in a system of relations with other signifiers and how no one can be completely in control of language and its meaning. According to Lacan, developments in the discipline of linguistics both shed light on what Freud was trying to say and provide a theoretical framework for reinterpreting Freud. In rereading Freud in this way, Lacan construes many of Freud's terms, including castration and the Oedipus complex, as signifying something about the way language and culture work.

Before Lacan, "phallus" and "penis" were interchangeable terms, although "phallus" was often regarded as the more delicate term. But Lacan used "phallus" to designate what he called the Symbolic, which is language and culture. In other words, the phallus is the symbol of the effect that language has on the development of human subjectivity. The phallus and the penis therefore are not the same thing. The penis is the actual male organ. The phallus is a symbol of language and culture.

But precisely what Lacan means by the phallus is subject to a number of different interpretations. According to one view, the phallus is a symbol of coming into culture, of learning to speak. And this act of becoming a human subject involves a kind of castration, a loss of the phallus. Like object-relations theorists, Lacan emphasizes the preoedipal phase of a child's development. In particular, Lacan is interested in how human subjectivity originates in a traumatic loss, a loss necessitated by the differentiation of the baby from the (m)other. This loss occurs as a person enters into culture, and through it human desire originates. Human desire always seeks and fails to restore the wholeness that preceded the origin of subjectivity. Lacan thus recasts the terms of Freud's oedipal theory. The phallus symbolizes desire for the mother and wholeness which can never be realized once a subject has entered culture. At the same time it points to the effects of language, the fact that once we have entered language it leaves its mark on us. Lacan calls this experience of entering into language a castration. To be human is to be castrated, and men and women share the lack of the phallus.[29]

Lacan's phallus, therefore, is not a penis. But what precisely is it? A number of feminist writers have pointed out that the phallus and the penis cannot be conceptually separated, since the phallus always carries semantic associations to the penis. As Jane Gallop writes: "The penis is what men have and women do not; the phallus is the attribute of power which neither men nor women have. But as long as the attribute of power is a phallus which refers to and can be confused (in the imaginary register?) with a 'penis,' this confusion will support a structure in which it seems reasonable that men have power and women do not" (1982, 97).

For this reason, I refuse the Lacanian distinction between a phallus and a penis. I intentionally call God's penis a phallus so as to reject the problematic assumptions upon which Lacanian theory rests. In other ways, however, I find Lacanian theory to have anticipated some of the results of this analysis. In particular, there is a convergence between his claim that the phallus must be veiled and the veiling of the divine phallus I explore. Indeed, I would argue—using Lacanian terminology—that the penis in some instances also has to be veiled. Unlike Lacan, I do not attribute this veiling to a generalizable and univeral process. Rather, it arises from the contradictions of masculinity in a specific symbolic order. Nevertheless, as we shall see, there are parallels between Lacan's claim that the veiling of the phallus is directly related to the entrance of a subject into language and my own argument that the veiling of the divine phallus is linked to the emergence of the seminal word, what Lacan would call the Logos. There is obviously a great deal more to be said about these tantalizing Lacanian intersections than I can say in the present context. I hope someday to come back to them. But for now, let us return to Freud.

Chapter Two

Analytic Phallusies

The "sexual libido" took over the role of a deus absconditus, *a hidden or concealed god. . . . Yaweh and sexuality remained the same. The name alone had changed and with it, of course, the point of view: the lost god had now to be sought below, not above.*

CARL JUNG, Memories, Dreams, Reflections

Most interpreters of Freud's *Moses and Monotheism* dismiss it as one of his least interesting analytic works. It is the product of his old age, written while his health was deteriorating, and during a time when the tenuousness of the psychoanalytic movement in Vienna and the vulnerability of Jews to anti-Semitism were much on his mind.[1] Because the substantive claims of *Moses and Monotheism* have been dismissed, attention has recently focused instead on what this work says about Freud's own Jewishness.[2] The fact that Freud initially intended to call *Moses and Monotheism* a historical novel signifies, according to some, that he did not regard this as a serious historical work on the Jewish religion.

But I would argue that while many of the historical claims in *Moses and Monotheism* are absurd, Freud formulates a number of illuminating analytic questions about the relationship between the deity's gender and religious practice. Indeed, most of my own analyses can be construed as a way of thinking about questions that *Moses and Monotheism* poses, particularly in the third essay of the book. This is the essay that

Freud could not bring himself to publish in Vienna during the rise of Nazi Germany and that he himself recognized as containing the essential parts of his arguments.[3] For example, at the end of his second essay, Freud says that the central contentions of his argument have not yet appeared. "Beyond this [the second essay], there would be a very great deal to discuss, to explain and to assert. Only thus would an interest in our purely historical study find its true justification" (1939, 52). Several times he indicates that he views the claims of the first two essays as primarily historical in nature and not interesting from an analytical perspective. In the preface to the third essay, which was published only after his flight to England, Freud tells us that he withheld this essay because of his fear of how the Catholic church might react to the psychoanalytic movement. This worry was probably legitimate, for Freud has some very new things to say about the nature and origin of Christianity. However, casting doubt on his own motivations, he reminds us that *Moses and Monotheism* in many ways retraces ground that he has covered already in *Totem and Taboo*.[4]

Everything points to the third essay as one of fundamental concern to Freud: it contains his central psychoanalytic claims about monotheism, and he worried most about its publication. There are a number of new claims in this section that do not appear in his other writings on religion. In the context of reviewing his historical argument about Moses' Egyptian origin and murder, Freud develops at length his understanding of psychological latency and repression, which he regards as parallel to the development of monotheism. Just as childhood memories come back to an adult, so the primal deed against Moses and the religion of Moses undergo a repression and resurface in the history of the Jews. It is here that Freud recounts his theory of original parricide developed in *Totem and Taboo*, but he takes it a step further. In totemic religion, the father is hidden in the symbol of an animal. The worship and eating of the animal expresses in indirect form the reverence for and fear of the father. But with monotheism, Freud argues, the presence of the father behind God is made explicit: "The first step away from totemism was the humanizing of the being who was worshipped. In the place of the animals, human gods appear, whose derivation from the totem is not concealed. . . . The male deities appear first as sons beside the great mothers and only later clearly assume the features of father-figures. . . . The next step [the development of monotheism], however, leads us to the theme with which we are here concerned—the return of a single father-god of unlimited dominion" (1939, 106).

Monotheism, according to Freud, was the first religion to recognize the father behind the image of God. "The re-establishment of the primal father in his historic rights was a great step forward but it could not be the end." Freud them proceeds to contrast the Mosaic religion with the Christian religion. If the Mosaic religion is the Father religion, Christianity is the Son religion. Christ the Son took the place of the Father. In some ways, Christianity represents a regression in Freud's view, for it abandoned the centrality of the father God, ended strict monotheism, endorsed superstitions, and retarded intellectual development. But in other respects, he sees the myth of Christ's resurrection as a return of the primal father. Through the crucifixion of the son, Christianity atoned for the original sin, the murder of the father. Based on this interpretation, Freud believed he had uncovered one of the reasons for anti-Semitism: While Christians acknowledged their original sin, namely, killing the father God, Jews never would (ibid., 86–90).

Another of Freud's new claims concerns the Jews' distinctive spirituality. According to Freud, a conceptual, cultural, and moral revolution occurred when Moses introduced the Jews to an abstract conception of God. By prohibiting the making of divine images, Moses helped the Jews to triumph over the senses since they now no longer envisioned God in human form (144). This triumph of spirituality over the senses was an instinctual renunciation which, like all such renunciations, Freud views as a sign of maturation and progress. The Mosaic prohibition on images raised God and the Jews to a higher level of spirituality and moved the Jews to a superior position to those who remained in bondage to the senses. Freud thus sees a direct relationship between this transformation of a people and the renunciations of instinctual gratifications which a boy must accomplish on the way to maturity: "The religion which began with the prohibition against making an image of God develops more and more in the course of centuries into a religion of instinctual renunciations. It is not that it would demand sexual *abstinence*; it is content with a marked restriction of sexual freedom. God, however, becomes entirely removed from sexuality and elevated into the ideal of ethical perfection. But ethics is a limitation of instinct" (148).

It is here, in my judgment, that Freud makes his most interesting observations about monotheism. Freud sees a connection between the fatherhood of God, the prohibition on images, sexual renunciation, and the triumph of the spirit over the senses. He understands the prohibition on images in terms of the gender of God, specifically God's fatherhood, and he sees that prohibition as linked to masculine renunciation. Like Freud, I also argue that there is a connection between the image of God the father, the prohibition on material images of God, and sexual renunciation, as I will show in the following chapters. But where Freud regards the prohibition on images of God as linked to a triumph of spirituality over the senses, I regard it as a means of coping with the dilemmas raised by the father's body. Ironically, my own account of monotheism and the centrality of the homoerotic dilemma is Freudian through and through. But it is a Freudian reading of monotheism that Freud himself did not develop.

It is curious that Freud did not think about the body of the father God. In part, he was surely misled by the long tradition that claimed that the God of the Jews did not have a body. But given Freud's willingness to depart from conventional wisdom about monotheism and about most other things that he interpreted, this explanation by itself cannot account for his failure to speculate about the father's body in his account of monotheism. Indeed, the human father's sexual body is central to Freud's account of the Oedipus complex. There is thus an important tension in Freud's account of monotheism. He describes monotheism as discovering the image of the father that had earlier been disguised in the symbols of animals, but at the same time he claims that Moses introduced an idea of God with no imaged content. Thus Freud's account of monotheism is contradictory: on the one hand he asserts that in monotheism the father is rediscovered behind the image of God; on the other hand he insists that what is discovered is a conceptual idea of God. Rizzuto notes how Freud seems unaware of his conceptual leap from paternal image to the intellectual idea of God.[5] "Freud does not seem to be aware that in talking about an abstract idea [of God] and instinctual renunciation he makes a major shift—at once descriptive, conceptual, logical, theoretical and historical. The introduction of this new notion meant abandoning the beautifully built theory of object representation implicit in his previous formulations" (1979, 25–26). Because he does not recognize this departure in his thinking, Freud provides no explanation for the banning of the father's image.

Ironically, Freud had all the theoretical resources to account for this disappearance of the father's body, for he was well aware of the potential for homoerotic desire between father and son. Freud postulated an original bisexuality in the newborn that only later was organized along heterosexual lines through the Oedipus complex. But there were two versions of that complex. In one version, the one most familiar to readers and the one central to *Totem and Taboo* and *Moses and Monotheism*, the male child desires his mother, and because of that desire becomes afraid of his father castrating him, an event Freud believed occurred repeatedly in history. Out of narcissistic attachment to his organ, a boy represses his desires for his mother and ends the competition with his father. This is the successful resolution of the Oedipus complex.

But Freud explored another variant on this process, what he called an "inverted" or "passive" Oedipus complex.[6] In this version, the boy wishes to be castrated so as to replace his mother and become the object of his father's affections. This desire to become a woman and take the female position is, if development is not arrested, also surmounted. The narcissistic connection to his penis again helps the boy to renounce this desire for his father and to identify with him instead, taking a heterosexual love object. If for some reason these homosexual feelings become fixed, they may cause paranoia or other disorders.

Although the relationship between the image of God and homosexual longings for the father are not taken up in *Totem and Taboo* or in *Moses and Monotheism*, Freud analyzed them in other contexts, most notably his case studies. In his 1911 study of Daniel Paul Schreber, for example, Freud explores a case of paranoia that involves homoerotic feelings toward a father God. According to Freud, Schreber's case illustrates what goes wrong if a boy does not successfully resolve his oedipal desires for his father.

Freud's analysis of this case is based on Daniel Schreber's personal memoirs of his hospitalizations and treatments in two asylums written between 1900 and 1902 (Schreber 1955).[7] Schreber was a well-respected judge, at one point presiding judge of the superior court in Leipzig. During his hospitalization Schreber developed a detailed theology in which he imagined that God wished him to be transformed into a woman. According to Schreber's theology, the soul is in the nerves of the body and after death returns to God, who is made up of nerve alone. In returning to God, the soul-nerves go through a purification and gain a state of blessedness in which there is uninterrupted enjoyment combined with contemplation of God. A soul's happiness lies in continual reveling in pleasure. When describing his own transformation into a woman, Schreber refers to this as "soul voluptuousness."[8] Schreber believes there is an upper and lower God. The rays of the lower God, Ariman, can "unman" human men.[9] Schreber believes the end of the world order is imminent and that he alone will survive this transition. He views himself, interestingly enough, as the Eternal Jew, who once unmanned will become the vehicle to reproduce the species. At first Schreber believes that his doctor, Dr. Flechsig, is behind the plot to turn him into a woman. But later he sees God as the major force behind his unmanning. Schreber becomes aware of changes in his own body, of his increased "soul voluptuousness" and indications that his male organ is retracting: "The "soul voluptuousness" had become so strong that I myself received the impression of a female body, first in my arms and hands, later in my legs, bosom, buttocks and other parts of my body" (1955, 148). Schreber is initially horrified by this unmanning but subsequently comes to see it as his right and duty to cultivate feminine feelings.

In Schreber's memoirs, Freud saw a classic illustration of his theory of paranoia, which had already been worked out in some detail (Chabat 1982, 34). According to Freud, Schreber's case demonstrated the warding off of homosexual wishes. Paranoia develops because of the inability to accept what Freud regards as a contradiction: that I (a man) love (a man). The wish is suppressed, reversed, and then enters consciousness as an external perception: "I love this man" becomes "This man wants to harm me." Schreber's paranoia was set off, Freud claims, by an outburst of homosexual libido, occasioned when his wife was away on vacation. Freud finds confirmation of this interpretation in Schreber's report that the onset of the illness was accompanied by twelve nocturnal pollutions in one night. The presence of Schreber's wife, Freud speculates, served as an antidote to the attractive power of the men about him, and her absence thus brought on his outburst of homoerotic desire. Freud goes on to argue that for Schreber the image of God is in fact a disguise first for Dr. Flechsig, who in turn is a surrogate for Schreber's father. Indeed, Freud notes that Schreber's father was a prominent physician. When Schreber accuses God of understanding nothing about living men and knowing only how to deal with corpses, he is in fact maligning his father's skills as a doctor. Freud suggests that God becomes the vehicle whereby Schreber can disguise and hence allow into consciousness his own desires for his father. God (Father) wants me to be transformed into a woman. Schreber's fear of castration by his father became a wish to be transformed into a woman, a wish first resisted but then made tolerable by the substitution of God for father (Freud 1911, 63, 45, 55–56). God, then, is a concept through which repressed homosexual feelings are finally acknowledged and accepted.

Freud's reading has been criticized on numerous grounds, and the assumption that behind paranoia lies repressed homosexuality has been largely abandoned in analytic circles.[10] Moreover, it turns out that Schreber was subjected to childhood abuse that may very well explain many of his symptoms and fantasies.[11] Nor are Schreber's memoirs necessarily to be dismissed as the ravings of an ill man. Some commentators see a sophisticated critique of gender relations in Schreber's desire to become a woman, and a poignant theological critique of a religious system that does not make God the father accountable to any rules outside himself.[12] Still, Freud's analysis of Schreber's case is relevant here for two reasons: first, it shows that Freud was well aware of homoeroticism toward the father and its expression in symbols of God, and second, it suggests that—whatever the merits of Freud's understanding of Schreber's case—his insights about religion in this context have more general applicability.

The Schreber case is not the only place in which Freud works out these issues. In his analysis of the "Wolf Man," Freud also writes about how the image of God allows for the expression of homoerotic attachments to the father that otherwise must be repressed.[13] Here Freud sees repressed homosexual wishes expressed in the young boy's childish theological questioning: Did Christ have a behind and did he shit? "We catch a glimpse of his repressed homosexual attitude in his doubting whether Christ could have a behind, for these ruminations could have no other meaning but the question whether he himself could be used by his father like a woman—like his mother in the primal scene" ([1914] 1918, 64). Freud ponders these same themes again in "A Seventeenth-Century Demonological Neurosis" ([1922] 1923), in which he explores how homoeroticism is involved in a painter's pact with the Devil.

The purpose of this detour into Freud's case studies is not to endorse his theory of homosexuality or his analyses of these cases. Indeed in important ways, Freud's theory of homosexuality is wrongheaded. Because Freud was reading homosexuality within a heterosexual framework, he mistakenly assumes that homosexual desires necessarily feminized the male who has them. That is not true: homoerotic desire occurs in men who by all criteria are as masculine as heterosexual men.[14] And yet Freud is right in diagnosing the way in which heterosexual imagery is sometimes imposed on homosexual relations. When procreative heterosexuality dominates the cultural system, the sexual relationship between men may be cast in heterosexual terms, especially when femininity is associated with subordination as it was in ancient Judaism.[15] What these case studies show, however, is how deeply

Freud had thought about the issue of homoeroticism and its relationship to the image of the father God. Freud published the Schreber analysis in 1911 and wrote the case of the Wolf Man in 1914 (it was published in 1918). Clearly, the homoerotic and religion were on his mind during the period he was writing *Totem and Taboo*, which was published in 1913.

In any case, the theory of religion that Freud works out in his case studies provides a way to account for the disappearance of God's body, which Freud detects but leaves unexamined in *Moses and Monotheism*. In linking my own reading of monotheism to Freud's, it is important also to mark the difference. Freud sees the idea of God as making possible the expression of repressed homoerotic wishes. Because God is a spiritual projection, loving him is less threatening than loving a father of flesh and blood. Homoerotic love is transferred to an idealized and disembodied image of the deity, and the son's homoerotic attachment to the father is sublimated and expressed in idealized love. My analysis of monotheism suggests that the image of the father God's body must be prohibited or veiled so that it does not provoke homoerotic desires. In other words, images of God do evoke an image of the father's body and hence potentially arouse homosexual desire. In this view, God turned his back to Moses, not to allow for the sublimation of homoerotic impulses—although this may have been an ineluctable result of the metaphor—but to prevent Israelite men from facing them. Because God's back was turned, Israelite men did not have to confront the maleness of the father God they loved.

Of course, Freud views symbols of the deity as reflecting actual psychic tensions in a young child, and I see these conflicts occurring in religious myth. I am reluctant to make the Freudian move from myths to psyche. That the cultural imagination could not permit the thought of a homoerotic relationship with God does not mean that individual Israelite men repressed homoerotic desires. All we can say is that this religious culture held up an image of procreative heterosexuality as an ideal and repressed images that would mock that ideal. This is a notion of repression in a different sense than Freud meant. It is not the banishing of an idea from the conscious to the unconscious because of an individual's inability to deal with it. It is a cultural avoidance of certain ideas that undermine a reigning paradigm, in this case of masculinity.

Moses and Monotheism

It was not just ancient Jews who could not face the implications of the maleness of God. As we've seen, Freud could not bring himself to think about the possible homoerotic relationship of the Jewish male to the father God, even though he had already considered the issue in his earlier writings. However, Freud's failure to develop his homoerotic theory of religion in *Moses and Monotheism* is not entirely surprising since that work represents Judaism as a distinctively masculine religion whose psychological effects make good men.[16] It is no wonder that Freud could not pursue the idea that homoeroticism lies at the heart of monotheism. To do so would have undercut the force of his argument about the inherent masculinity of the Jewish religion.

There are various ways of interpreting Freud's masculinization of Judaism. Van Herik and Rieff see it as a form of Jewish triumphalism.[17] But it is more likely a defensive posture on Freud's part, an attempt to deny the common association between femininity, passivity, and Jewishness. That Judaism was identified with femininity in European imagination has been amply demonstrated by both Gilman and Geller, who show how this association also plagued Freud's own identity.[18] Geller in particular has explored how Freud's fears about the Jews' femininity enters into his discussion of circumcision in *Moses and Monotheism*. We know that Freud struggled with the "negative" connotations of Judaism from a now famous story that Freud's father related to him as a young adolescent. In a letter to Karl Abraham, Freud tells how he and his father used to take walks together. On one of these walks, his father recounted how different things were for Jews than when he was young. To illustrate, he told Freud how a Christian had once knocked off his fur cap and said, "Jew get off the pavement." "And what did you do?" asked the young Freud of his father. "I went into the roadway and picked up my cap" was his quiet reply.[19] Given the situation in which Freud wrote *Moses and Monotheism*, amid the rise of Nazi Germany, the increasing victimization of the Jews, and Freud's own declining health, it is hardly surprising that he was worried about Jewish passivity, which for him was connected to femininity.[20]

But it was not just the femininity of Jews and Judaism that upset Freud. The problem of a male's femininity was entangled for Freud in the issue of homosexuality. To be a homosexual in Freud's eyes was to be passive and dependent, and to take a male as an object of desire. We know that Freud was troubled by what he regarded as his own homosexual tendencies, particularly in regard to two of his most intimate and subsequently problematic relationships: with Wilhelm Fliess and Carl Jung. We see from Freud's letters that he was involved in thinking about and mastering his own homosexuality between 1910 and 1912, the same period in which he was working on writings that most involved the issue of homoeroticism. While traveling in Rome, Freud wrote to Carl Jung in a letter dated September 24, 1910:

> My travelling companion is a dear fellow, but dreamy in a disturbing kind of way, and his attitude towards me is infantile. He never stops admiring me, which I don't like, and is probably sharply critical of me in his unconscious when I am taking it easy. He has been too passive and receptive letting everything be done for him like a woman, and I really haven't got enough homosexuality in me to accept him as one. These trips arouse a great longing for a real woman. A number of scientific notions I brought with me have combined to form a paper on paranoia, which still lacks an end, but takes quite a step forward in explaining the mechanism of the choice of neurosis.[21]

The paper Freud is referring to is his work on Schreber. So at the very time that Freud was working on Schreber's homosexuality, he was insisting that he had overcome his own. The man Freud was traveling with was Sándor Ferenczi. Freud recognized and resisted Ferenczi's desire for more intimacy and dependence than Freud wanted. After the trip, Ferenczi in fact apologized to Freud for his behavior. Freud responds as follows on October 6:

> You not only noticed, but also understood, that I *no longer* have any need to uncover my personality completely, and you correctly traced this back to the traumatic reason for it. Since Fliess's case, with the overcoming of which you recently saw me occupied, that need has been extinguished. A part of homosexual cathexis has been withdrawn and made use of to enlarge my own ego. I have succeeded where the paranoiac fails.[22]

Then on October 17, he writes again to Ferenczi: "You probably imagine that I have secrets quite other than those I have reserved for myself, or you believe that my secrets are connected with special sorrow, whereas I feel capable of handling everything and am pleased with the greater independence that results from having overcome my homosexuality."[23] Freud thus understood Ferenczi's desires as homosexual in nature and explained to him that since the Fliess affair he had overcome such desires. Fliess was one of Freud's most intimate companions. Some even speculate that there was sexual activity during their meetings (Rosenberg 1978, 194). But for the present purposes, whether Freud was involved in physical intimacy with other men is beside the point. What is important here is that he viewed himself as having homosexual tendencies which he had to master. The mastery of those impulses, he believed, would lead him to ego strength.

But Freud's fears about his homosexuality did not disappear. He voiced them again after a now famous fainting spell at a meeting in Munich on November 24, 1912, in which he was carried into the next room by Jung. This was the second time Freud had fainted in Jung's presence. The first occurred in 1909 as they set off on a trip to the United States, as Jung was talking about prehistoric corpses that had been discovered in Copenhagen cemeteries. Most interpreters have followed Jung's and Jones's interpretation and construed Freud's fainting episodes as reflecting his fear of death or his anxiety about the future of his ideas in the hands of Jung, who at that point seemed to be Freud's designated successor.[24] Freud seemed to see them differently. He writes, "Repressed feelings, this time directed against Jung, as previously against a predecessor of his, naturally play the main part."[25]

One suspects that the predecessor he refers to is Fliess. Indeed, a similar incident occurred in the same Munich meetingroom in the 1890s when Freud was with Fliess. Regarding this incident, Freud commented to Ernest Jones that there was "some piece of unruly homosexual feeling at the root of the matter."[26] Freud's recognition of and efforts to suppress his homosexual impulses go a long way to explaining the avoidance of the issue of homoeroticism in *Moses and Monotheism*.

Thus, it is significant to note that just prior to Freud's second fainting spell in Jung's presence, he and Jung were discussing monotheism.[27] The conversation revolved around a paper by Karl Abraham ([1912] 1955) on the ancient Egyptian Amenhotep IV (Ikhnaton). In his essay, Abraham anticipated many of the concerns Freud would later take up in *Moses and Monotheism*, for he gives an analytic account of monotheism's origin. When Freud fainted, Jung was disagreeing with him about whether there was a father complex behind the creation of this monotheistic religion, a point Abraham had made in his paper. Jung argued that the religious reform of Ikhnaton was not directed against his father, that in fact the reformer held the memory of his father in honor.[28] What connection is there between the subject under discussion and the fact that Freud himself associated this fainting spell with repressed feelings of homosexuality? It is possible that these repressed feelings were not just about Jung, and Jung's threat to Freud's work, but also in some way about the topic of monotheism and the father God. This of course is speculation. But as we shall see, there are other pieces of evidence that suggest Freud's overall discomfort with this topic.

Consider first the subject matter of Abraham's paper. Abraham points to several aspects of Ikhnaton's psychic development that are relevant to understanding his religious revolution. According to Abraham's analysis, Ikhnaton's primary libidinal attachment was to his dominant mother. It was this attachment that led to the new pharaoh's monogamy, an unusual practice in Egypt. But Abraham sees the father complex as the central force in Ikhnaton's religious revolution. After his father's death, Ikhnaton becomes ruler of Egypt and orchestrates a transition from the polytheistic worship in which the god Amon dominates to the exclusive worship of Aton. In the process of this transition, Ikhnaton removes the names of both the god Amon and his father from all monuments. Abraham interprets this religious revolution as a rebellion against the father.

The erasure of Amon is thus an attempt to erase the memory of Ikhnaton's father. But Ikhnaton has not completely overcome his dependence on paternal authority. The new god, Aton, is an idealized father that supplants his real father. Abraham goes on to suggest that Ikhnaton's teachings not only contain essential elements of Jewish monotheism, but are in many ways in advance of it. Ikhnaton does not imagine his god as corporeal, like the old gods, but as spiritual and impersonal. He therefore forbids all pictorial representations of this god. Moreover, Ikhnaton makes Aton the one and only god, in transparent imitation of the uniqueness of the father: "He thereby became the precursor of Moses and his monotheism, in which the one and only god unmistakably bears the features of the patriarch, the sole ruler of the family" (Abraham [1912] 1955, 287).

Clearly, Abraham provided a suggestive analytic theory about the origin of monotheism. It is startling, then, that Freud does not even mention the essay once in *Moses and Monotheism*.[29] That Freud forgot or overlooked this essay by one of his favorite pupils, an essay he had read and commented upon in his correspondence with Abraham, seems to confirm the ambivalence suggested by the fainting spell. Abraham's essay in fact points to a major lacuna in Freud's own account, which explains how Moses, a devotee of the Aton religion, imposed monotheism on the Jews. In this way, Freud never provides an analysis of how monotheism developed. Rather, he presupposes its existence and explores its effects.

Moses and Monotheism thus picks up the story where Abraham's essay leaves off. It tells the story of what happens to monotheism after the revolt against Ikhnaton. Indeed, if we read *Moses and Monotheism* against the backdrop of Abraham's essay, Freud's Moses is a high-ranking prince in Ikhnaton's retinue. This identification flows naturally from Freud's extended argument at the beginning of *Moses and Monotheism* that Moses is of Egyptian royal origin and that Moses' murder in fact parallels and repeats the overthrow and death of Ikhnaton, whose end, like Moses' own, is wrapped in mystery (1939, 23, 25). Indeed, Freud seems to regard Ikhnaton's religious revolution as the historical "moment" when totemism shifted to monotheism, for as he points out, Egyptian religion prior to Ikhnaton involved worship of all kinds of animals. It is clear that Freud regards his thesis of Moses' Egyptian origins to have far-reaching implications: "It will be better to suppress any inferences that might follow our view that Moses was an Egyptian" (ibid., 17). Some readers of Freud view his argument about Moses' Egyptian origin as reflecting his desire to deny his own Jewish origins,[30] but as is now evident, there is an analytic repercussion as well: Jewish monotheism originated out of the family situation of Ikhnaton, and this family dynamic is erased in Freud's essay.

Abraham's account of monotheism is much closer to the analysis of religion that Freud developed in his studies of Schreber, the Wolf Man, and the possessed painter and that he elsewhere stated in a more theoretical way (Freud 1914b). Like this early Freud, Abraham sees both sides of the Oedipus complex operating in montheism: the rebellion against the father and the honoring of and need for the father. He also sees the spiritualization of the father and the removal of the father's image as permitting an acknowledgment of the dependence on the father's love. It would not be difficult at all, in fact, to read Freud's analysis of the Schreber case into Abraham's essay on Ikhnaton. Abraham himself saw a connection between his own essay and that case study. In exploring the meaning of the sun, which served as the symbol of the deity Aton, Abraham cites Freud's argument in the Schreber case that the sun is a father symbol:

> [As a sign of Ikhnaton's] unusually strong inclination to subli-
> mate, we find that the warmth of the sun has a second signifi-
> cance; it becomes the symbol of the all-embracing love of

Aton. . . . This symbolism is well known to us from the dreams of both normal and neurotic persons. Furthermore, in the pathology of neurosis abnormal feelings of heat and cold are very common. They are closely related to the eroticism of such patients, to which only a passing reference can here be made. (Abraham [1912] 1955, 289)

Freud's account of monotheism ignores the dependent, loving side of the Oedipus complex. He completely erases the love of God, which is connected to the father's love. As van Herik notes, "In *Moses and Monotheism* the firmly authoritative and therefore psychically educative, qualities of Moses and his god overshadow the loving protective and consoling character of fathers and god as they are portrayed in *The Future of an Illusion*" (1982, 178). It is striking, then, that Freud sees the absence of the sun symbol as the single most important difference between Jewish and Egyptian monotheism. Clearly he wishes to give an account of monotheism without a symbol of the father's love.[31]

Traces of Freud's ambivalence toward the father's love in Abraham's essay are already evident in a letter to Abraham dated June 3, 1912. In general, Freud writes approvingly of the essay and seems to accept much of the argument.

> I have read your Egyptian study with the pleasure that I always derive both from your way of writing and way of thinking, and should like to make only two criticisms or suggestions for alteration. In the first place you express the view that when the mother is particularly important the conflict with the father takes milder forms. I have no evidence of this, and must assume that you have had special experience in regard to it. As the matter is not clear to me, may I ask you to have another look at this passage? Secondly, I have doubts about representing the king so distinctly as a neurotic, which is in sharp contrast with his exceptional energy and achievement, as we associate neuroticism, a term which has become scientifically inexact, with the idea of inhibition. We all have these complexes, and we must guard against calling everyone neurotic. If we have warded them off, we should be spared the name. (Abraham and Freud 1965, 118)

In response, Abraham declares his intention to revise his manuscript in light of Freud's criticism. We have to assume that the essay Abraham actually published is more heavily weighted toward the conflictual side of the Oedipus complex than the original draft. Freud's criticism of Abraham's paper, however, is consistent with my suggestion that he was disturbed by the theme of father love. Freud wanted Abraham to develop more fully the conflict between father and son, the direction in which Freud later took his own analysis of monotheism. Moreover, just two years before Abraham's essay, Freud had himself written a historical case study involving a male subject impelled by a relationship with a dominant mother. In this study of Leonardo da Vinci, Freud argues that the artist's early libidinal attachments to his mother were responsible for homosexual impulses which were displaced into the artist's work. When Abraham emphasizes the libidinal attachments of Ikhnaton to his mother, the sublimation of Ikhnaton's need for dependence onto the idea of God, and the centrality of the loving sun, his analysis points rather directly, at least in Freud's own terms, to homoeroticism as a factor in monotheism's production. Although Abraham himself never drew this conclusion in the published paper, I suspect his interpretation of Ikhnaton's relationship to the loving sun god troubled Freud.

Freud's avoidances were not limited to his response to Abraham's essay on monotheism. Quite similar tendencies are exhibited in his own analysis of Michelangelo's statue *Moses*, which he first visited in 1901 and became fascinated with again on his unsettling trip to Rome with Ferenczi in 1912. Many commentators have noted that Freud both identified with Moses and viewed him as a father figure. As the founder of psychoanalysis constantly struggling with the apostasy of his disciples, Freud saw himself as a new Moses. But Moses also scowled judgmentally at Freud the son, who had broken a sexual commandment, who had surmounted his unconscious fears of punishment by the ancestral God, and who had abandoned the religion of his father.[32]

Freud's analysis of Michelangelo's *Moses* is in fact one of his strangest pieces. He initially resisted publishing it and had to be persuaded to do so by his colleagues—even then, it only appeared anonymously.

This reaction anticipated his hesitation about publishing the third essay of *Moses and Monotheism*.[33] The Michelangelo essay purports to be an illustration of the power of psychoanalysis to explain art, but as such it is a disappointment. Freud completely ignores the way in which this piece of art may reflect the psychosexual development of the sculptor, in dramatic contrast to his earlier analysis of Leonardo da Vinci in which he explores in detail the relationship between the artist's work and his homosexual impulses.[34] Paradoxically, he goes on at length about why *Moses* represents the subordination of human passion to a higher service.

In contrast to many other interpreters who see Moses as about to throw down the tablets of the law in reaction to Israel's idolatry, Freud argues that the sculptor depicts Moses as having already checked his rage. In an initial fit of anger, Freud says, Moses drew his right hand across his body and grasped his beard. But he then subsequently drew it back across his body to catch the tablets that nearly fell from under his right arm. The traces of this movement are still visible: the forefinger of Moses' right hand is still in his beard, caught by a violent movement that has now subsided. The tablets of the law, now upside down, have just been kept from falling (see plate, Part III). Freud argues that Michelangelo "has added something new and more than human to the figure of Moses; so that the giant frame with its tremendous physical power becomes only a concrete expression of the highest mental achievement that is possible in a man, that of struggling successfully against an inward passion for the sake of a cause to which he has devoted himself" (1914a, 233). It is doubtful that Freud's interpretation of the statue is correct since Moses was to be paired with Saint Paul and was more likely an idealized character study (Liebert 1983, 209). But we should notice the similarity between Michelangelo's Moses, as Freud interprets him, and Freud's Moses in *Moses and Monotheism*. In the statue, Moses the lawgiver saves the tablets of the law by an instinctual renunciation of anger; in *Moses and Monotheism*, Moses institutes an instinctual renunciation of desire through the prohibition on images.

Despite having described his Michelangelo piece as an attempt to discern the artist's intention and his inner motives, when Freud finally gets around to specifying the inner motives from which Michelangelo operated, his reflections are startlingly banal. Indeed, he offers a historical rather than psychoanalytic perspective:

> We have now completed our interpretation of Michelangelo's statue, though it can still be asked what motives prompted the sculptor to select the figure of Moses, and so greatly altered Moses, as an adornment for the tomb of Julius II. In the opinion of many these motives are to be found in the character of the Pope and in Michelangelo's relations with him. Julius II was akin to Michelangelo in this, that he attempted to realize great and mighty ends, and especially designs on a grand scale. He was a man of action and he had a definite purpose, which was to unite Italy under the Papal supremacy. He desired to bring about single-handed what was not to happen for several centuries, and then only through the conjunction of many alien forces; and he worked alone, with impatience, in the short span of sovereignty allowed him, and used violent means. He could appreciate Michelangelo as a man of his own kind, but he often made him smart under his sudden anger and his utter lack of consideration for others. The artist felt the same violent force of will in himself, and, as the more introspective thinker, may have had a premonition of the failure to which they were both doomed. And so he carved his Moses on the Pope's tomb, not without a reproach against the dead pontiff, as a warning to himself, thus, in self-criticism, rising superior to his own nature. (1914, 233–34)

It is a disappointing conclusion for an essay that promises something on the order of the discovery of the Oedipus complex behind Hamlet. Perhaps this was why Freud published it anonymously. Readers might have wondered why the essay avoided a psychoanalytic interpretation had they known its true author. In the introductory footnote to the essay, Freud writes that "the editors have decided to print it, since the author, who is personally known to them, moves in psycho-analytic circles, and since his method of thought has in point of fact a certain resemblance to the methodology of psycho-analysis" (ibid., 211).

This may be Freud's little joke, but it could also be serious. Freud may be acknowledging here that the piece is atypical, for it leaves off its analysis precisely where psychoanalysis usually begins. Indeed, when reflecting on his decision to publish the piece anonymously, Freud writes that "only much later did I legitimize this non-analytical child." This is a "non-analytical child" because Freud does not actually perform an analytic interpretation. Even when he reflects on Michelangelo's motives, he is careful not to endorse the explanation, which he says is the "opinion of many." But is it his own opinion? How would Freud the analyst go about explaining the artist's motives? Surely Freud's essay does not live up to his own judgment that "if a biographical study is really intended to arrive at an understanding of its hero's mental life it must not. . . . silently pass over its subject's sexual activity or sexual individuality" (1910, 69).

It is significant that Freud suppresses the psychosexual dimensions of Michelangelo's life, given the wealth of information available about the artist. Two biographies were written by close intimates of Michelangelo, and hundreds of letters and poems survive that give a full picture of the artist's life.[35] Indeed, we know more about Michelangelo than any other artist before the nineteenth century. There is a wealth of information available on the relationship of Michelangelo to his father, although not about his relationship to his mother or wet nurse. We know that Freud read the biography of Michelangelo by Giorgio Vasari (1568) because he cites it on several occasions in his Leonardo essay.[36] We do not know how much Freud knew about Michelangelo's intense, passionate relationships with men. Since this information was available in the books Freud read on Michelangelo, it is reasonable to suppose that he was aware of some of it and that he knew he could have discovered more if he so chose. In fact, in a letter written in 1935 to an American mother whose son was homosexual, Freud tells her that "homosexuality is assuredly no advantage, but it is nothing to be ashamed of, no vice, no degradation, it cannot be classified as an illness. . . . Many highly respectable individuals of ancient and modern times have been homosexuals, several of the greatest men among them (Plato, Michelangelo, Leonardo da Vinci, etc.).”[37] That the information available readily lends itself to psycho-analytic interpretation is evident by the recent study of Liebert (1983), who explores among other things the homoerotic implications of Michelangelo's creations, such as his depiction of Noah's nakedness in the Sistine Chapel (see plate, Part II) and its repetition in the *Children's Bacchanal.*

By failing to discuss the way the art work reflects the sculptor's psychosexual conflicts, Freud can pass over in silence the question of how the artist's *Moses* might reflect his homosexual impulses. Does Freud believe it is only anger that Michelangelo's *Moses* is repressing, or is there another impulse as well, an impulse of the artist? When we re-read Freud's analysis of *Moses* in light of his silence about Michelangelo's psychosexual impulses we discover some notable lapses for a master analyst who usually pays such careful attention to insignificant details. Most dramatically, Freud barely comments on the position of Moses' left hand, although he spends several pages analyzing the position of the right hand. Indeed, as Freud notes earlier in his essay, the left hand perplexes interpreters: He cites Jakob Burckhardt who complains that “the celebrated left arm has no other function in reality than to press his beard to his body.” About the left hand Freud has only this to say: “The hand is laid in the lap in a mild gesture and holds as though in a caress the end of the flowing beard. It seems as if it is meant to counteract the violence with which the other hand has misused the beard a few moments ago” (1914a, 214, 230). Freud's brevity here is odd. His account of the left hand makes no sense in terms of his own interpretation, which presupposes that Michelangelo caught Moses at the end of a violent movement whose traces are still evident. If this is so, why would the left hand be *gently* holding the beard? Moreover, given Freud's propensity to see sexual meanings, it is striking that he has almost nothing to say about Michelangelo's positioning of the left hand in Moses' lap above the groin, surely significant in an artist who was preoccupied by the male nude and who had homosexual tendencies (Liebert 1983, 115).

Let us pursue this matter of the neglected left hand a bit further. Freud was familiar with Fliess's theory of the connection between bisexuality and bilaterality. Fliess regarded left-handedness and the left side of the body as the locus of the feminine in men and believed that all left-handed people showed characteristics of the opposite sex. Although Freud was influenced by Fliess's notion of bisexuality, he questioned his friend's theory of left-handedness. In a series of letters to Fliess between 1897 and 1901, Freud indicated that he was testing the left hand of his own patients.[38] Fliess apparently also thought that Freud might be left-handed: Freud writes, "I had the impression, furthermore, that you considered me to be partially left-handed; if so, you would tell me, since there is nothing in this bit of self-knowledge that might hurt me. It is your doing if you do not know every intimate detail about me; you have surely known me long enough. Well, then, I am not aware of any preference for the left hand, either at present or in my childhood; rather I could say that years ago I had two left hands." While Freud denies his left-handedness in this letter, he does not disclaim his bisexuality, the apparent reason for Fliess's interest in the possibility of ambidextrousness in Freud. In a subsequent letter, however, Freud seems to confirm Fliess's assumption, describing a test he gives himself for left-handedness: "The button business, which has received my fullest recognition, stands out like an oasis in the desert. In the carriage I already convinced myself, by unbuttoning my clothes, that you were right." Jeffrey Masson comments that "Freud may mean that since he is able to unbutton his clothes with his left hand, he is latently left-handed and therefore, in Fliess's view, latently homosexual as well" (1985, 296 n. 3). It is also interesting to note that in an 1898 letter to Fliess, Freud refers to Leonardo da Vinci: "Leonardo—no love affair of his is known—is perhaps the most famous left-handed person. Can you use him?" Here, then, is a link between the theme of left-handedness and Freud's later essay on Leonardo's homosexuality, in which he writes that "Leonardo's physical beauty and his left-handedness might be quoted in support" of the view that both male and female dispositions are biologically operative (Freud 1910, 136). Given that Freud is still toying with this idea in 1910, it is significant that the left hand plays so little a role in his analysis of Moses two years later.

There is one final oversight in Freud's discussion of Michelangelo's *Moses* that bears some scrutiny. As Eva Krüll has pointed out (1986, 186–87), the *Moses* of Michelangelo may actually depict Moses after he has come down from the mountain a second time. This is suggested by the horns which Michelangelo sculpted on Moses' head. The assumption that Moses had horns after he descended a second time is based on what is commonly thought to be a mistranslation of a biblical passage in Exodus 34, an issue to which I will return in chapter 6. But Freud has nothing whatsoever to say about these horns. Even apart from the obvious question of their possible sexual significance, there is the fact that they appear after Moses has gone up the mountain and seen God. Once again Freud has avoided the issue of the father God's body.

To what extent does this denial of the male relationship with the father God reflect Freud's own avoidances of his father? Although much has been written on Freud's relationship with his father, the focus has tended to be on the competitive side of the Oedipus struggle and not on the possibility of a passive complex, that is, on Freud's wishes or fantasies for intimacy with his father. It is beyond the scope of this inquiry to explore this issue fully. But there are several things that may be indicative of Freud's feelings toward his father.

In his letters to Fliess, for example, Freud writes of what he calls his father's "perversion," by which he means his father's seduction of Freud's siblings, including his brother. On February 8, 1897, Freud writes that "unfortunately, my own father was one of these perverts and is responsible for the hysteria of my brother (all of whose symptoms are identification) and those of several younger sisters. The frequency of this circumstance often makes me wonder" (Masson 1985, 230–31). At this point Freud has not yet abandoned his seduction theory and is still convinced that behind hysteria lies a real seduction. Moreover, Freud only moves away from the seduction theory as he begins his own analysis and faces his own psychosexual conflicts (Krüll 1986, 56, 68ff.). In a letter to Fliess, Freud reports that among the reasons for changing his mind is the "surprise that in all cases, the *father*, not excluding my own, had to be accused of being perverse" (Masson 1985, 264; emphasis in original). From this, Freud develops his Oedipus theory, in which the child fantasizes his or her seduction. Did Freud's abandonment of the seduction theory correspond to having to face the possibility of *his own* seduction by his father, what he will later refer to as the inverted or passive Oedipus complex? There is no way of knowing. But in the same letter to Fliess in which he explains why he no longer believes the seduction theory is valid, Freud tells a joke in which he depicts himself as a naked woman. "A little story from my collection occurs to me: 'Rebecca, take off your gown, you are no longer a bride.' "[39] The overt meaning of the joke is that Freud, having now abandoned his seduction theory, has lost his opportunity for fame and hence is without his bridal gown. But given the associations of femininity and homoeroticism for Freud, this identification of himself with Rebecca is revealing of how he views himself in relation to his father. Krüll has suggested that this joke might allude to Rebekka, the mysterious second wife of Jakob Freud (1986, 136–37). If so, then Freud has placed himself in the role of his father's wife.

One of Freud's famous dreams following his father's death may also point to a similar theme. In his "You are requested to close the eyes" dream, Freud recounts a dream that occurred the night after his father's funeral.

> I found myself in a shop where there was a notice up saying "You are requested to close the eyes." I recognized the place as the barbers to which I go every day. On the day of the funeral I was kept waiting, and therefore arrived at the house of mourning rather late. The family were displeased with me, because I had arranged for the funeral to be quiet and simple, which they later agreed was the best thing. They also took my lateness in rather bad part. The phrase on the notice-board has double meaning. It means "one should do one's duty toward the dead" in two senses—an apology, as though I had not done my duty and my conduct needed overlooking, and the actual duty itself. The dream was thus an outlet for the feeling of self-reproach which a death generally leaves among the survivors. [40]

This dream has been extensively analyzed as reflecting oedipal struggles with Jakob Freud. But did Freud perhaps also understand this dream as reflecting his wish to avoid what he would later call inverted oedipal fantasies? Closing the eyes is like a prohibition against seeing the images of the father God. When we consider that in the Jewish observance of mourning, in the period between death and the funeral, the corpse undergoes a ritual cleansing, a *taharah*, Freud's dream can be interpreted as a wish not to see or imagine his father's naked body. It is not often the case that a family member performs the *taharah*, nor is it clear that this procedure was followed in the case of Jakob Freud. Still, Freud would have known about the ritual, and his dream could reflect his desire to close his eyes to his father's body. And what about his tardiness in the barbershop? Freud associated cutting the hair with castration and hence feminization (Freud 1910, 96). Why in his interpretation of this dream does he have nothing to say about going to the barber, an act that is forbidden by Jewish law during the period of mourning?

How Freud may have understood this dream is pure speculation. In the end it does not matter whether he actually had homoerotic feelings for his father. The important point is to see that Freud's writing about monotheism is characterized by the same repression I have suggested is operating in his religious tradition. Because he could not or would not think about why the image/body of the father God had to be veiled, Freud did not face the issue of the son's erotic desires for the father.

It is time, then, to return to *Moses and Monotheism* and to the prohibition on images. In light of the preceding analysis, Freud's understanding of this prohibition seems restrained. He argues that it represents an attainment of an intellectual and spiritual conception of God and an instinctual renunciation of human appetites. A concept of the deity without an image is a triumph over sensuality. It is this general renunciation that develops into sexual renunciation. Yet Freud himself is aware that the two types of renunciations are of a different order: "An advance in intellectuality consists in deciding against direct sense-perception in favour of what are known as the higher intellectual processes. . . . The rejection of a sexual or aggressive instinctual demand seems to be something quite different from this" (1939, 117–18). And again several pages later he acknowledges discrepancies in his argument:

The religion of Moses forced upon the people an advance in intellectuality/spirituality which, important enough in itself, opened the way, in addition, to the appreciation of intellectual work and to further renunciations of instinct. . . . This is what we have arrived at. And, though we do not wish to take back any of it, we cannot hide from ourselves that it is somehow or other unsatisfying. The cause does not, so to speak, match the effect; the fact that we want to explain seems to be of a different order of magnitude from everything by which we explain it. May it be that all the investigations we have so far made have not uncovered the whole of the motivation but only a certain superficial layer, and that behind it another very important factor awaits discovery: In view of the extraordinary complexity of all causation in life and history, something of the sort was to be expected. (123)

Freud then goes on to refer again to the repression and repetition of Moses' murder, as if this answers the question. But clearly he recognizes that there is a missing conceptual link in the shift from a prohibition on images to a sexual renunciation, a link his analysis does not reveal. If he had reflected at all on the connection between the prohibition on images and scopophilia (sexual pleasure in looking), which plays a profound role in his theory, he might have had to recognize that the prohibition against seeing the father's body leads to a renunciation of a desire for the father.

There is one other indication that Freud may have had in mind the homoeroticism between father and son while he was writing *Moses and Monotheism*. In developing his analogy between monotheism's emergence and his psychological concept of latency, Freud briefly reviews his theory of psychosexual development. He then pleads that since he cannot give a multitude of examples to back up his claims, he will cite but one case to illustrate the point. Significantly, it is a case that involves the passive oedipal complex of a boy who witnessed his parents in an act of sexual intercourse (ibid., 78–80). Initially the boy responded to the event with an aggressive masculinity, identifying with his father and making sexual overtures to his mother. This behavior continued until his mother forbade him to touch his penis and threatened to inform his father. This threat had a traumatic effect on the boy.

He gave up his sexual activity and altered his character. "Instead of identifying himself with his father, he was afraid of him, adopted a passive attitude to him and, by occasional naughtinesses, provoked him into administering corporal punishment; this had a sexual meaning for him, so that he was thus able to identify himself with his ill-treated mother." Although Freud does not make the connection explicit, the boy's renunciation of his sexuality is precisely what Freud claims occurs as the consequence of a prohibition on images in monotheism. Tellingly, the boy loses the sensitivity in his penis after assuming a passive role in relation to his father.

In conclusion, consider again Freud's claim that the prohibition on images was analogous to the discovery of paternity. Both, he suggests, were triumphs of the spirit or intellect over sensuality. The prohibition on images forced people to conceptualize rather than image God. Similarly, Freud believes paternity is based on reason and not the senses. In his view, the father of a child must be inferred, whereas the mother is always obvious. But in light of the foregoing, Freud's claim about paternity now sounds a lot like a wish. To construe paternity as spiritual is to imagine a father as a nonsexual being without a body. Yet Freud's entire Oedipus complex presupposes a boy's understanding of his father as a sexual being with a penis like his own. Indeed, the boy fears castration because he believes he poses a threat and competition to his father's sexual relationship with the mother.[41] Freud's linking of the prohibition on images to the discovery of paternity thus suggests that what is true of one is true of the other: he wishes to imagine both a human father and a divine father without an organ of reproduction.

PART II

God's Body: The Divine Cover-Up

The Drunkenness of Noah by Michelangelo. Sistine Chapel, Vatican.
Photograph from Alinari/Art Resource, New York.

Chapter Three

The Averted Gaze

After all the rest, as I have said, Moses tells us that man was created after the image of God and after His likeness (Gen. 1:26). Right well does he say this, for nothing earth-born is more like God than man. Let no one represent the likeness as one to a bodily form; for neither is God in human form, nor is the human body God-like. No, it is in respect of the Mind, the sovereign element of the soul, that the word "image" is used.

PHILO, On the Creation

The law of Moses . . . nowhere prescribed the belief that God is without a body, or even without form or figure, but only ordained that the Jews should believe in his existence and worship Him alone: it forbade them to invent or fashion any likeness of the Deity, but this was to insure purity of service; . . . Nevertheless, the Bible clearly implies that God has a form, and that Moses when he heard God speaking was permitted to behold it, or at least its hinder parts.

SPINOZA, A Theologico-Political Treatise

To ASK ABOUT THE anatomical sex of the Jewish God is to formulate a question that strikes most interpreters of Judaism as absurd. For, as we've seen, it is assumed that the Jewish God has no body. Raphael Patai is illustrative of how this ancient assumption has continued into the modern period. The God of the Jews, he writes, "being pure spirit . . . is without body, he possesses no physical attributes and hence no sexual traits. To say that God is either male or female is therefore completely impossible from the viewpoint of traditional Judaism" (1967, 21).

But in fact matters are much more complicated than this, for on a number of occasions various Israelites are said to have seen God. And in these "God sightings," or "theophanies," which is the more technical term for them, various Israelite leaders see the deity in what appears to be a human form. But it is a human form in which the sex of God is carefully obscured. The question of God's genitals was an extremely delicate one for ancient Jews, a question to which any answer would have been troubling and disconcerting. And it is in part an attempt to sidestep this question that explains why the divine body is so carefully veiled. This is an example of what I call a cultural avoidance, a desire to evade or perhaps even an inability to imagine a question because of the difficulties engendered by its answer.[1]

God Sightings

The literature of ancient Israel contains a number of reports in which someone sees God. In one early Israelite myth, for example, God

> said to Moses, "Come up to the Lord, with Aaron, Nadab, and Abihu, and seventy elders of Israel, and bow low from afar. Moses alone shall come near the Lord; but the others shall not come near, nor shall the people come up with him." . . .
>
> Then Moses, Aaron, Nadab, Abihu and seventy elders[2] of Israel ascended and they saw (*wayyirĕʾû*) the God of Israel: under His feet there was the likeness of a pavement of sapphire, like the very sky for purity; Yet he did not raise His hand against the leaders of the Israelites; they beheld (*wayyeḥĕzû*) God and they ate and drank. (Exod. 24:1–3, 9–11)

This myth, which most scholars attribute to an old Israelite tradition, contains "some of the most astonishing and inexplicable verses" of the

Hebrew Bible.[3] It is clearly the explicit sighting of God that is so surprising. But in addition, there are a number of textual and linguistic problems interpreters have puzzled over in attempts to locate this myth historically and make sense of it.[4] It is not at all clear, for example, whether the verses describing the sighting of God (9–11) belong to the same story as the earlier verses in which God tells Moses, Aaron, Nadab, and Abihu to come up to the Lord (1–2). In the first set of verses God directs Moses alone to come near the Lord, while the latter verses describe all of the leaders seeing God. Interrupting these two parts of the story is a sacrifice in which Moses sprinkles blood on the people (3–8). Many interpreters view both the sacrifice and the eating of a meal in the presence of God as two different accounts of how the covenant with God was ratified. It is also surprising that this myth includes Nadab and Abihu in the group that ascends the mountain. In later biblical sources, Nadab and Abihu are described as sons of Aaron, and hence of priestly lineage (Lev. 10:1 and Exod. 6:23). Moreover, they are the two sons of Aaron who die for offering a strange fire before the Lord (Lev. 10:1–3). Rabbinic commentaries blame their death on the fact that they gazed at God in an inappropriate manner. But these later references to the two may be an elaboration of the earlier myth. Interpreters have therefore debated whether Nadab and Abihu are interpolations intended to legitimate a priestly presence at this spectacular event or simply mythic figures whose significance is now lost. The pavement of sapphire which Moses and the elders see and the meal they eat in front of God have also perplexed readers. But about the key point of the myth, that leaders of Israel saw God, interpreters have little to say.[5]

In another early myth, Moses alone requests permission to see God. But here, God only permits Moses to gaze on him from behind. This incident occurs after the Israelites have worshiped the golden calf. In anger God declares, "If I were to go in your midst for one moment, I would destroy you." Moses is particularly worried about the implications of this declaration: "You have not made known to me whom You will send with me. Now if I have truly gained Your favor, pray let me know Your ways that I may know You and continue in Your favor." God promises, "I [literally, 'My face'] will go in the lead." Yet Moses still remains ill at ease: "Unless You go ['Your face goes'] in the lead, do not make us leave this place. For how would it be known that I have gained Your favor, I and your people?" Once more God reassures Moses that he does indeed have divine favor, at which point Moses unexpectedly says, "Oh let me behold Your Glory (Kavod)!" This request seems to have little to do with Moses' desired reassurances on behalf of the people (Childs 1974, 594). And God answers, "I will make all My goodness pass before you ['before your face'] as I proclaim the name Lord before you. . . . But you cannot see My face, for man may not see Me and live."

> And the Lord said, "See, there is a place near Me. Station yourself on the rock and, as My presence (Kavod) passes by, I will put you in a cleft of the rock and shield you with My hand until I have passed by. Then I will take My hand away and you will see My back; but My face must not be seen." (Exod. 33:21–23)

This myth seems to represent a different set of assumptions than the previous myth, which implies that Moses and other Israelite leaders see the deity from the front. Here God says that no one may see the divine face and live. Moreover, the myth in which Moses sees God's back may belong to an older tradition embedded here in the larger story about Moses asking for divine reassurance on behalf of the people (Childs 1974, 596; Noth 1962, 257).

Various prophets are also reported to have sighted the deity in dreams or visions. The prophet Amos sees God standing by the altar (Amos 9:1); Job sees God at the end of his long ordeal (Job 42:5); and the prophets Micaiah (1 Kings 22:19), Isaiah (Isa. 6:1–2), Ezekiel (Ezek. 1:26–28), and Daniel (Dan. 7:9–11) see God seated on a throne. The visual content of these God sightings either is not reported at all (Amos, 1 Kings, Job) or is reported in an apparently censored version (Isaiah, Exodus 24). But enough information is conveyed to make it clear that the deity is imagined in human form. Isaiah, for example, sees that "the skirts of His robe filled the Temple. Seraphs stood in attendance on Him. Each of them had six wings; with two it covered its face, with two it covered its legs and with two it would fly." Ezekiel and Daniel are the most explicit about what they have seen. Ezekiel reports that when the heavens opened, he saw four creatures of strange configuration. For twenty-five verses, he describes these creatures, and then in what is undoubtedly the climax of the passage, he describes what he saw above them:

> Above the expanse over their heads was the semblance of a throne, in appearance like sapphire; and on top, upon this semblance of a throne, there was the semblance of a human form. From what appeared as his loins up, I saw a gleam as of amber—what looked like fire encased in a frame;[6] and from what appeared as his loins down, I saw what looked like fire. There was a radiance all about him. Like the appearance of the bow which shines in the clouds on a day of rain, such was the appearance of the semblance of the Presence of the Lord. When I beheld it, I flung myself down on my face. And I heard the voice of someone speaking. (Ezek. 1:26–28)

A similar scene appears to Daniel in a dream, an image influenced by the earlier visions of Isaiah and Ezekiel. Daniel first sees four beasts and then the figure of the deity:

> Thrones were set in place, and the Ancient of Days took His seat. His garment was like white snow, and the hair of His head was like lamb's [or clean] wool. His throne was tongues of flame; its wheels were blazing fire. A river of fire streamed forth before Him; thousands upon thousands served Him; myriads upon myriads served him; the court sat and the books were opened. (Daniel 7:9–10)

As we shall see, such dreams, visions, and sightings of God are reported as well in the apocalyptic, merkavah, and rabbinic literatures, which developed along with and after the biblical literature.

All of the myths involving God sightings exhibit a discomfort about describing the deity's image. In most God sightings, such as those of Amos, Job, and Micaiah, the deity is not described at all or very little content of the vision is reported. When Moses and the elders go to the top of the mountain, the narrator describes only what is under God's feet. When Ezekiel describes God on the chariot, he couches his description in repeated qualifications that show a discomfort with describing God as a human figure: "such was the appearance of the semblance of the Presence of the Lord." And Daniel's sighting of God, although showing no explicit ambivalence, occurs in a dream, possibly a less direct medium of experience.

It is the nature of this ambivalence that has been subject to alternative interpretations. What does this veiling of the divine body mean?

Making Sense of God's Body

Those favoring a metaphoric interpretation construe references to God's form as a special kind of religious language that is to be taken figuratively. The descriptions of the deity are just metaphors, or literary tropes. Interpreters thus point out how Israelites used various metaphors to talk about God. God is described as "a lion" (Hos. 13:8), "a rock" (Deut. 32:4, 15, 18, 30, 31), and "a mother bear" (Hos. 13:8), among other things. Their argument is that Israelites did not actually think of God in human form, but simply used the human body, as they did rocks and lions, to conceptualize the deity. No one would say that Israelites actually thought God was a lion, rock, or mother bear, this reasoning goes, so why make the assumption that they actually thought of God in human form? For example, when God leads the children out of Egypt with "a strong arm" (Exod. 3:19–20, 13:9) the reference is to the power of the deity, which is symbolized by the outstretched arm. Mettinger puts it this way: "We must make a distinction that is hard to express in English terminology: the distinction between *the mental concept* of God . . . and *the express form* in which this concept is communicated in texts. . . . When the Old Testament texts mention God's 'hands' or 'eyes,' we designate this as an anthropomorphic (i.e., human-like) representation. However, such representations may be symbolic adumbrations of a *Gottesvorstellung* (mental concept) that is much more sophisticated than this" (1978, 204–5).[7] In other words, the metaphor is just a vehicle for a more sophisticated conception and hence does not indicate how Israelites actually imagined God. God's appearance and essence is in fact beyond human description and comprehension. The references to the deity's body parts are used figuratively to conceptualize what otherwise cannot be communicated.

This line of interpretation, however, may be anachronistic, particularly in dealing with the earliest myths in which the Israelite leaders see God. A vast historical distance exists between ancient Jews and interpreters of modern sensibilities, making it impossible to say whether Israelites and ancient Jews had symbolic understandings of these myths. Specifically, the metaphoric interpretation does not allow for the possibility that Israelites could actually have believed God had or appeared in human form. For these reasons, some interpreters prefer a literal reading. They argue that many Israelites and Jews believed God actually had a body. The restraint in describing God stems not from a desire to avoid anthropomorphisms, as the advocates of the metaphoric interpretation suggest, but from the acknowledgment of God's transcendence or otherness (Barr 1959). Awe and fear of the deity underlie the hesitation about describing God's form.

> It is stated a few times that no man can look upon God (Exod. 33:20; Judg. 13:22); but this does not mean that God has no form, but rather that his divinity is so terrible that whoever sees him cannot remain alive. . . . Even if a few anthropomorphic expressions are to be understood metaphorically, the fact remains that God is often described in human terms and that the most distinct anthropomorphisms are found in the earliest strata of the Old Testament. Nevertheless, the universal prohibition on images (Exod. 20:4) places the strictest possible limitations upon anthropomorphism. . . . This prohibition expresses plainly the transcendence of God to a degree not found in any of the other ancient religions. (Ringgren 1966, 69–70)

If the metaphorical and literalist strategies of interpretation define the ends of a spectrum, the developmental perspective falls somewhere in between and attempts to reconcile them. Like literalists, developmentalists admit that the earliest biblical sources reflect primitive or naïve notions of a God in human form.[8] These early accounts are said to indicate that ancient Israelites initially believed God had a body, but naïve conceptions of God were eventually outgrown as the Israelite religion developed. According to this view, Israelites repudiated gross anthropomorphisms over time and gradually came to think of God as an invisible and formless being. This more sophisticated conception arose as a natural consequence of Jews reflecting on the idea of God. Some interpreters argue that the beginnings of this intellectual development are already evident in passages that represent God anthropomorphically.[9] According to the developmental view, even the earliest sources exhibit an inchoate discomfort with anthropomorphism that would later intensify.

Not all those who favor a developmentalist interpretation understand it as an organic process of spiritualization. Although some view these changes as connected to a developing emphasis on God's transcendence, others, such as Mettinger, see them as the result of the profound cognitive dissonance brought about by the Temple's destruction and the Babylonian exile in the early sixth century B.C.E.[10] Whereas previously, Israelite theology could imagine God enthroned on the ark above the cherubim, such images became incomprehensible after the Temple had been desecrated and Israel exiled.[11] Postexilic writers therefore articulated a theology in which God's presence was no longer tied to one location.

Each of these interpretations can account for the ambivalence about sighting God and each has evidence to support it. The question, then, in interpreting myth, is how can one know when a face is just a face?

When Is a Face Just a Face?

Those who adopt the metaphoric interpretation point to the explicit way in which God's body is used as a literary device. For example, in the myth in which Moses sees God's back, God promises Moses, "My face will go before you," an expression which obviously means that

God will lead the Israelites. In this case, the face of God functions as a synecdoche for God's whole being. In other passages as well, the face of God is a metaphor for divine presence. Thus "seeing God's face" or "appearing before God's face" means visiting the sanctuary (Exod. 23:15, 17, 34:23; Deut. 16:16, 31:11; Isa. 1:12; Ps. 42:3).[12] Similarly, when one turns to God in a time of trouble one seeks the "face of God" (Ps. 24:6; 2 Sam. 21:1; Ps. 27:8, 105:4). When God ceases to attend to the human world, the divine face is hidden (Deut. 31:17; Isa. 8:17, 64:6; Ps. 10:11). Since the face of God is clearly a metaphor in these other contexts, there is no reason to take it literally in the God-sighting passages either. When God tells Moses that no one can see the divine face and live, the point is that no one may see the divine *presence*. The myth underscores this point when God tells Moses that he will see the divine glory. The term for "glory" (*kavod*), or "presence," as many interpreters translate it, is a way of evoking God's closeness without ascribing to God a specific form. The face, back, and even the hand of the deity's presence are merely metaphors to describe the indescribable:

> There is the unequivocal affirmation in the early epic traditions that Moses spoke to God "face to face" (Exod. 33:11; Deut. 34:10) and "mouth to mouth" (Num. 12:8) and that he beheld "the likeness of the Lord" (Num. 12:8). Nonetheless, this anthropomorphic language must be discounted as hyperbole. The "face" of the Deity must refer to His Presence rather than His form, since "you cannot see My face, for man may not see Me and live" (Exod. 33:20; cf. Judg. 6:22f, 13:22), a view that Israel shares with its Canaanite neighbors (e.g., UT 2 Aqht 2.45). (Milgrom 1990, 365)[13]

Interpreting the references to God's body metaphorically also helps account for what otherwise would be glaring contradictions between narratives. According to one passage, Moses went into the tent of meeting and "the Lord would speak to Moses, face to face, as one man speaks to another" (Exod. 33:11). If taken literally, this statement obviously negates the claim that Moses may not see God's face and live, which appears only nine verses later (Exod. 33:20). It is only by con-struing the first statement metaphorically, as saying that God spoke to Moses in an unmediated manner or as one equal to another, that the two descriptions can be reconciled. Thus the textual clarification that Moses and God spoke "as one man speaks to another" itself signals a figurative reading of the phrase "face to face."[14] It could be, of course, that these two statements derive from different traditions and simply contradict one another. Nonetheless, at some point the two state-ments (Exod. 33:11, 33:20) were joined together, and what may have enabled them to be joined, and perhaps even have motivated their coming together, was the possibility of construing God's face meta-phorically.

The story of Moses, Aaron, Nadab, and Abihu's ascent to the top of the mountain is the most difficult for interpreters favoring a meta-phorical interpretation. Even in this case, however, some interpreters insist that an actual sighting of the deity is *not* involved. The Septua-gint, the translation of the Hebrew Bible for the Greek-speaking world, already softens the anthropomorphic implications of this myth. Instead of "they saw the God of Israel," the Septuagint has "they saw the place where the God of Israel stood." And instead of "they beheld God," the Septuagint has "they appeared in the place of God." The Septuagint also translates "Yet He did not raise his hand against the leaders of the Israelites" as "nobody was missing."[15] In this way, both the sighting and anthropomorphisms are removed. Mai-monides, for his part, argues thus: "Know that the three words *to see* [ra'oh], *to look at* [habbit], and *to vision* [hazoh] are applied to the sight of the eye and that all three of them are also used figuratively to denote the grasp of intellect. . . . Every *mention of seeing*, when referring to God, may He be exalted, has this figurative meaning—as when Scrip-ture says: *I saw the Lord* (1 Kgs. 22:19); . . . *I beseech thee, let me see Thy Glory* (Exod. 33:18); *And they saw the God of Israel* (Exod. 24:10)."[16] Modern readings also propose emendations to the words for seeing. Some read the word for seeing in verse 10 (from the stem r'h) as mean-ing "they feared" (from the stem yr'). And the second word for seeing (hazah) in verse 14 is interpreted by some in terms of an Arabic cognate (*hada*) to mean "stay before," that is, "in the presence of." What motivates these modern emendations is the assumption, based on the other myths involving God sightings, that the deity cannot be seen. Clearly modern ambivalence about seeing God is here projected onto the ancient myths.[17]

The myth in Exodus actually lends itself more readily to a literal reading. Indeed, the myth goes out of its way to emphasize that the Israelite leaders saw God, repeating the idea two times. It is often on the basis of this myth in particular that literal and developmental interpreters take their stand. Literalists see here evidence of an embodied notion of the deity that persisted throughout Israelite religion. Developmentalists argue that this embodied view of God eventually gave way to a more spiritualized image. Nicholson, for example, writes that "it could not of course be expected that the statement that the representatives of Israel saw God would pose the same problem for modern commentators as it did for ancient translators and exegetes. But it may be claimed that modern commentators have either failed to see or at best have underestimated the significance of this feature of Exodus xxiv 9–11. Yet it is surely the most emphasized aspect of the passage as a whole" (1974, 91). Even some of the most ardent supporters of the metaphorical interpretation give in on this one. After dismissing all the other visions as ecstatic experiences or as lacking "sensorial perception of their bodily eyes," Terrien admits, "In this narrative, on the contrary, the setting is topographically concrete, the human witnesses are many, and the visual perception of the Godhead, twice affirmed (vss. 10 and 11), is made even more explicitly sensorial by its sequential climax 'they ate and drank'" (1978, 135).

It is true that the narrator of this myth averts the gaze by describing only the sapphire pavement on which the deity stands, but this may be an act of censorship on the narrator's part. The myth suggests that the Israelite leaders themselves were permitted to see the deity directly and from the front; but their privilege is not shared with the listeners or readers in the way that Ezekiel's vision is.[18] Instead, the eyes are directed to what is under the deity's feet. Interpreters understand the sapphire pavement as a representation of the heavens or a reference to the ark upon which the divine presence rested in the sanctuaries.[19] As mentioned earlier, most interpreters construe the eating and drinking that takes place on the mountain as a covenantal meal, although it might also be understood as a joyous celebration of the sighting of God.[20]

Embodied meanings of images cannot be easily dismissed even from passages that seem obviously metaphorical. Consider again the story in which Moses sees God's back. If "face" means "presence," then what does "back" mean and what did Moses see when he saw God's back? If it means "absence," then how can Moses *see* an absence? Not one commentary I consulted notes that the word "backside" is in fact used elsewhere to describe the backsides of both oxen and men. In the description of the Temple built by Solomon, for example, there is an image of a molten sea supported by twelve oxen, "Three looking toward the north, and three looking toward the west, and three looking toward the south, and three looking toward the east; and the sea was set upon them above, and all their hinder parts (*'ăḥōrêhem*) were inward" (1 Kings 7:25). In Ezekiel, the same term is used regarding men: "And He brought me into the inner court of the Lord's house, and, behold, at the door of the temple of the Lord, between the porch and the altar, were about five and twenty men, with their backs (*'ăḥōrêhem*) toward the temple of the Lord, and their faces toward the east; and they worshipped the sun toward the east" (Ezek. 8:16). Clearly, the term "backside" applied to God is used in a very concrete sense to refer to the human body. Furthermore, the fact that "face" stands for God's whole being ("My face will go before you") does not preclude the deity's having an embodied form. Indeed, the very same expression is used to describe a human military leader who leads his troops into battle (2 Sam. 17:11). Indeed, God's hiding the divine face from Moses is reminiscent of Pharaoh's charge to Moses: "Be gone from me! Take care not to see me again, for the moment you look upon my face you shall die" (Exod. 10:28). A literal face can be hidden as well as a metaphorical one.

The doubts about whether Israelites actually saw the face of God cannot be put to rest. There is a teasing uncertainty about this image, an uncertainty that may be another symptom of the ambivalence interpreters have detected. Perhaps the sources wish to create a doubt about whether God has a face and whether it has been sighted. This confusion is itself a veil, one that entraps modern readers in the myths' own questions and diverts their attention from other questions that should not be asked.

Consider, for example, the fact that Moses and God are said to have spoken "mouth to mouth" (Numbers 12). God is the one who describes the relationship this way. What prompts the deity to do so is the challenge to Moses by his siblings, Miriam and Aaron. The story begins with the report that Miriam and Aaron are angered because Moses has married a Cushite woman. The precise nature of their worry is not clear, but their anger leads them to question Moses' authority: "Has the Lord spoken only through Moses? Has He not spoken through us as well?" Upon hearing this challenge, God calls Moses, Aaron, and Miriam to the tent of meeting and descends there in a pillar of cloud. To Aaron and Miriam God declares:

> Hear these My words: To a prophet among you, I the Lord make Myself known through a vision (*marĕʾāh*), I speak to such a one in a dream. Not so with My servant Moses; he is trusted throughout My household. With him I speak mouth to mouth, plainly and not in riddles and he beholds the likeness of the Lord. (Num. 12:6–8)

Like "face to face," "mouth to mouth" lends itself to a metaphorical interpretation, suggesting God spoke to Moses "in an unmediated manner." The point seems to be that God speaks to Moses more directly than to other prophets, who are addressed through visions or dreams.

Yet the incident with Miriam and Aaron undercuts this reading precisely as it makes it possible. If the purpose of this story is to explain why Moses has more authority than his brother or sister, then God should only speak to them in visions or dreams. Yet God calls Miriam, Aaron, and Moses and speaks to all of them directly. The passage thus requires a different understanding of Moses' authority. The claim that

Moses "beholds the likeness of God" thus becomes pivotal. Moses is differentiated from other prophets not just because God speaks to him directly, but because Moses is permitted to gaze upon the deity. And if seeing God is what distinguishes Moses, then a more embodied reading of "mouth to mouth" rises to the surface. In short, Moses is distinguished from other prophets by seeing God when God speaks.

Possible support for such an interpretation comes from the story of Jacob fighting with "a man" of divine origin (Gen. 32:25–33).[21] At the end of this story, Jacob calls the place Peniel, meaning "face of God," and declares that he has seen the face of this being and lived to tell about it. In this case, seeing the face is no metaphor. Jacob has not only seen but actually touched this being and has a permanent injury lest he come to doubt the reality of the incident. His experience is confirmed in his reunion with Esau after a twenty years' absence in Paddan-Aram. In a touching scene, the brothers meet and embrace. When Esau declines his brother's offer of gifts, Jacob responds, "No, I pray you; if you would do me this favor, accept from me this gift; for to see your face is like seeing the face of God (*Elohim*), and you have received me favorably." Seeing his brother's face after all this time is as miraculous (and perhaps as frightening) as seeing the face of God.

It does not seem accidental, however, that as soon as doubt about the existence of a divine face has been set aside, an equivocation of another sort emerges in its place. Specifically, it is not at all clear whose face Jacob has actually seen. Has Jacob struggled with a divine being or with God? The ambiguity has shifted from the reality of the face to the nature of the being whose face has been sighted. Yet the effects of the ambiguity are the same: it is no longer certain whether Jacob has seen the face of God.[22]

Uncertainties are thus part of the very fabric of these ancient narratives. The inherent ambiguity of the sources makes it impossible to know when the body of God is meant to evoke an image and when it is the vehicle for an idea. It is as if the closer we get to God's face, the less certain we are that it is God we are seeing.

It is important, then, not to dismiss the ambiguities, contradictions, and doubts. Although they may originally arise from the juxtaposition of conflicting traditions, read in a single narrative they serve certain cultural purposes. Doubts about which words are to be construed as metaphor and which are meant to be taken literally create a veil of language which keeps the deity's figure in the dark. The myths themselves seem to entrap readers or listeners in a labyrinth of questions from which there is no escape.

A Way out of the Framework

On the question of God's body, the three strategies of interpretation—the metaphoric, the literal, and the developmental—have tended to determine the bounds of the inquiry. Other answers are not possible until other questions are imaginable. And one of the questions that the governing framework has made unthinkable is the nature of the deity's sex.

This is most obvious of the metaphoric interpretation, which has generally been the dominant mode of understanding references to God's body. Having in effect done away with the deity's body as an issue, the very thought of divine genitals is unintelligible. But those who interpret ancient Jewish sources metaphorically are importing what were originally Greek ideas into their reading. Specifically, they are assuming that Israelites and Jews shared the Greek philosophical commitment to an incorporeal God.

It is not difficult to understand how this conflation of Jewish and Greek history came about. Jews and Greeks were themselves involved in a process of Hellenizing Jewish culture from the third century c.e. onward. Judaism was repackaged in a way that made Jewish beliefs and practices palatable to both Jews and non-Jews in a Hellenized world. For example, dietary restrictions, which never before had been given an explicit rationale, were now seen as embodying moral values.[23] The appeal and power of Greek culture led many Jews to adopt the idea of a disembodied God. For example, in the earliest Greek account of Jewish history, Hecataeus of Abdera (c. 300 b.c.e.) explained that Moses "did not fabricate any image of the gods because he believed that god was not anthropomorphic; rather the heaven which encompassed the earth was the only god and lord of all" (Gager 1972, 26–27; Stern 1974, 28). Eventually philosophers such as Philo and Maimonides systematically read Jewish tradition in light of Plato and Aristotle, a reading so powerful that it continues to find devotees among modern interpreters. But the question is whether Jews discovered these ideas independently, as Greeks and many Jews came to believe, or whether these ideas were imposed upon earlier sources, thereby distorting our understanding of them. Many interpreters assume that even prior to contact with Hellenistic civilization Jews developed certain religious conceptions analogous to those of the Greek philosophers. In particular, Jews, like the Greeks, rejected polytheism as well as the belief in embodied deities. The evidence cited for this Jewish discovery are those sources that are said to exhibit ambivalence about God's body.

But this argument is implausible from the outset. The Greeks left an explicit record of their growing intellectual discomfort with their mythology and its images of the gods. There is no evidence that the ancient Israelites produced any explicit philosophical writings challenging the idea of gods in human form. All the evidence in the case of Israel is indirect, from narratives whose meaning is open to question. One cannot assume, therefore, that the process whereby Israelites came to reject the mythologies of other ancient Near Eastern peoples proceeded in the same way and with the same sorts of concerns that shaped the revolution in Greece. In many analyses of ancient Israel, there is an assumption of a gradual, natural, and somewhat intuitive discovery of the philosophical or religious problems of thinking about God as an embodied being, but this assumption must be questioned. Embedded in this depiction of Israel's "natural philosophy" is a chauvinism that makes Israel inherently more philosophical than other peoples.[24]

This argument from plausibility, of course, does not by itself undermine the standard interpretations of Israelite religion or ancient Judaism. But it does begin to chip away at an edifice that has otherwise seemed immovable. And it creates the possibility of seeking other ways to explain the ambivalence about seeing the deity's figure. How might we read these ancient Jewish sources if we remove the Greek lenses through which their interpretations have often been refracted?

Asking whether Jews really believed God had a body is not in the end a very productive question.[25] It leads down a road that has already been much traveled and whose alleys and detours are already well explored. But even more problematic, as we've seen, the sources themselves are evasive about when references to God's form are to be taken literally or not. As I've suggested, that is one of the ways these sources successfully divert attention from a deeper question that cannot be imagined. What I wish to do, then, is refuse the age-old question of whether these images are literal or metaphorical. In setting this question aside, we can gain a new ground and formulate a new set of questions.

The question I want to ask is not whether Jews really believed God had a body but why, when they imagined God in a human form, that form was so carefully veiled and why it was veiled in the particular way it was. This question remains relevant whether the images are taken literally or figuratively. In other words, it shifts the focus of discussion away from the nature of the belief to the use of the images. How are images of the body employed to represent God and what kinds of limitations are imposed on their use?

To frame the question this way draws immediate attention to the fact that the human body is the preferred image for picturing what it is like to see God. It is important to dwell on this point for a moment. To say the body is simply a metaphor like "God the lion" or "God the rock" is to fail to take seriously the distinctive context in which images of the body are used. The ancient Judaic sources after all have special significance. They depict the exceptional cases of religious leaders who were privileged to see God. Whether the writers or readers actually believed God had a body is really not very important. The point is that when they described seeing God, they evoked a human form. The image of the human body is thus of a different order than other metaphors that are used to refer to God. The comparison of God to a lion does not conjure up the image of a lion because this image is not used in contexts that describe God sightings.[26] But when Moses is said to have seen the divine back, and Isaiah the divine robes, and Ezekiel the divine figure, the sources evoke a human image. The human body, then, is the privileged image for imagining what it might be like to gaze on the deity.

Moreover, visual images used in contexts in which a character in the narrative or myth is said to have seen something invite the reader or listener to take up the perspective of the character who sees. Thus, while the image of God as a lion who preys on Israel's enemies conveys an idea of God's strength and ferociousness, the description of Moses *seeing* God's back invites us to picture a human figure striding past.

God's Body and Other Private Matters

There is no doubt that the sighting of God, as well as other divine beings, was imagined to be a fearful and dangerous experience. This sense of danger of course was a consequence of an encounter with the transcendent Other or the realm of the sacred.[27] Presumably, the fear engendered by a sighting of God was also inspired by the simple fact that it was regarded as an extraordinary occurrence (Janowitz 1992). Yet these factors do not seem to explain why the sighting of certain parts of God's figure were considered more dangerous than others. If the problem is sacrality or the experience of the nonordinary, then any part of the divine figure should pose the same danger. Why may the gaze fall on the feet and back and not the front or face?

Some of the later sources, which imagine God as a figure seated on a throne, provide a partial explanation. Seeing God is like seeing the king, a privilege granted only under special circumstances.[28] It would be an affront to stare into the king's face. Lowering the eyes or bowing in obeisance, the gaze falls on the deity's feet. These actions signify a lack of parity between God and humans as well as an ultimate barrier to divine and human intimacy. One can never look on God's face the way one human does with another. Indeed, there are many biblical stories of figures who bow or prostrate themselves in respect or fear of another person (2 Sam. 9:6; 1 Kings 1:23; Isa. 45:23; Ps. 95:6), and the failure to bow sometimes signifies a serious insult (Esther 3:1–6). Israelite literature also imagines many religious figures falling on their faces when God appears: "Exalt the Lord our God and bow down to His footstool. He is Holy" (Ps. 99:5).

It thus seems self-evident that the aversion of the gaze from the deity's face (Exodus 33) and to the feet (Exodus 24) is an act of deference.[29] But other cultural meanings may be at work in this same set of distinctions. As I've argued elsewhere, culture is a palimpsest of meanings, in which one layer can be superimposed on another. Myths and rituals are powerful precisely because they contain a variety of messages simultaneously (Eilberg-Schwartz 1990, 119–40).

The aversion of the gaze, I've suggested, also reflects an ambivalence about God's sex. Specifically, the gaze is averted from precisely those parts of the deity's body that play a critical role in our judgments about a human figure's sex, namely, the front and face. Because these parts of the deity's body are veiled, it is as if the whole question of this being's sex posed a fundamental danger that could not be faced. Furthermore, the turning of the divine figure and the diversion of the gaze from the midsection to the feet may represent an act of modesty, both on the part of the deity who turns away and on the part of the Israelites who avert their eyes.

This is not to say that the divine genitals would actually have been exposed if God had not turned away or their gaze not been diverted. In Israelite imagination, God was presumably clothed, as is suggested by the robes in the theophany of Isaiah. But the turning of the back, whether or not the being is clothed, symbolically represents a hiding of the very spot by which sexual identification can be confirmed. This interpretation makes the most sense of the fact that the deity is represented as turning away from Moses. Surely there are easier ways to hide the face than by turning the whole body around? Might God's elaborate choreography also hide something else? In fact, the text itself not only allows but actually encourages this understanding. The word that is rendered as "my face" (*pānāy*) is more equivocal than translations suggest. *Pānāy* can also mean "my front side."[30] When God says to Moses, "I will take My hand away and you will see My back (*'āḥōrāy*);

but *Pānāy* must not be seen," it is certainly plausible to understand the deity to be presenting the backside in order to hide the divine front side. Indeed, Ezekiel, who has a direct frontal view of the deity, rivets his gaze on God's loins. His description proceeds from the loins up and the loins down, rather than from one end to another, as if his eyesight is irresistibly drawn back to the midsection of the deity's body. If Ezekiel's description is any indication of what more circumspect texts dared not imagine, it is the deity's midsection that is most prominent on a frontal view. The erotic overtones of this vision played an important role in esoteric doctrine in early rabbinic mysticism, as I discuss in chapter 7.

The hiding of the face can be understood to serve a double purpose. On the one hand, it is itself a veiling of God's sex, since the face is one of the key places in which sexual identity can be displayed. It is thus significant that in none of the God sightings, even those that are most detailed about the divine figure, is God explicitly represented with a long flowing beard, even though we learn the color of the hair on the deity's head (Dan. 7:9). We have no indication, then, that God has facial hair, a common characteristic of males in general and in the ancient Near East in particular. The Canaanite god El, who is so similar to Yahweh, is normally described and represented in art with a long flowing beard (Cross 1973, 16, 35), so it is curious that Yahweh's face cannot be seen and no mention is made of a beard.

At the same time, the hiding of the face is also a diversion. That is, the whole question of God's genitals has been deflected to the extremities of the body and replayed there. This helps explain the ambivalence about whether God's face was ever seen. The diversion of the gaze to the feet reflects an analogous process. The feet also draw attention away from the deity's midsection. Moreover, the term "feet" is an occasional euphemism for penis (Isa. 7:20; Ruth 3:7; possibly Exod. 4:25). And covering the feet is apparently a euphemism for urination (Judg. 3:24; 1 Sam. 24:4).[31] Lest I be misunderstood, I am not suggesting that the reference to the divine "feet" is meant euphemistically in this particular myth, although it comes to have this meaning in later sources. But it does provide evidence from ancient Israel of how the desire to avoid referring to the penis is deflected onto the body's extremities.[32]

Thus far I have suggested an alternative way of thinking about the cover-up of God's body. It is impossible to prove that this interpretation is true. On the other hand, it meets as many of the criteria for a plausible interpretation as the alternatives: it accounts for the same range of evidence and rests on defensible assumptions about the nature of myth and religious symbols. But this alone is not enough. It must also account for other kinds of evidence within the Hebrew Bible, linking up with and offering insight into other issues in the understanding of Israelite religion and ancient Judaism. At this point, my alternative interpretation remains to be made plausible through a cumulation of evidence in the next chapter, but for now, let me conclude by pointing to an interesting instance of how the ancient avoidance of God's body is evident in a modern book of children's biblical stories that I bought for my daughter.[33]

Does God Have a Big Toe, by Marc Gellman, is a series of imaginative interpretations of biblical myths designed to bring the Hebrew Bible alive for young Jewish children. Of particular interest is the chapter "Does God Have a Big Toe," which is a retelling of the Tower of Babel story. In this retelling, all people lived in one place and spoke one language until a little girl named Arinna asked her mother a difficult question: "Mommy, I have a big toe, and you have a big toe, and Daddy has a big toe. Does God have a big toe?" (1989, 43). According to the story, everything would have been fine and dandy had Arinna's mother explained that "God is not a person. God is special and invisible and wonderful and God is the creator of the universe. God has made each of us in God's image. But God is not a person. And that is why God does not have a big toe." But Arinna's mother was too busy to answer and told Arinna to ask her father. Arinna's question goes unanswered by both her father and grandfather. Finally, a family friend directs Arinna's question to the king. The king takes the question seriously and decides to build a tower to heaven to find the answer. God intervenes by changing people's languages and dispersing them so the tower cannot be built. The story ends with Arinna and her family leaving Babel as part of the dispersal. While riding on a cart, Arinna formulates a new question, and it is with this question that the story ends: "Mommy, I have a belly button, and you have a belly button, and Daddy has a belly button. Does God have a belly button too?"

One could not hope to find a more perfect reiteration of the dynamics encountered in the Israelite myths. The idea that God has a body naturally leads a child to ask about the nature of that body. The question is made trivial by being placed in the mouth of a child. Yet this childish curiosity about God's body has dire consequences for humanity and leads directly to the dissolution of the original human unity. Everything would have been fine had the childish curiosity been satisfied with the right answer, with the claim that God is not a person and therefore does not have a big toe. It is significant, too, that the big toe is the focus. As in the case of Moses and the elders, a diversion is at work, as if the real question cannot yet be fully imagined. Questions about the big toe are safe since Mommies and Daddies both have big toes. That other questions lurk in the child's mind is evident by the final question about God's belly button, a question that, like the gaze of Ezekiel, is fixed considerably closer to the genitals. The child is only curious, as any child might be, exploring each part of her body and wondering if God has one too. It is surely only a matter of time before the question of the genitals comes to mind and puts in doubt the assurance that all of us are made in the image of God.

Chapter Four

Indecent Exposures

*Noah, the tiller of soil, was the first to plant a vine-
yard. He drank of the wine and became drunk,
and he uncovered himself within his tent. Ham,
the father of Canaan, saw his father's nakedness
and told his two brothers outside. But Shem and
Japheth took a cloth, placed it against both their
backs and walking backwards, they covered their
father's nakedness; their faces were turned the
other way, so that they did not see their father's nakedness. When Noah woke up from his wine and
learned what his youngest son had done to him, he
said, "Cursed be Canaan; the lowest of the slaves
shall he be to his brothers." And he said, "Blessed
be the Lord, the God of Shem; let Canaan be a
slave to them."* Genesis 9:20–25

In the myth that serves as epigraph to this chapter, the waters of
the flood have subsided, and Noah, his wife, children, and their
spouses have left the ark. Noah plants a vineyard and becomes drunk;
during his drunken stupor, he lies naked in his tent. When Ham reports what he has seen to his virtuous brothers, they turn their backs
and avert their gaze. This myth has many striking similarities with the
story in which God turns his back to Moses (Exod. 33:12ff.).[1] God
turns away so that Moses will not see what should not be exposed, just
as Shem and Japheth walk backwards to avoid seeing their father's genitals.

The myth of Noah's exposure is crucial in making sense of why God's body must be veiled, but before investigating its parallels with the Exodus myth, let me clarify my grounds for comparing them. Some would say that simply because both stories are part of the biblical text they can be used to interpret one another. And there is some truth in this position, since whatever the origins of these sources, they are now part of one literary whole. But a historical sensitivity requires additional grounds for the comparison. It is in fact unclear whether these two myths originally derive from a common source. There is general consensus that the Noah myth is from the J source, a written or oral tradition developing between the tenth century and the late eighth century B.C.E. in Judah, the southern kingdom of Israel's divided monarchy. There is less certainty about the myth of God turning the divine back on Moses. Some source critics view this myth as deriving from the J source as well. Others regard it as belonging to the E source, a tradition from the northern kingdom of Israel between 922 and 722.[2]

Is there justification for linking these two myths, even if they do derive from different literary or oral traditions? I believe there is, for other biblical sources associate the loss of the father's honor with the exposure of his nakedness, suggesting that this idea was not limited to one writer or tradition in ancient Israel. In fact, the father's nakedness becomes a metaphor for other acts that dishonor the father. In the Holiness Code (Lev. 17:1–26:46), for instance, incest with one's mother is several times described as uncovering the father's nakedness (Lev. 18:7–8, 20:11) in language reminiscent of the Noah incident: "Your father's nakedness, [that is,] the nakedness of your mother, you shall not uncover; she is your mother—you shall not uncover her nakedness." The prophet Ezekiel (22:10) also refers to the sin of "uncovering one's father's nakedness," when speaking of incest between a son and his mother.[3]

It is clear, moreover, that in the Holiness Code "uncovering the father's nakedness" is not a euphemism. It does not replace but supplements and therefore interprets the phrase "uncovering the mother's nakedness." Why would incest between a son and his mother be described as "uncovering his father's nakedness"? Interpreters tend to take "the father's nakedness" as being an indirect reference to the woman's nakedness. Levine, for example, understands it as " 'the nakedness reserved for your father, belonging to your father.' Only one's father has access to one's mother's sexuality" (1989, 120). But this argument fails to consider that the exposure of the father's nakedness is itself an act of dishonor. In short, even if we cannot presuppose a literary dependence on the Noah myth in these legal sources, they clearly share its basic assumption: that it is disgraceful for a father's nakedness to be exposed. And this assumption appears to have had some general currency in ancient Israel; it is not limited to one author or one period of time. This makes plausible the suggestion that worries over the father's honor lie behind the story of God's turning his back to Moses, even if that myth does not derive from the same tradition as the myth of Noah.

The comparison of the two myths both takes for granted and provides support for the conclusion that God is imagined as a father figure and that the veiling of God's body is necessary for the same reasons that a father's nakedness should be covered. That is not to say, of course, that God is always imagined as a father or even in masculine images, as we discussed in chapter 1. But the image of God the Father is one of the popular masculine images that Israelite literature employs to conceptualize the deity. This is not surprising if one recalls that Israel's conception of Yahweh was deeply indebted to and sometimes identified with the Canaanite deity El, who was routinely thought of as a father God (Cross 1973; M. S. Smith 1990). The frequent description of God as "the god of your fathers" or God of your father Abraham or Isaac or Israel (Jacob) also links the deity closely to the role of fatherhood (Gen. 26:24, 28:13, 31:5, 29, 42, 32:10, 43:23, 46:1, 3; Exod. 3:13, 15, 16, 4:5, 15:2, 18:4; Deut. 1:11, 4:1, 26:7; Jos. 18, 3; Ps. 75:10, 81:2; Ezek. 8:28).[4] The fatherly image of the deity expresses God's loving care for Israel, as well as an expectation that the people Israel will honor and be loyal and obedient to him. In the Blessing of Joseph, an early source, there are a series of divine epithets, including the following: "By the strength of the Shepherd, the Stone of Israel, by El, your Father who helps you" (M. S. Smith 1990, 16–17). The fatherhood of God is particularly well developed in Jeremiah 2:27. Here the image of a heavenly father is associated with God's role as creator. God the father, not the mother, is the one who gave birth to Israel.[5] A similar use of the image appears elsewhere: "Children unworthy of Him . . . Do you thus requite the Lord, O dull and witless people? Is not He the Father who created you, Fashioned you and made you endure?" (Deut. 32:5–6). And again: "But now, O Lord, You are our Father: We are the clay and You are the Potter" (2 Isa. 64:7). "Have we not all one father? Did not one God create us? Why do we break faith with one another, profaning the covenant of our fathers" (Mal. 2:10). Jeremiah also evokes the fatherly image to describe God's protective relationship to Israel in "her" youth. God declares to Israel, "You had the brazenness [forehead] of a street woman, you refused to be ashamed. Just now you called to me, 'Father! You are the Guide of my youth" (Jer. 3:4). Jeremiah goes on to use the image of divine fatherhood to evoke loyalty: "I had resolved to adopt you as My child, and I gave you a desirable land . . . and I thought you would surely call Me 'Father,' and never cease to be loyal to Me" (Jer. 3:19). And finally Jeremiah employs the father image as a symbol of God's everlasting commitment to and love for Israel. The remnant of Israel "shall come with weeping, and with compassion will I guide them. I will lead them to streams of water, by a level road where they will not stumble. For I am ever a Father to Israel, Ephraim is My firstborn" (Jer. 31:9).

According to Deuteronomy, the divine father expects obedience just like a human father: "Bear in mind that the Lord your God disciplines you just as a man disciplines his son. Therefore keep the commandments of the Lord your God: walk in His ways and revere Him" (Deut. 8:5). The abundant instructions of guidance to sons in Proverbs also plays on this linkage of the human father and the father in heaven. Indeed, there is an ambiguity in many of these passages as to whether the speaker is a father addressing a son or God addressing men: "Once I was a son to my father, the tender darling of my mother. He instructed me and said to me 'Let your mind hold on to my words; keep my commandments and you will live'" (Prov. 4:3–4; see also Mal. 1:6; 2 Sam. 7:14; Ps. 89:27). Eichrodt summarizes the image of

God as father this way: "For God's election of Israel means that he has adopted her, and so indeed become the Father of his people; and this position is seen to be the foundation both of his claim to obedience from his son, and of the son's confidence in his Father's loving concern, a concern which is held with increasing emphasis to include the bestowal of pardon" (1967, 2:475).

It is important to note here, too, that in these ancient texts the concept of human fatherhood is already extended beyond physical kin relationships. Joseph describes to his brothers his role in Egypt as "a father to Pharaoh, Lord of all his household, and ruler over the whole land of Egypt" (Gen. 45:8). Similarly, Micah says to the Levite who visits him, "Stay with me and be a father and a priest to me" (Judg. 17:10). A similar usage of the term father is found in Judges 18:18 and Isaiah 22:20. In all of these cases, fatherhood is associated with a position of power, an ability to give guidance, and a position that entails respect. Fatherhood even in the human realm stands for the relationship between a group of people and a ruler, protector, and guide, and the relationship of God to Israel clearly draws on these metaphorical uses. As a parental figure, God offers protection and demands obedience.

The cover-up of the divine father's body, then, is analogous to the hiding of the human father's nakedness in the story of Noah. What neither Israel nor Noah's virtuous sons dared imagine was the phallus of the father. But if we look to other religious traditions, we may see how the genitals of the deity have been considered a reasonable matter for speculation. Jesus' penis, for example, is depicted in a wide range of medieval art, as Steinberg (1983) has shown, arguing that the emphasis on his penis is part of what expresses Jesus' humanness. Furthermore, Jesus' foreskin became a sacred relic and an object of veneration in medieval Christianity (Bryk 1970). Indeed, one medieval nun believed the foreskin of Jesus was used as a wedding ring in her marriage to Christ (Bynum 1989, 164). Early Buddhist sources describe the Buddha's body as having seven marks, including a penis that is retractable like that of a horse (Dayal 1975, 302).[6]

Nor should we assume that the Buddha and Jesus are exceptional cases because of their semi-human, semi-divine status. Full-fledged gods, such as the Greek gods Poseidon, Apollo, and Zeus, are frequently sculpted in Greek art with their penises fully displayed. Greek myth tells how the god Ouranos, the god of the sky, was castrated by his son Kronos. Ouranos' manhood falls into the seas and from it Aphrodite is born. Zeus's sexual exploits are the theme of many Greek myths as well (Kerényi 1951). The erection of Siva is also the subject of much Hindu mythology. The erect phallus of Siva, "the erotic ascetic" as Doniger calls him, is a symbol of the power to spill the seed as well as to retain it (O'Flaherty 1973). Hindu mythology tells of wives of Pine Forest sages who touch Siva's erect phallus. In another myth a woman finds an amputated phallus and, thinking it to be Siva's *linga*, takes it home and worships it. At night she takes it to bed for her pleasure. A Hindu textbook on aesthetics says that Siva riding on a bull should be portrayed ithyphallic (erect) and the end of the phallus must reach the limit of the navel. In still another myth, Siva castrates himself because there is no use for this *linga* except to produce creatures who have already been created. The divine phallus is also of concern in ancient Near Eastern mythology. Sumerian stories, for example, tell how the god Enki masturbates, ejaculates, and fills up the Tigris with flowing water and how he uses his penis to dig irrigation ditches, an important aspect of the Sumerian agricultural system. And perhaps most directly pertinent to the present discussion is the penis of El, whose sexual exploits and erection are the subject of religious poetry, as we shall see later in this chapter (Cross 1973, 23).

As these examples suggest, the divine phallus has been a religious matter in other traditions. Why was this not the case in ancient Israel?

The Father's Nakedness

The myth of Noah's nakedness tells us nothing about why it is so problematic for sons to gaze on their father's genitals. It takes this prohibition as a given that needs no explanation. Some ancient and modern commentators speculate that Ham has committed a homosexual act or castrated his father.[7] They point out that when a son commits incest with his mother it is referred to as "uncovering the father's nakedness" (Lev. 18:22). Since in this context "uncovering the father's nakedness" is a metaphor for heterosexual incest, they conclude that seeing the father's nakedness must refer to homosexual incest in the Noah story.[8] But as noted earlier, the relationship between these texts can be reversed: The laws of incest in the Holiness Code share the assumptions of the story of Noah's nakedness, a story that speaks of the father's honor. By alluding to that story, the law underscores how son-mother incest, like the father's indecent exposure, dishonors the father. More to the point, if the Noah myth is about a homosexual act, why did the other brothers walk backwards and turn their heads? Their behavior only makes sense if looking upon the father's nakedness is itself considered a sin. Otherwise, why should they bother to avert their gaze?[9] The myth of Noah's nakedness therefore makes most sense as a condemnation of the father's exposure before his sons.

One reason for the prohibition was clearly the honor due to a father. It was disrespectful to see Noah naked, particularly in his vulnerable drunken state. To avert the gaze was to respect the father's honor.[10] It is important to take note of Noah's state here. In Israelite imagination, the father's nakedness was connected with shame when the father was the passive object of someone's gaze.[11] A father was not dishonored if he intentionally exposed his nakedness. It was his prerogative to do so. The narrator of the Noah story has no apparent difficulty with a servant or son grasping a patriarch's penis while taking an oath, as evident in two other stories, both of which also come from the J source (Friedman 1987, 248–49). In the first (Gen. 24:1–4), it is Abraham who orders his servant Eliezer, "Put your hand under my thigh and I will make you swear by the Lord, the God of heaven and the God of the earth that you will not take a wife for my son from the daughters of the Canaanites among whom I dwell, but will go to the land of my birth and get a wife for my son Isaac. . . . So the servant put his hand under the thigh of his master Abraham and swore to him as bidden." In the second story (Gen. 47:29–31), Jacob asks his son Joseph, "Do me this favor, place your hand under my thigh as a pledge of your steadfast loyalty: please do not bury me in Egypt." Joseph replies, "I will do as you have spoken." And Jacob says, "Swear to me." "And he swore to him." As many interpreters have noted, the word "thigh" is sometimes used in ancient Jewish sources as a euphemism for the penis.[12] In each of these cases, the patriarch has exposed his nakedness intentionally in the process of asserting his power and status. The penis is the symbol of the patrilineage itself. Noah, by contrast, has been viewed in a drunken stupor, a shameful act.

That exposure and shame are deeply entwined in Israelite culture is also evident in another Israelite myth from the same source: the myth of Adam and Eve. As the familiar story goes, the first human couple become aware of their own nakedness after eating from the tree of knowledge against the express wishes of God. As some interpreters have pointed out, this story may be read as a kind of ascent of the human from the realm of the animal (Oden 1987, 92–105). If it is read as a story about the move from animality to humanity, then Adam and Eve are not simply becoming differentiated from animals; they are becoming more like God. What characterizes this differentiation is an emerging awareness of their nakedness and a desire to cover their sexual organs.

Prior to their eating from the tree, Adam and Eve are in some sense like animals: "The two of them were naked . . . yet they felt no shame." Whether they are sexually active like animals is left unclear. After they eat of the fruit, their eyes are opened and they perceive that they are naked. They then sew together fig leaves and clothe themselves. The realization that they are naked and the desire to cover their genitals is meant to distinguish these first humans from animals.

Why is it the serpent who represents the animal realm from which Adam and Eve emerge? Freud has influenced many to see the snake as a symbol of the penis, but I suggest its significance lies elsewhere. One of the most striking features of serpents is the periodic shedding of their skins. Because it regularly sheds its covering, the serpent may be a symbol for both transformation and the lack of shame in the animal world.[13] The serpent who periodically undresses becomes the vehicle by which Adam and Eve learn that they are naked and must clothe themselves. That this meaning may be present in the narrative is also suggested by the description of the snake, who is called the shrewdest ('*arum*) of all the wild beasts (Gen. 3:1). Many interpreters have noted that the Hebrew term "shrewdest" is a pun on the word "naked" which appears one verse earlier in the description of Adam and Eve ('*arumim*), but they have not generally pursued the connection to its logical conclusion. The snake's shedding of its skin makes it the most naked/shrewdest of all animals, and its otherness to the humans is underscored at the end of the narrative, with God making skin garments for Adam and Eve and clothing them (Oden 1987, 99–105). The snake sheds its skin and the humans learn to put skins on. In this myth, then, the first humans reject the habits of the serpent/animal world.[14]

In their ascent out of animality, the first couple also become more like God. Ironically, it is the serpent who first suggests the possibility. Although God has told Adam that eating of the fruit will cause death, the serpent tells Eve, "You are not going to die. God knows that, as soon as you eat of it, your eyes will be opened and you will be like God [or divine beings] who knows good and bad." One is at first tempted to dismiss the serpent's statement as a devious lie. And yet as the narrative unfolds, the serpent becomes more and more credible. When God looks for Adam in the garden, Adam hides because he is naked. "Who told you that you were naked?" asks God. "Did you eat of the tree from which I had forbidden you to eat?" Eating from the tree of knowledge did indeed open human eyes as the serpent had foretold. Finally, the narrative concludes with explicit confirmation of the serpent's suspicions. After clothing Adam and Eve with skins, God says, "Now that the earthling has become like one of us, knowing good and bad, what if it should stretch out its hand and take also from the tree of life and eat, and live forever?" (Gen. 3:22). The "punishments" of the story also fit this interpretation, for they are designed to complete the separation of the human and animal world. The snake loses its feet and must crawl on its belly. Although the myth does not say so explicitly, the snake also loses the ability to speak, which the tale presupposes. Both Adam and Eve are punished in ways that make them human. Eve is condemned to continual sexual desire and childbearing, differentiating her from animals, which go into heat on a periodic cycle. And unlike animals, Adam must earn his food through the sweat of his brow. Humanness is thus a mixed blessing.

Becoming like God is equated with becoming aware of how to differentiate good and bad. There are a variety of interpretations of what this statement means. At the most abstract, knowledge here is construed as moral knowledge. But there is also a more concrete way to read this myth. Awareness of one's genitals and shame about their exposure is also considered part, and perhaps the most basic element, of what it means to know the difference between good and bad. Read quite literally, then, Adam and Eve may become more like God because they learn to have shame about their nakedness and to cover their genitals. Covering themselves is thus an act of *imitatio Dei*. This reading may seem farfetched because we have long been conditioned to think of God as lacking a body. But if, as the various sources I point to throughout this book suggest, God is imagined as having a human figure that is veiled, this understanding may be true to what the myth says. At the most explicit level, the myth depicts the awareness of nakedness as what differentiates humans from animals *and* what links humanity to divinity.

Support for this interpretation of the garden of Eden story comes from the Sumerian epic *Gilgamesh*, which tells a parallel story about a figure named Enkidu. In this myth, the god Anu creates Enkidu as a foil for Gilgamesh, the king of Uruk, who is terrorizing human civilization. Enkidu is a wild man who lives with animals. As the story unfolds, Gilgamesh instructs a hunter to take a woman to entrap Enkidu, for he knows that once Enkidu embraces her the wild beasts will reject him. This is in fact what happens. Enkidu lies with her for seven nights, and at the end of that time he returns to the hills. But the animals now flee from him, and Enkidu can no longer follow them, for he has lost his swiftness. "Enkidu was grown weak, for wisdom was in him and the thoughts of a man were in his heart."[15] When he returns to the woman, she says, "You are wise, Enkidu, and you have become like god. Why do you want to run wild with beasts in the hills?" She shares her clothing with Enkidu and teaches him to eat bread and drink beer.

Sexual knowledge is thus the key moment in Enkidu's transformation from a wild thing into a human being.[16] Like Adam and Eve, this knowledge makes Enkidu more like the gods. In both cases, a woman initiates the transformation.

Note as well that beer is introduced in the Enkidu story as a symbol of culture, and Enkidu in fact becomes drunk on this new beverage.[17] This may provide an interesting and unexpected bridge between the story of Adam and Eve and the story of Noah. Noah's drunkenness may be, at least in part, a sign that culture, represented by the availability of fermented products, has been reestablished once more after the flood. Only this time, the refounding of culture also involves a prohibition on seeing one's father's nakedness. Both the Adam and Eve story and the myth about Noah closely link the emergence of culture to sexual awareness and restriction. And in becoming cultured, all of these characters are in some sense more like God.

To summarize, then, the myths of Noah and Adam and Eve regard shame about nakedness as a foundational moment in the emergence of human culture. The myth of Noah shows that this general human concern is regarded as particularly important for protecting the father's honor. Noah, as the only father to survive the flood and, hence, the paradigmatic father of humankind, must have his dignity protected. To be uncovered is to reintroduce a state of disorder. Culture is preserved by the virtuous sons who cover their father's nakedness.

The link between nakedness and shame, between being human and being covered, suggests one reason why the divine father's body must be veiled. But the question remains as to why the father's nakedness is regarded as so shameful in the first place? Why is the prohibition on seeing the father's nakedness regarded as essential to human culture? As I suggest below, this prohibition seeks to ensure that heterosexual desire remains the norm.

The Gaze and Homoeroticism

Within a culture that defines heterosexuality as the norm, the male gaze is properly directed to women alone. Men should not look at men, and boys should learn not to desire their fathers. A great deal of cultural theorizing has paid attention to the mechanisms by which heterosexual incest is prevented.[18] But the focus on heterosexual incest ignores the question of how the social prohibition on incest between sons and fathers develops. In other words, how are sons taught to desire people like their mothers, not like their fathers? What role does the repression of father-son incest play in promoting heterosexual desire? Although Freud tended to emphasize the taboo on heterosexual incest in his writings about the Oedipus complex, he did develop a theory of how homosexual incest comes to be prohibited. As we saw in chapter 2, Freud argued that a child has a polymorphous sexuality that is only organized along heterosexual lines by the forces of the Oedipus complex. In the passive version of this complex, the son wishes in some sense to become a woman so that he can be the object of his father's desires. But his narcissistic attachment to his penis makes him repudiate these wishes and identify, not with his mother, but with his father.

Freud's notions about an infant bisexuality appear problematic to those who assume that the object of desire is determined by one's biology. But the many forms that sexuality takes cross-culturally suggests that culture plays a very substantial factor in organizing desire. Take, for example, the Sambia studied by Gilbert Herdt (1982, 1987).[19] To become a man among the Sambia involves a period of ritualized fellatio between younger and older males. During the period of initiation, which lasts for many years, a younger man performs fellatio on an older man so as to ingest his semen and thereby gain his own manhood. At the end of this period, most Sambian men marry and carry on strictly heterosexual relationships. Instances such as this suggest that Freud was essentially correct that desire is shaped by familial and cultural symbols.

One need not embrace Freud's theory of infant bisexuality or even the idea that children have sexual desires for parents to find a relevant insight about culture and how it operates in the myth of Noah. The prohibition against a son seeing his father's nakedness symbolically expresses and thereby institutionalizes heterosexual desire as a norm. The story of Noah is after all a second creation story, a telling of what human culture was and what it should be after its destruction in the flood and rebirth in Noah's line. In this new beginning, heterosexual desire is reconstituted once more. In Genesis 2:23–24, a story from the same author as the myth of Noah (J), heterosexuality has already been presented as the norm. God decides that "the earthling should not be alone" and takes a piece of Adam's side to create a second creature. Thus emerges male-female complementarity. But in the refounding of culture after the flood, another erotic relationship potentially disrupts male-female relations: that of sons and fathers. The prohibition against seeing Noah's nakedness deals with this potential disruption.

This interpretation of the Noah myth assumes that male-male sexual activity was considered problematic in Israelite culture, an assumption supported by the ancient texts. The Holiness Code treats male-male sexual acts as an abomination (Lev. 18:22), punishable by death (Lev. 20:13).[20] The language of the code is significant: "Do not lie with a man as one lies with a woman; it is an abhorrence." The description of the sin is consistent with Israelite attempts to keep the perceived natural order in place.[21] This prohibition against male-male sexual acts appears among a list of sexual and other offenses, including various kinds of incest, bestiality, intercourse with a woman who is subject to menstrual pollution, and dedicating one's child to Molech. It is not entirely clear what unites this list. But many of these acts pose a threat to the integrity of Israelite lineage (incest or adultery) or waste Israelite "seed" (male-male sexual acts, intercourse with women during menstruation, bestiality, offering one's children to Molech).[22]

It is also significant that this list of prohibitions begins and ends with the injunction not to imitate the ways of the Egyptians or the Canaanites, both groups who are said to be descendants of Ham (Gen. 10:6).[23] In ancient Israelite imagination, male-male sexual acts were considered something alien and hence were linked to the stereotyping of its proximate others, the Canaanites. The association of homosexual activity with Canaanite practice in the Holiness Code thus lends support to my interpretation of the Noah story. In the cursing of Canaan for his father's sin, the Canaanites are condemned as an immoral line.[24] The same strategy is used to defame the Moabites and Ammonites, who are descended from the incestuous union of Lot and his daughters (Gen. 19:30–38), which repeats in significant ways the story of Noah and his son Ham. Lot and his daughters have fled the city of Sodom after it has been destroyed by God. Lot gets drunk on two successive nights, and during his drunken stupor, his daughters have intercourse with him. Their children are the ancestors of the Moabites and Ammonites. Israel, then, is depicted as one of the few genealogical lines untainted by sexual perversion. [25]

The association of homosexual desire with the Canaanites may also be suggested in the story of Sodom and Gomorrah's destruction, a story told by the same narrator as the myth of Noah's nakedness (Genesis 19). In this story, God visits Lot in the form of two angels. The men of Sodom and Gomorrah gather outside Lot's door and demand, "Bring them out to us, that we may know them." It's well recognized, of course, that the biblical term "to know" frequently connotes sexual intimacy (Gen. 4:1, 17, 25, 19:5, 8, 24:16, 38:26; Num. 31:17, 18, 35; 1 Sam. 1:19; Judg. 11:39, 21:11, 19:22, 25; 1 Kings 1:4). The action of these men confirms the wickedness of Sodom and thus explains God's prior decision to destroy the population (Gen. 18:20). Lot, however, protects his guests and refuses to turn them over to the men outside his door. [26] He begs the men of the city, "Do not commit such a wrong. Look, I have two daughters who have not known a man. Let me bring them out to you and you may do to them as you please; but do not do anything to these men, since they have come under the shelter of my roof." The description of the daughters as two "who have not known a man" links knowing and sexual intercourse and thus calls for a similar reading of the men's desire that Lot "Bring them out to us, that we may know them."

Traditionally, this story has been interpreted as denigrating Canaanite culture by linking it with homosexual desire. But recently some interpreters have argued that the overriding point of the story may instead be to condemn rape and to valorize the obligations of hospitality. [27] On this interpretation, the men of Sodom are condemned, not for homosexual desire, but for their intentions to turn Lot's guests into objects of a violent sexual act. Lot is a virtuous host in protecting his guests. According to this interpretation, heterosexual rape was less problematic in the culture depicted by the Lot story, for Lot offers the men his daughters instead of his guests. But I find unconvincing the argument that the daughters are simply chattel to be disposed of at will. The narrator condemns Lot's actions, as evidenced by the ironic twist that Lot is subsequently seduced by his own daughters. Lot is hardly treated by this narrator as a virtuous person.

But even if this story is not interpreted as a condemnation of homosexual desire, it is clear that in general Israelite culture viewed male-female complementarity and heterosexual desire not simply as a norm, but as part of the fabric of creation. This is evident in the way that both stories of creation (Genesis 1–2) posit a complementarity between men and women that belongs to the natural order. In the second story of creation, moreover, the union of man and woman is imagined as recuperating a person's lost half. This presumptive heterosexuality is underscored by the hundreds of male-female relationships that are mentioned in the Hebrew Bible and by the use of heterosexual imagery to describe the relationship between God the husband and Israel the wife. One male-male relationship in the Hebrew Bible, that between David and Jonathan, may be homosexual, but that example is dubious.[28]

Interpreters of the Lot story have tended to minimize the fact that it is *men of God* that the men of Sodom desire to know. To be sure, the men of the city assume that the visitors to Lot's house are human men, but the narrator knows otherwise. They are in fact divine beings sent by God, and earlier in the narration they seem to be equated with God (Gen. 18:1–3). From the narrator's (and hence the reader's) standpoint, the men of Sodom desire to have intimacy with divine men. The story is therefore not just about the impropriety of homosexual rape, but also about men desiring "divine men."[29] This desire reverses another hierarchy, that between heaven and earth. Lot's offer of his daughters is thus an attempt to turn the desire of human men away from men of God back to appropriate objects: human women, a theme to which we will return.

Those who think Ham has committed a homosexual *act* with his father are partially right. There is an element of homoeroticism in the Noah story. Ham has looked upon his father's nakedness, but gazing is enough to generate desire. That "the gaze" and desire are intimately linked has been amply demonstrated by recent art and film critics. John Berger in his *Ways of Seeing* describes the relationship of the gaze, power, and heterosexual desire in European paintings of the nude. "Men act and women appear. . . . Men look at women. Women watch themselves being looked at. This determines not only most relations beween men and women but also the relation of women to themselves. The surveyor of woman in herself is male: the surveyed female. Thus she turns herself into an object—and most particularly an object of vision: a sight" (1972, 47, 54).

Laura Mulvey makes similar arguments in an influential essay about film. It is the male heterosexual gaze that directs the view of the camera. The film's viewers are thus invited to gaze upon women as objects of desire. "The male figure cannot bear the burden of sexual objectification. Man is reluctant to gaze at his exhibitionist like" (1989, 20).[30] For similar reasons, it is considered erotic when a woman removes her glasses in films. She is casting off her position as spectator and becoming instead the object of the gaze (Doane 1982, 82–83).

The male gaze and desire were also linked in the ancient Israelite imagination. Abram, for example, worries about the beauty of Sarai as they enter Egypt, and his fears are born out when the Egyptians see Sarai's beauty and take her into Pharaoh's court (Gen. 12:11, 14). Shechem, son of Hamor, sees Dinah and rapes her (Gen. 34:2); Judah sees the daughter of a Canaanite woman and he marries her and cohabits with her (Gen. 38:2). From his rooftop, David sees Bathsheba bathing and desires her (2 Sam. 11:2–4). There are, of course, exceptions to the male who gazes. Potiphar's wife, for example, casts her eyes on Joseph and desires him (Gen. 39:7), but the narrator condemns her behavior. Indeed, this reversal of desire signifies the harlot (see Ezek. 23:26). An interesting exception is the Song of Songs in which the woman's gaze is not problematic (5:10). But in biblical texts, the desirous gaze and the gaze that beholds beauty is generally the gaze of a man looking at a woman. It may be on occasion a woman who gazes at a man, but it is never a man gazing at another man. [31] Thus the prohibition on Ham's seeing his father is intended to direct the male gaze away from the male to the female body. Furthermore, it is Noah's passivity, his taking of what was regarded as the female's position, that makes the viewing of his nakedness so problematic.

Love the Lord your God

An Israelite male who gazed at God was like Ham, who looked at his naked father. Israelite men were expected to be Semites, virtuous sons of Shem who avert their gaze from their father in heaven. It stands to reason that a desiring relationship between a male God and human men would pose difficulties in the culture of ancient Israel, which treated male-female complementarity as an ideal and condemned male-male sexual acts as an abomination for which they lose title to their land or worse (Lev. 18:22, 20:13). This is one of the reasons that the sexual features of God had to remain veiled. For Moses or other male Israelites to have seen God would be a misplacement of the male gaze. Evidence for the potentially troubling homoerotic relationship with God has thus far been from two directions: the circumspection with which Israelite myth handles the issue of God's body and the similarity between one of these God-sighting myths and the myth of Noah's nakedness. But there is other evidence of the erotic relationship between men and God.

Prophetic literature frequently imagines the relationship between Israel and God as a marriage: God is the husband to Israel the wife. This metaphor is used more frequently and extensively than other personal metaphors. [32] The eighth-century prophet Hosea seems to have been the first to develop this imagery fully, although there is some earlier Israelite evidence for the use of the metaphor. [33] Hosea is instructed by God to marry a woman who is promiscuous and with whom Hosea has several children. This marriage is clearly intended to parallel the marriage between God and Israel. "So intricately combined and blended are the two stories—of God and Israel, and Hosea and Gomer—that it is impossible to tell always where one stops and the other picks up" (Anderson and Freedman 1980, 3). The marriage metaphor serves several functions: it interprets the covenant between God and Israel as worthy of commitment and it casts idolatry as tantamount to the act of an adulterous wife: "For she is not my wife and I am not her husband—and let her put away her harlotry from my face and her adultery from between her breasts" (Hos. 2:4). Hosea views God's relationship to Israel in the period of the desert as an idyllic time before Israel's adultery with other gods. But Hosea also envisions a time when the relationship between God and Israel will be restored: "In that day—declares the Lord—you will call [Me] Ishi [my husband], and no more will you call Me Baali [My Husband Baal]" (Hos. 2:18).

The prophets Jeremiah and Ezekiel, apparently influenced by Hosea, also develop the marriage metaphor (Anderson and Freedman 1980, 46–47). "I accounted to your favor the devotion of your youth, your love as a bride—how you followed Me in the wilderness" (Jer. 2:1). Jeremiah also uses the image of adultery: "Now you have whored with many lovers: can you return to Me?" (Jer. 3:1). According to Ezekiel, God finds Israel as an abandoned baby and takes her under his care. Eventually she reaches maturity, and in one graphic image, about which I have more to say later, God is represented as having sexual intercourse with her (Ezek. 16:7–8). But after this espousal, Israel whores with other gods:

> You built yourself an eminence and made yourself a mound in every square. You built your mound at every crossroad: and you sullied your beauty and spread your legs to every passerby, and you multiplied your harlotries. You played the whore with your neighbors, the Egyptians big of phallus—you multiplied your harlotries to anger me. (Ezek. 16:24–26)

This prophetic image of Israel whoring after other nations or gods (Hos. 4:12–15, 5:3, 6:10, 9:1; Isa. 1:21; Jer. 2:20; Ezek. 6:8, 16:23; 2 Isa. 57:7) appears also in the deuteronomic literature (Exod. 34:15; Deut. 31:16; Judg. 2:17), and allusions to the same imagery occur elsewhere (Num. 15:39; Lev. 17:7, 20:5; Ps. 106:39; Mic. 1:7; Nah. 3:4).

The images of an unfaithful wife (*ma'al*) (Num. 5:11–27) equate idolatry and adultery (Adler 1989, 124). Fidelity to God is thus analogous to a legitimate relationship involving the appropriate form of sexual expression.

Israelite religion was unique among ancient Near Eastern traditions in applying the metaphor of marriage to the relationship between God and a collectivity. No other god in the ancient Near East was said to be husband of the people. Interpreters have tended to view the metaphor of whoring after other gods as a response to Canaanite fertility practices which involved the *hieros gamos*, the marriage of Baal with nature. But this interpretation is no longer compelling.[34]

These images, which cast the relationship between God and Israel in heterosexual terms, obviously have several effects: to interpret the covenant as demanding the fidelity and commitment of a marriage relationship, and to support the dominance of the man in that relationship. The man is to his wife as God is to Israel. But the heterosexual metaphor, which works so well when speaking about Israel as a collectivity, ignores a critical fact. The primary relationships in Israelite imagination were between a male God and individual male Israelites, such as Moses, the patriarchs, and the prophets. The images of a female Israel, then, were addressed primarily to men and conceptualized their male relationship to God.[35] Men were encouraged to imagine themselves as married to and hence in a loving relationship with God. A homoerotic dilemma was thus generated, inadvertently and to some degree unconsciously, by the superimposition of heterosexual images on the relationship between human and divine males. In other words, the metaphors of God married to Israel spill over into other symbolic registers where God is imagined in relationship to individual men.

This lack of compartmentalization is visible in the texts in several ways. It appears, for example, when Israelite men assume the position of God's wives, a point developed in more detail in chapter 6. It is evident as well in the mixing of metaphors within scriptural passages. This shifting of symbolic registers is evident in both Hosea's and Jeremiah's use of these images.

Hosea, for example, does not initially describe his listeners as God's wife. Rather, they are children of Israel the mother: "Rebuke your mother, rebuke her—for she is not My wife and I am not her husband" (Hos. 1:4).[36] "But do not both mother and children represent Israel?" asks Wolff perceptively (1974, 33). Yes, indeed, for as Mays writes, "The children are the individual members of Israel, which is represented by the mother as a corporate person. The individual and collective ways of thinking are juxtaposed to create flexibility in the allegory" (1969, 37). In the course of this passage, moreover, the identification of the listeners with the position of "children" is gradually loosened. Instead of saying "I will disown you," God says, "I will also disown her children: for they are now a harlot's brood." For thirteen verses, God speaks about Israel the adulterous wife in the third person. And then suddenly,

> And in that day—declares the Lord—*you* will call [Me] Ishi, and no more will *you* call Me Baali. For I will remove the names of the Baalim from *her* mouth, and they shall nevermore be mentioned by name. . . . And I will spouse *you* forever: I will espouse *you* with righteousness and justice, and with goodness and mercy, and I will espouse *you* with faithfulness. (Hos. 2:18–22; italics added)

The listeners are thus no longer personified as the children of the promiscuous wife, but are themselves the adulteress who returns in fidelity and remarries her husband.[37] This shifting of pronouns (you, her) is characteristic of prophetic discourse in general. But it obviously serves some very distinctive purposes in this case. It enables Hosea to distance his listeners from the image of the faithless wife (your mother, her) and to identify with the image of the faithful wife (I will espouse you), and to see themselves as either wife or children of God. God is both Israel's father and "her" husband.[38]

A similar shifting of metaphors occurs in Jeremiah: "I accounted to your favor the devotion of your youth, your love as a bride—how you followed Me in the wilderness. . . . declares the Lord" (Jer. 2:1). In the next declaration, however, Israel is no longer in the position of wife: "Hear the word of the Lord, O House of Jacob, every clan of the House of Israel! Thus said the Lord: What wrong did your fathers find in Me that they abandoned Me and went after delusion and were deluded? They never asked themselves, 'Where is the Lord, Who brought us up from the land of Egypt?' " (Jer. 2:4–6). In one sense, the shift signals that God is speaking to different generations. The wife imagery is used to describe the period of the wilderness. The subsequent generation, now called fathers, lived in the land of Israel but forgot the God who had brought them out of Egypt. But as we have seen, Jeremiah also describes this latter period with the image of a faithless wife: "Now you have whored with many lovers: can you return to Me?" (Jer. 3:1). A few verses later, moreover, Jeremiah juxtaposes the image of the faithless woman with that of children who call to God as father: "And you defiled the land with your whoring and your debauchery and when showers were withheld and the late rains did not come, you had the brazenness of a street woman, you refused to be ashamed. Just now you called to Me, 'Father! You are the Guide of my youth' " (Jer. 3:2–4).

Remember that these images were addressed at least in part to Israelite men, who were to imagine themselves both as lovers of God and as God's children. God the father is also God the lover. The homoerotic resonances, however unintentional, lie just beneath the surface and threaten to break into consciousness. Consider Jeremiah's loincloth parable: God commands Jeremiah to buy a cloth of linen and to put it around his loins. After wearing it, Jeremiah is commanded by God to take it to Perath and cover it up there in a cleft of the rock. When God orders Jeremiah to dig it up, he finds the loincloth is ruined:

> Thus said the Lord: Even so will I ruin the overweening pride of Judah and Jerusalem. This wicked people who refuse to heed My bidding, who follow the willfulness of their own hearts, who follow other gods and serve them and worship them, shall become like that loincloth, which is not good for anything. For as the loincloth clings close to the loins of a man, so I brought close to Me the whole House of Israel and the whole House of Judah— declares the Lord—that they might be My people, for fame, and praise and splendor. But they would not obey. (Jer. 13:8–11)

The principal meaning of this passage is obviously to condemn Israel's lack of fidelity to God. But not far beneath is the exceedingly erotic conception of Israel's relationship to God as the cloth covering God's loins. When that image is juxtaposed to images of Israel following other gods, an act that Jeremiah himself compares to adultery, it leaves little doubt that Israel is expected to cling to God's loins. The Psalmist's longing for God evokes similarly passionate overtones:

> God, You are my God; I search for You, my soul thirsts for You. My body yearns for You, as a parched and thirsty land that has no water. I shall behold You in the sanctuary, and see Your might and Glory. Truly Your faithfulness is better than life; my lips declare Your praise . . . I sing praises with joyful lips, when I call You to mind upon my bed, when I think of You in the watches of the night. (Ps. 63:2–9)

There are as well several myths that ponder the potentially erotic relationship between individual humans and male divine beings. I have already mentioned the desire of the men of Sodom "to know" the men of God who visit Lot. Another example is the perplexing myth in Genesis 6:1–4 (J), which recounts how the "sons of God"

> saw how beautiful the daughters of men were and took wives from among those that pleased them—The Lord said, "My breath shall not abide in man forever, since he too is flesh; let the days allowed him be one hundred and twenty years."—It was then, and later too, that the Nephilim [Fallen Ones] appeared on earth—when the divine beings cohabited with the daughters of men, who bore them offspring. They were the heroes of old, the men of renown.

This story takes for granted the presence of other divine beings beside God, a view that is found elsewhere in the Bible (Ps. 29:1, 82:1; Deut. 33:2–3; 1 Kings 22:19–22).[39] Perhaps it is the fragment of a larger mythology that is now lost. But even if it is, why has it survived and what point does it make in this context? What is interesting, for the present purposes, is how it imagines the relationship between heaven and earth in heterosexual terms. The divine males have intercourse with human females. The narrator gives no indication of finding fault with this action, even referring to the offspring as men of renown, although the placement of this story before the flood reflects an editorial judgment that the incident contributes to God's decision to wipe out humanity (Hendel 1987, 16).[40] Nor does this narrator appear to imagine female divine beings for the male humans, as some Gnostics later would. In any case, the myth takes for granted that a male heterosexual gaze is directed from heaven to earth, glossing over the anxiety of what kind of relationship men have with a male god, an anxiety expressed more directly in the story of Sodom and Gomorrah.

We now see that the story of Sodom intersects in interesting ways with the myth in which God turns his back on Moses, for like the men of Sodom who want "to know" the men of God, Moses desires "to know" God. In the long introduction to the myth, Moses says, "Now if I have truly gained Your favor, pray let me know Your ways that I may know You and continue in Your favor" (Exod. 33:13). As in the Sodom story, the term "knowledge" may sustain an erotic overtone. Moses' desire to know God is deeply connected with his desire to see God's glory, to know God in a way that he has not known the deity before. It is true that the term "to know" is a covenantal idiom (Amos 3:2). But the possible allusion to sexual intimacy cannot be dismissed. To really know God is more than knowing God's name or the divine nature. Moses has long ago learned the personal name of God, "I will be Who I will Be" (Exod. 3:14). Now he wants something more. Vriezen, writing with a very different purpose, describes the concept of knowing God this way:

> The Old Testament itself always speaks about knowing God (da'ath 'elohim) without specifying what it fundamentally means. . . . The knowledge of God embraces much more than a mere intellectual knowledge . . . knowledge is living in a close relationship with something or somebody, such a relationship as

to cause what might be called a communion. For that reason sexual intercourse can be called "knowing" and *da'ath 'elohim* (the knowledge of God) and *chesed* (solidarity, communion) can be used as parallels. (1970, 153–55)

Eichrodt makes a similar point about the use of the word knowledge by the prophet Hosea: "It cannot be overlooked that the highly significant story of his marriage, which stands at the beginning of his message, and was the means by which Yahweh gave him a new understanding of God's relationship with Israel, also gives the word y-d-ʿ [to know] the warmer tone of inward intimacy . . . the *response [of] love and trustful surrender* awakened by the unmerited love of God. Because God 'knows' his people, that is to say, he has introduced them into a permanent relationship of the closest mutual belonging, that same people for their part have both the ability and the obligation to embrace him in 'knowledge'; that is, in a loving affection which results in the permanent demonstration of loyalty and kindness" (1967, 2:292–93). This potentially erotic relationship between Moses and God will be developed in more detail later. For now the point is simply to note how Moses' desire to know God leads to a veiling of God's body, to a covering of the divine face and a presentation of the divine back.[41] God will not entirely satisfy Moses' desire.

It may be significant, too, that in this same myth God says, "I will make all My goodness (*ṭûbî*) pass before you as I proclaim the name Lord before you." Interpreters typically read "goodness" as referring to divine attributes or qualities since the "goodness" of God is a well-developed theological concept (Ps. 31:20, 145:7; Jer. 31:12). Childs, for example, sees this usage as indicating that "God is no longer seen primarily in terms of a visible appearance." He goes on, "Of course, the usage in v. 19 is unique and without an exact parallel, but the concern is clearly to define God's revelation in terms of his activity toward Israel" (1974, 596). But is it so clear that God's goodness refers to the divine qualities? The word "goodness" can also mean beauty (Hos. 10:11; Zech. 9:17) and may therefore refer to the beauty of God. The usage of *ṭûbî* is only unique if these parallels are ignored. Moreover, in its adjectival form, this word is used to mean pleasant or agreeable and to describe the physical beauty of women and men (Gen. 6:2, 24:16, 26:7; Exod. 2:2; 1 Sam. 9:2; 2 Sam. 11:2; Esther 1:11, 2:3, 7; Dan. 1:15) (Brown, Driver, and Briggs 1975, 373, 375). In one context, the term is associated with erotic desire, namely, when David spies Bathsheba bathing naked (2 Sam. 11:2). Yet translators and interpreters have generally resisted taking the reference to God's goodness as a reference to the deity's beauty. At the very least there is an ambiguity here. And the ambiguity in the meaning of both "knowledge" and "goodness" suggests that God's turning of his back to Moses may incite desire as much as it acts to deflect it.

Scandals of Monotheism

The problem of human men's desire for a male God may have been intensified by a specific factor in Israel's developing religious thought: namely, the impulses toward exclusive worship of one God. The story of Israel's emerging monotheism is complex and still subject to dispute. Contrary to earlier views, Israel did not always believe in the existence of one God alone. This radical form of monotheism developed relatively late in the mid sixth century B.C.E. Indeed, it now appears that Israel's religion was henotheistic or monolatrous.[42] Monolatry, the worship of a single high god, recognizes the existence of other deities and even incorporates some of them as lower gods in a pantheon. There is evidence in Israelite literature of sacrifices to other gods who were understood to be subordinate members of Yahweh's pantheon. By the eighth century, if not earlier, these other forms of Israelite worship had come under prophetic attack and were condemned for the first time. In other words, what previously had been acceptable in Israelite worship was increasingly decried as an inappropriate form of syncretism. This initiated changes that ultimately led to the exclusive worship of one God and the radical monotheism of the fifth century.

There is also archaeological evidence that during the earlier pe-

riod—when Israel was worshiping a variety of deities—some Israelites may have imagined Yahweh with a consort named Asherah, a deity also known as well from the Canaanite pantheon. Inscriptions
from Kuntillet 'Ajrud refer to "Yahweh and his Asherah."[43] There is
ongoing debate about whether these inscriptions actually refer to the
goddess as a divinity or to the survival of her symbol, the tree. In turn,
these debates have stimulated a rethinking of biblical passages that
condemn worship of Asherah. Do these passages indicate that the
worship of Asherah was widespread in ancient Israel or simply presuppose the use of the tree symbol, now called asherah, in Israelite cult? A
variety of technical linguistic and historical arguments are marshaled
on both sides of the debate. Some interpreters argue that polemics
against Asherah are located exclusively in the relatively late biblical
writings of the Deuteronomist (late seventh century). The absence of
such polemics in earlier writings signifies that Asherah worship was
unchallenged in the period of the monarchy. Other interpreters disagree. They contend that although Asherah was considered a consort
of Yahweh during the early period of the judges, by the time of monarchy (1000 B.C.E.) Israel had repudiated Asherah worship and was
moving toward an exclusive relationship with Yahweh.

These arguments about the development of monotheism add another dimension to the investigation of the relationship between
ancient Israelite men and God. Homoerotic overtones to the human-
divine connection cannot be traced only to the emergence of monotheism. For example, the Greek myth of Ganymede tells how Zeus in
the form of an eagle abducts a young beautiful boy, a myth that may
have served to legitimate the homoerotic relations between older and
younger men widely accepted in Greek society.[44] But as Israel's religious imagination became more restricted in its ability to imagine God
with a lover, the divine phallus became more problematic. Without a
lover, the concept of a divine phallus became meaningless. What, to
put it bluntly, would a male monotheistic God do with a phallus? Furthermore, as Israel took on a metaphoric role as God's lover, the erotic
aspects of the divine-human relationship were heightened.

It is interesting, therefore, that the myths of the God sightings at
Sinai, which many date to the eighth and ninth centuries B.C.E., are

recorded during the period in which an exclusive commitment to Yahweh is believed to have emerged.[45] In other words, as God loses a divine partner, it becomes disturbing to visualize the divine body. Thus we find that the metaphors of marriage are first applied to the relationship between God and Israel by Hosea, the prophet who is also credited with having initiated the turn toward a more monotheistic worship of Yahweh. Significantly, Ezekiel's vision of God comes after these developments. His vision is by far the most explicitly erotic of the God sightings, describing God from the loins up and the loins down. It is as if Ezekiel gives us the erotic version of the myth in which God turns his back to Moses. What I am suggesting, therefore, is that the homoeroticism that was always latent in Israelite theology was intensified by the emerging exclusive worship of Yahweh.

Though the Kuntillet 'Arjud inscriptions seem to suggest that Israelites did imagine Asherah as a goddess and hence as a lover of Yahweh, the Hebrew Bible makes no overt mention of Yahweh and a divine lover.[46] This distinguishes Yahweh in a critical way from the god El, the senior god of the Canaanite pantheon. Despite the many similarities between these gods (Cross 1973; M. S. Smith 1990, 7–12), there is a crucial difference. No biblical sources speak about Yahweh's sexuality. Canaanite poetry ponders El's penis and his relationship with his chief lover Asherah:

> [El walks] the shore of the sea,
> and strides the shore of the deep . . .
> Now they are low, now they rise
> now they cry "Daddy, daddy,"
> and now they cry "Mama, mama."
> El's "hand" grows long as the sea,
> El's "hand as the flood."
> Long is El's "hand" as the sea,
> El's "hand" as the flood . . .
> El, his rod sinks.
> El, his rod sinks.
> El, his love-staff droops.
> He raises, he shoots skyward.

He shoots a bird in the sky;

he plucks and puts it on the coals.

El would seduce the woman.

Lo the women explain:

"O mate, mate, your rod sinks,

your love-staff droops. . . .

The women are El's wives, El's wives and forever. . . .

The women are [El's wives],

El's wives and forever.

He bends, their lips he [kis]ses,

Lo, their lips are sweet,

sweet as grapes.

As he kisses, they conceive,

as he embraces they become pregnant.

They travail and give birth to Dawn and Dusk.

(Pope 1955, 38–39)[47]

What is significant about this poetry is how explicitly El's sexuality is conceptualized.[48] This frankness about the divine phallus is possible in part because of the articulation of a full pantheon of sexually active deities. But it is not just the veiling of Yahweh's phallus that distinguishes him from El. It is also the veiling of any reference at all to his physical maleness. One of the striking features of El in both iconography and myth is his long flowing beard. By contrast, as we have seen, Yahweh is nowhere mentioned with a beard, even in his vivid description in the book of Daniel.[49] Only on one coin minted in the Persian period do we find a depiction of a bearded deity which may be a representation of Yahweh (Meshorer 1967, no. 4).

This contrast between the sexual El and the desexualized Yahweh may provide a clue to the story of Israel's idolatry with the so-called golden calf (Exodus 32). In this familiar story, Moses has gone up the mountain to receive the Ten Commandments. He has been away for a long time and the people are impatient and ask Aaron to make a golden calf. It is in fact not a calf that Aaron makes but a bull.[50] The children of Israel dance around it and say, "These are your gods, O Israel." Interpreters generally construe the passage as a polemic against the religious shrines of Jeroboam in Bethel and Dan, which competed with the Temple in Jerusalem. Instead of duplicating the Temple exactly, Jeroboam had replaced the cherubim that support God's throne with bulls. Possibly Jeroboam chose the bull as a symbol of strength and virility, linking Yahweh with El, whose primary symbol was the bull.[51] The Israelite apostasy was not, however, in the association of Yahweh and El, for they were already linked in Israelite imagination. The problem was the reintroduction of El's sexuality as an aspect of Yahweh. Whether the bulls were images of Yahweh or simply platforms for him analogous to the cherubim, they connected Yahweh with an image of virility. In Genesis 49, a single reference to the "bull of Yahweh" appears in a blessing that also seems to refer to Asherah (M. S. Smith 1990, 16–17). The plural "these are your gods, O Israel" could thus be a double entendre. It may refer to Jeroboam's bulls. But it may also allude to the fact that the symbol of a virile bull carries along with it an expectation of a fecund female. In any case, the bull symbol, whether of Yahweh himself or simply a footstool, is far more sexual than the cherubim.

To summarize, then, the idea of a divine phallus and of divine maleness in general became more and more incoherent as Israelite religion tended toward an exclusive relationship with one God. In ancient Israel, the very idea of a penis presupposed the existence of an other, an other of the opposite sex, with whom some sort of satisfaction could be achieved and reproduction be assured. The idea of divine genitals was therefore potentially disruptive unless God was imagined with a lover, and the biblical writers never conceptualized God as sexually active with anyone but Israel. As we have seen, the solution of imagining Israel as a metaphorical woman generated other dilemmas: as part of this collectivity, Israelite men were placed in a potentially homoerotic relationship with God. The phallus of God thus represented a scandal in this religious mythology. By diverting the gaze from bodily parts of the deity, particularly from the front and genitals, the myths skirted the conceptual problem that lay at the heart of a system which did not imagine its God in sexual relations with other gods. This avoidance eventually made the entire body of the deity a problem.

Chapter Five

Genital Speculation

For I am God, not man.   HOSEA 11:9

THUS FAR, WE HAVE focused our attention on those myths involving God sightings, but there are other sources which suggest not
only the masculinity of God but even God's anatomical maleness.
Consider the extended metaphor comparing Israel to an adulterous
wife of God, Israel's faithful husband (Hos. 2:4–3:5). As noted before,
a time is envisioned when fidelity will be restored to this relationship.
In that time, God promises Israel

> I will espouse you forever: I will espouse you with righteousness
> and justice, and with goodness and mercy, and I will espouse you
> with faithfulness; then you shall know the Lord. (Hos. 2:20–21)[1]

This metaphor allows, even encourages, an analogy between sexual
intercourse and the covenantal relationship. As is evident from other
sources (Deut. 20:7, 28:30), in ancient Israel intercourse was expected to follow espousal promptly, so that if a man had espoused a
woman and had not "taken her" he was released from his duty of serving in the army (Deut. 20:7). It was also regarded as a travesty if a man
espoused a woman but another man had intercourse with her first
(Deut. 28:30). Hosea's concluding hope that Israel will "know" the
Lord thus alludes to sexual intercourse that completes the act of espousal.[2]

The prophet Ezekiel provides a still more explicit depiction of the sexual relationship between God and Israel. In this case, God first discovers Israel as an abandoned baby, cares for her, and watches her mature:

> Your breasts became firm and your hair sprouted. You were still naked and bare when I passed by you and saw that your time for love had arrived. So I spread My robe over you and covered your nakedness and I entered into a covenant with you by oath—declares the Lord God; thus you became Mine. (Ezek. 16:8)

This passage comes the closest of any to imagining God as an anatomically male deity. Most interpreters sanitize it and ignore its sexual overtones. They construe "spreading a robe" over the naked Israel as a symbol of marriage, as an act of acquiring the woman as a wife, or simply as protecting her.[3] But the sexual meanings in the passage are conveyed in a number of ways. First, the very same language is employed when Ruth goes to her kinsman Boaz (Ruth 3:3–9). Naomi, once Ruth's mother-in-law and now her friend, has instructed her to "note the place where he lies down, and go over and uncover his feet and lie down. He will tell you what you are to do."

> She went over stealthily and uncovered his feet and lay down. In the middle of the night, the man gave a start and pulled back— there was a woman lying at his feet. "Who are you?" he asked. And she replied, "I am your handmaid Ruth. Spread the 'corners' [wings] of your robe over your handmaid, for you are a redeeming kinsman."

The "uncovering of the feet" is a double entendre, suggesting that Ruth has exposed Boaz's genitals.[4] When Ruth asks him to cover her with his robe, the implication is that both espousal and intercourse are taking place. Indeed, the image of spreading the corners of his garment refers to how he hitches up his loose robe and covers her during intercourse.

God's promise that he "will enter" into a covenant with Israel carries similar sexual overtones. In Hebrew, "coming in" is sometimes used to describe intercourse (e.g., Gen. 38:9, 15). And the expression "coming into a covenant," though occasionally used in other contexts (1 Sam. 20:8; Deut. 29:11; Jer. 34:10), is not a typical way of expressing the idea of making a covenant. The expressions "cutting a covenant" and "establishing a covenant" are used more frequently by Ezekiel (16:62, 17:13, 34:25, 37:26). Finally, in a similar parable about God marrying two sisters (Israel and Judah) who had earlier whored in Egypt, Ezekiel has God say, "they became Mine, and they bore sons and daughters" (23:4). The birth of children here makes explicit the idea that divine intercourse has occurred with the feminized nations of Israel and Judah.

Some interpreters view Ezekiel's imagery as bordering on pornographic and dismiss it as a product of his idiosyncrasies (Cooke 1951; Eichrodt 1970). From another perspective, however, Ezekiel is simply stating more boldly what is already implicit in the thought of Hosea and Jeremiah. God's intercourse with Israel is simply the mirror image of Israel's "whoring" after other gods or other nations. If Israel's relations with other gods and nations is sexual, then fidelity to God may be sexual as well.

What is it about these particular contexts that allows what is otherwise unthinkable—God's sexual body—to surface? It is not just the personification of Israel as a woman that enables the divine penis to be conceptualized. It is also the use of a particular kind of religious language. Nowhere is anyone said to have seen God. These passages are thus similar to those in which God is represented as a rock or a lion. They call forth a set of ideas (covenant, fidelity, etc.) much more readily than they do an image of a man and woman making love. In part, this is because Israel is not actually a woman, but a collection of people personified as a woman. And the act of intercourse is itself a metaphor for the covenantal relationship between God and Israel. The idea of God cohabiting with Israel is fundamentally different than the idea of Zeus having sex with Hera. Since Zeus and Hera are imagined in human form, and since their coupling does not stand primarily for a conceptual idea, their intercourse more readily and naturally evokes a visual image. But when divine intercourse stands for a committed relationship between a deity and a people, the visual image recedes.

The Ezekiel passage is as close as we get to a graphic image of God having sexual intercourse. But even here the sex of the deity remains veiled, for in this case the gaze emanates from God and alights on the body of the female Israel. The divine body is behind the look and not the object of it. This represents a critical shift of perspective. In sources examined in the previous chapter, the gaze was that of a male figure looking at God. But the tables have now been turned, and the origin of the gaze has a great deal to do with how much is seen.

To borrow an insight from film criticism, there are multiple perspectives from which a narrative or myth enables a spectator to imagine. As Laura Mulvey notes, "There are three different looks associated with cinema: that of the camera as it records the pro-filmic event, that of the audience as it watches the final product, and that of the characters at each other within the screen illusion" (1989, 25). In the narratives and prophetic pronouncements of Israelite religion, there are also typically three vantage points: the perspective of an omniscient narrator who sees and tells all, the perspective of God (who is ironically less omniscient than the narrator), and the perspective of some character in the narrative.[5] In the Ezekiel texts in which sexual intercourse is depicted, the narrator's standpoint has become submerged in the perspective of the deity. In other words, it is through God's eyes that we gaze on the beauty of the young woman Israel. And in seeing this woman through the deity's eyes, the deity's body is not observed. To be sure, there are numerous other occasions when the narrative voice in prophetic literature collapses into that of God's. But the point is that this shift of perspective in Ezekiel allows a graphic depiction of God's intercourse, and it is because God's perspective is shared with us that this sexual act can be imagined. Unlike the view of an omniscient spectator, which would encompass the entire primal scene, our divine perspective keeps the male body out of sight. What we find here is consistent with what we discovered earlier: when the gaze is focused on bodies and beauty, it is typically the male who is doing the looking, the female who is the object of the gaze.

The reluctance to turn the gaze on the deity's sex is underscored by the delicate way God describes his intercourse with Israel: "With an oath, I entered into a covenant with you—declares the Lord God;

thus you became Mine." At the very moment God is about to join with Israel, the description takes leave of the metaphoric scene. God enters, not into Israel personified as a woman, but into a covenant with a collective people, and it is not with a phallus but through an oath that this bond is made. Significantly, God does not exhibit a similar delicacy when speaking about Israel's fornication with the Egyptians, whose big phalluses Israel is depicted as lusting after (Ezek. 16:26, 23:20), or Israel's masturbation with phallic objects (Ezek. 16:17).

The intrusion of the oath here has perplexed some interpreters since Israelite marriage did not involve the taking of an oath.[6] But as a diversion from God's phallus, its presence is not so surprising. The substitution of an oral promise for an act of sexual intercourse parallels the deflection of the gaze from the midsection and front of the deity to the face and back, discussed in chapter 3. This is not the only context in which the penis and the oath are associated. Recall that Abraham and Jacob are both Israelite patriarchs depicted as receiving solemn oaths from subordinates who grasp the patriarch's penis (Gen. 24:2, 47:29–30). To be sure, the parallels are not exact. In the human cases, it is the more powerful man who asks for the oath and the underling who must swear and grasp. In the Ezekiel passage, the divinity swears allegiance to the subordinate people, who are imagined as a nubile young woman. On the other hand, this young woman really stands for those who were the primary actors in covenant with God, Israelite men. The similarities are thus stronger than they might at first appear.

Paradoxically, while the anatomical maleness of God is never fully conceptualized, God is sometimes imagined not only in feminine imagery but as anatomically female. Phyllis Trible, for example, has noted how God is imagined as a pregnant woman (Isa. 42:14), a mother (Isa. 66:13), a midwife (Ps. 22:9), and mistress (Ps. 123:2), and she goes on to argue that on several occasions this imagery seems to ascribe anatomical femaleness to God. "Hearken to Me, O house of Jacob, all the remnant of the house of Israel, who have been borne by me from the womb, carried by me from the womb; even to your old age I am he and to gray hairs I will carry you. I have made, and I will bear; I will carry and I will save" (Isa. 46:3–4). Trible remarks that "the imagery of this poetry stops just short of saying that God possesses a womb." She argues also that in one passage God is represented as saying to Ephraim that "my womb trembles for him" (1983, 38, 45). Virginia Mollenkott points out that Zion cries, "The Lord has forsaken me, My Lord has forgotten me," and God responds, "Can a woman forget her baby, or disown the child of her womb? Though she might forget, I never could forget you" (1986, 20). In Isaiah 42, Yahweh cries out, "Like a travailing woman I will groan; I will pant, I will gasp at the same time" (ibid., 15). These passages, too, come very close to suggesting that metaphorically God is a mother with a womb. Similar imagery is evoked when Moses is overwhelmed by the Israelites' constant complaints: "Why have you dealt ill with Your servant . . . that You have laid the burden of all this people upon me? Did I conceive all this people, did I bear them, that You should say to me, 'Carry them in your bosom as a nurse carries an infant to the land that You have promised on oath to their fathers' " (Num. 11:11–13). In denying his own role as mother to Israel, Moses seemingly implies that it is God who is the mother who bore Israel and who should suckle the infant. There is also a possible association between breasts and the epithet "El Shaddai," one of the names used for God, a point noted by Trible (1986, 61) and Biale (1982; 1992, 26). The word Shaddai has the same consonantal structure as the word for breasts, though etymologically the two terms may derive from different stems. But in at least one passage there seems to be a deliberate play on the connection between the word breasts and the name El Shaddai (Gen. 49:25).

Some interpreters have cited such passages as evidence of God's partial androgyny, or at least of a balance of genders in the representation of the deity. In fact, there appears to be less reluctance in employing explicit metaphors of female anatomy for God than metaphors of male anatomy. This makes sense. Since the gaze is typically assumed to be male, and since it is male figures who are imagined to have seen God, the deity can be comfortably figured in metaphors that are anatomically female.

In the texts of ancient Israel, then, we are dealing with at least two kinds of God images: (1) visual descriptions of what is seen when a character looks upon God and (2) conceptual representations that describe God in contexts in which seeing does not take place. These conceptual representations are more likely to evoke ideas (covenant, fidelity, power) than specific mental pictures. When God's figure is described by one who sees him, the deity's sex is veiled by the aversion of the observer's gaze. The sex of the deity is allowed to emerge in conceptual representations partly because no one is looking. It is the disappearance of the gaze that allows the sex of God to be more fully imagined. Moreover, the deity's body is kept invisible by the conflation of the narrator's perspective with God's own.

Interpreters of Israelite religion have been intrigued by the question of how the images of God in the prophetic literature can be reconciled with the religious prohibition against material images of the deity. Some see a contradiction here: while the prohibition seems to imply that God is unrepresentable, the prophets depict God as being masculine. Others argue that there was never a reluctance to think about God anthropomorphically; hence the prohibition on images has to be interpreted differently (von Rad 1962, 1:218). In my view, the prophetic descriptions and metaphors also suggest that certain kinds of restraints were placed on imagining God as explicitly male, and these restraints require a rethinking of the prohibition against images.

The Veto on Images

The so-called aniconic impulse is often regarded as one of the most distinctive aspects of Israelite religion.[7] Its importance to Israelite religion is suggested by its appearance in the various versions of the Decalogue (Exod. 20:4; Deut. 5:8), as well as in various other legal codes, the Covenant Code (Exod. 20:20), the Holiness Code (Lev. 19:4), the list of covenant curses (Deut. 27:15), and the so-called ritual Decalogue (Exod. 34:17). Archaeological evidence confirms the literary record, showing a sharp discontinuity in anthropomorphic figurines of male deities between Late Bronze Age and Iron Age strata in early Israelite sites.[8] Whereas in the earlier period figures that may represent male and female deities are common, in the later strata only one male figurine has been unearthed. The standing goddess plaque, the main type of female cult image, seems to be entirely lacking.

There are various debates about the meaning of and historical development of the prohibition on material images.[9] Some view it as an original law that goes back to the Mosaic period, while others believe it originated in the eighth century under the influence of the prophetic critique of non-Israelite religious cults. A textual explanation for the prohibition is provided only in sources of a relatively late date (Deut. 4:12ff.), which were rationalizing an already well-established practice. According to these sources, the prohibition is related to the fact that Israel did not see God at Sinai but only heard a divine voice. Some interpreters argue that this shows that Yahweh's transcendence was thought to be compromised when he was represented in concrete form. Others regard the prohibition as an attempt to protect and reinforce the idea of a God who acts in history. On this view, an image would somehow infringe upon the freedom of the deity, since a living God cannot be put into a static form. Still others believe the rejection of images reflects Israel's rejection of magic; by proscribing images, which might be magically manipulated, control over the deity could be prevented. The prohibition is also understood as part and parcel of Israel's desire to reject the religious practices and cultures of neighboring peoples.

There are a number of difficulties with most of these suggestions.[10] In particular, most of these theories work within a quasi-developmental framework that imagines monotheism as emerging from a pagan or primitive background. There is also a striking impulse to spiritualize this religious prohibition. More compelling is Hendel's view that the aniconic tradition reflects Israel's early ambivalence about kingship. Since the representation of the deity on the throne or ark was used to legitimate human kingship, Israel's ambivalence about that institution may have been expressed in the rejection of images altogether (Hendel 1988). It is for this reason that Yahweh is not imagined enthroned on the ark. The pros and cons of these arguments, however, need not detain us any longer, for even if these other interpretations are correct, a practice as important as the refusal to make images always carries multiple meanings and serves many functions (Eilberg-Schwartz 1990, 119ff.).

One of these functions, I suggest, was to defuse the idea of God's maleness. Like the aversion of the gaze from the deity's figure in Israel's religious literature, the prohibition on material images kept the issue of God's sex from being fully confronted. In other words, this practice was rooted in the same ambivalence displayed in the early Israelite myths and prophetic texts. It was another way, perhaps the most important way, of glossing the difficulties generated by a male God partnered only by the collective Israel. This is not to say that any religious images crafted by ancient Jews would have represented the divine genitals. But the making of God images would have forced the Israelites to be explicit about the deity's secondary sexual characteristics, such as facial hair. As we have seen, archaeological remains indicate that male deities of the ancient Near East were frequently pictured as bearded figures riding on a cherub throne.[11] The prohibition on making images was thus consistent with the use of images in the prophetic writings. It was not anthropomorphism itself that was a problem for ancient Israel, but a specific problem posed by anthropomorphism: the deity's sex. The "veto on images" and the restraints at play in the prophetic writings were both responses to the same dilemma. And while I do not assume that these sexual dilemmas were the only motivations behind the prohibition on images, their influence contributed to its importance.

A number of scholars have approached this view tangentially. Thus, von Rad writes that "the idea of man as made in the image of God has also to be incorporated in this discussion [on the veto of images]. Israel herself to be sure drew no such connecting lines, but it can hardly be doubted that there is an inner connexion between the commandment [not to make images] and the image of God in man" (1962, 1:218 n. 70). In a christological vein, von Rad goes on to say "that the time had not yet arrived when God could be worshipped as man." Von Rad does not say why Israel cannot imagine worshiping God as man. Nor does he speculate about the nature of this inner connection between the veto on images and the image of God in man. But we have already come a long way toward making sense of these connections, and we shall return later to the question of why Christianity, unlike Judaism, was able to think of God as man.

The prohibition against material images, then, was not simply a rejection of syncretism. It was a specific way of protecting the honor of the father God. In what may be the earliest version of this prohibition (called the "Shechemite dodecalogue"), there is a direct association between this prohibition and the respect due to one's parents.

> Cursed be the man who makes a sculptured or molten image, abhorred by the Lord, a craftman's handiwork, and sets it up in secret. And all the people shall respond, Amen. Cursed be he who shames his father or mother. And all the people shall say, Amen. (Deut. 27:15–16)[12]

By not making images, a man—and the laws in Deuteronomy 27 are addressed specifically to men—respects God, his parent in heaven, just as he must honor his human parents. There are of course many ways in which boys can dishonor their parents (see, for example, Deut. 21:18–21). But as we've seen, the story of Noah suggests that averting the eyes from the father's nakedness is paradigmatic.[13] It is not just the father's honor, however, that is protected in the laws of Deuteronomy. The curses against a man who makes images and who dishonors his parents are followed by curses over one who removes a neighbor's landmark, who makes the blind go astray, who upsets the justice of the stranger, fatherless, and widow, who sleeps with an animal, who sleeps with his half sister or mother-in-law, who smites his neighbor in secret, or who takes a bribe to acquit the murderer of an innocent person. Much of this list concerns the violation of privacy, overstepping sexual bounds, the secretive performance of some shameful act. Some scholars even refer to this list as the "sexual dodecalogue" (Weinfield 1972, 279). Shaming the parents is thus regarded as analogous to these other shameful sexual acts.

The association between honoring one's parents and not overstepping sexual boundaries is operative in the Holiness Code as well. "If any man reviles (yěqalēl) his father or his mother, he shall be put to death; he has repudiated his father and his mother—his bloodguilt is upon him" (Lev. 20:9). [14] What follows this law is a list of sexual violations, beginning with adultery and shifting to adultery with one's father's wife: "If a man lies with his father's wife, it is the nakedness of his father that he has uncovered; the two shall be put to death—their bloodguilt is upon them." The admonition against cursing one's parents thus serves as a general introduction for a variety of sexual restrictions, including incest with one's mother, the act that counts as exposing one's father's nakedness. [15] Here again Israelite imagination links the ideas of honoring one's parents and staying within the bounds of proper sexual behavior.

The Shechemite dodecalogue, then, illustrates the nexus between three different kinds of prohibitions: against making material images of God, against dishonoring one's parents, and against violating various sexual norms. It is not merely the possible secrecy involved in setting up images that explains why that prohibition appears with the others. Nor does this law simply indicate that "no image of the godhead could venture to appear" (von Rad 1962, 1:215). Rather, it implies no representation of the God-body would be allowed. The prohibition on making images of Yahweh is thus another way of averting the son's gaze from Yahweh's figure. The "Semites" are asked to be like Shem, the virtuous son of Noah, and refuse to gaze at their Father's nakedness.

The veto on divine images is also tied to other demands. In the Decalogue (Exod. 20:1–6), for example, it is juxtaposed to the religious prohibition against worshiping other deities. There are signs that this passage reflects later editing, as many commentators have noted. Nonetheless at some point the prohibition on images came to be associated with the first commandment, which insists on God's exclusive relationship with Israel (Childs 1974, 405). [16] Why is the making of images singled out as the alien practice par excellence that should be avoided? As others have noted, Israelites had many practices and conceptions in common with their neighbors, such as sacrifices and the idea of covenant. What, then, was so problematic about divine images? [17]

As suggested earlier, there is a logic that leads from Israel's exclusive commitment to one God to the prohibition on images. Since Israel is forbidden to have any other gods, Yahweh cannot be imagined as having a sexual partner, and it is precisely at the moment when other gods are ruled out of Israel's imaginative universe that the problem of the divine sex becomes difficult. Hence the second commandment—the prohibition on images—responds to the problem generated by the first commandment. That is not to say, however, that the prohibition on images necessarily developed hand in hand with the prohibition against worshiping other gods. But the juxtaposition of these rules suggests that the ideas came to be linked and understood to support one another.

The religious prohibition against worshiping other deities intensifies and makes much more visible the potentially homoerotic relationship between Israelite men and God. Because God cannot have a divine sexual partner, Israel in effect becomes the equivalent of God's spouse. This is implicit in the language of the Decalogue, which imagines God as jealously guarding the exclusivity of his relationship with Israel. Thus the adjective "jealous" (qn') is used to describe the reaction that a man has when he suspects his wife of adultery (Num. 5:15, 18, 25, 29; Prov. 6:34, 27:4).[18] And because the deity's relationship with Israel is in fact a relationship with individual Israelite males, at the very moment the Decalogue personifies Israel as a wife, Israel is addressed by God in the first person maculine singular (Childs 1974, 394). You (masculine, singular) are my wife whose fidelity I guard, God says to each Israelite man. The prohibition on images is thus evoked precisely where the dilemma of a homoerotic relationship threatens to emerge.

The veiling of the father's body, then, takes a variety of forms in Israelite religion: the prohibition on making images, the aversion of the gaze of characters who see God, and the submerging of the listener's perspectives into the perspective of God. This cloaking of the deity's sex, the invitation to be a virtuous son of Noah, calls for a new way of thinking about what has traditionally been regarded as a growing Israelite discomfort with anthropomorphism.

The Name, the Face, and the Glory

Many interpreters cite a variety of plausible evidence to demonstrate growing Israelite reluctance about visualizing God in human form.

They contrast, for example, the earliest sources in which God's figure is sighted with later sources that seem troubled by such an idea. In particular, the book of Deuteronomy serves as an important contrast to the early narratives. Whereas the narratives in Exodus emphasize that Moses and the leaders saw God, in Deuteronomy, Moses declares to the children of Israel, "For your own sake, therefore, be most careful—since you saw no shape when the Lord your God spoke to you at Horeb out of the fire—not to act wickedly and make for yourselves a sculptured image in any likeness whatever, having the form of a man or a woman, the form of any beast on earth, the form of any winged bird that flies in the sky" (Deut. 4:15–18). The emphasis seems to shift from seeing the deity to hearing the deity's word.

A similar development is said to be reflected in the deuteronomic story about Elijah's flight for his life after having killed the prophets of Baal (1 Kings 19:1–14). Exhausted, he is awoken by an angel who feeds him. He then rises and "walks forty days and forty nights as far as the mountain of God at Horeb." There he goes into a cave, and spends the night, until God instructs him to come out "and stand on the mountain before the Lord."

> And lo, the Lord passed by. There was a great and mighty wind, splitting mountains and shattering rocks by the power of the Lord; but the Lord was not in the wind. After the wind—an earthquake; but the Lord was not in the earthquake. After the earthquake—fire; but the Lord was not in the fire. And after the fire—a soft murmuring sound. When Elijah heard it, he wrapped his mantle about his face and went out and stood at the entrance of the cave.

This incident is reminiscent of and was probably modeled on the story of Moses standing in the cleft of the rock and gazing on the deity from behind. The forty days and forty nights, the cave, and the covering of the face all point back to the earlier myth of Moses. Yet in contrast to Moses, Elijah sees nothing. He hears only a still, small voice.

Some scholars have argued that the increasing importance of intermediaries between humans and God, such as angels and a personified Wisdom, as well as an increasing reliance on indirect terms to refer to God, signal a growing discomfort with anthropomorphism.[19] The Deuteronomist writes, for example, about the Temple in Jerusalem as the place in which God "causes his name to dwell." God's name has taken the place of the divine presence. Given this developmental scheme, it is not surprising that later sources speak of God as completely incomparable: "To whom, then, can you liken God, What form compare him?" (Isa. 40:18). "To whom can you compare Me or declare Me similar? To whom can you liken Me, so that we seem comparable? . . . For I am God and there is none else, I am divine, and there is none like Me" (Isa. 46:5–9). God has apparently ceased to have analogies in the human world. And a notion of God in human form hardly seems compatible with the idea that "the whole world is full of his glory" (Isa. 6:3).[20] The developmental perspective, then, implies that over time or at some specific time there arose what interpreters regard as a more abstract notion of the deity. But there is an obvious and fundamental flaw in this argument. While it may be true that some sources exhibit reluctance to describe a God sighting, such sightings never cease in the literature of ancient Israel or the varieties of Judaism that follow. God sightings appear in sources dating from all periods of Israelite religion and continue throughout Second Temple forms of Judaism and into the late antique period and beyond.

Realizing the problem with the quasi-evolutionary view, some interpreters suggest other reasons for the shift in the deuteronomic writings. Mettinger (1979), for example, views the reluctance to imagine God as reflecting the need for a more transcendent God after the destruction of the Temple and the Babylonian exile in the early sixth century B.C.E. But I maintain that most of the evidence adduced in support of these other theories also lends weight to the alternative theory I have been developing. The language of the later sources represents another kind of theological deflection of the issue of God's sex.

The new theological terminology, for example, reveals at the conceptual level the sorts of restraints imposed by the aversion of the gaze from the front and midsection of God's body, discussed in chapter 3. Recall how the gaze was deflected from the midsection of the deity's body to the extremities, the feet, face, and back. In the later sources there is a concentration of theological terms referring to God's extremities. The face or countenance of God thus serves as a recurring image for God's care, protection, and concern (Eichrodt 1967, 2:35–38). In the priestly benediction (Num. 6:25–26), Aaron and his sons are to say to the children of Israel, "The Lord bless you and keep you. Let the Lord make his face shine upon you and be gracious to you. Let the Lord lift up his face upon you and grant you peace."[21] And when God anticipates how the Israelites will stray after alien gods and will forsake his covenant, he tells Moses, "Then My anger will flare up against them, and I will abandon them and hide My face from them" (Deut. 31:17–18; see also Deut. 32:20; Lev. 20:3, 5, 26:17). Examples of such facial imagery could be multiplied endlessly and have been studied extensively.

While it is easy to understand why interpreters see the emphasis on the deity's face as a sort of "spiritualization," it is more difficult to make that claim about "the deity's feet." Yet the feet of God are also an important vehicle for theological reflection (Wolfson 1992). "He bent the sky and came down, thick cloud beneath his feet" (2 Sam. 22:10; Ps. 18:10). The feet of God are a symbol of God's redemptive power: "Lift up Your feet because of . . . all the outrages of the enemy in the sanctuary" (Ps. 74:3). The sanctuary or ark in the Temple is regarded as God's footstool (Ps. 99:5, 132:7; Lam. 2:1; 1 Chron. 28:2). Ezekiel and Isaiah both describe the Temple as the place where God's feet rest (Ezek. 43:7; Isa. 66:1).

To be sure, these images carry a rich variety of theological meanings and cannot be explained simply as a response to the dilemmas posed for ancient Judaism by a male God. The face as the most present and expressive side of the human person obviously provides a ready way of talking about concern, disapproval, and anger. The feet of God evoke powerful images of a deity striding above in the heavens. Nonetheless, if the real worry were anthropomorphic representations of the deity, metaphors of God's face and feet would also be regarded as problematic. The authors of Deuteronomy do not draw back from references to God's outstretched arm and mighty hand (11:2, 26:8), God's heart (7:7), and his finger (9:10). If the focus of concern is in fact the deity's loins, then these metaphors draw attention away from the crucial part of the body, even if that body is simply a metaphorical one.

These theological images, of course, are more revealing than the actual God sightings. Whereas no one is allowed to see (or at least describe) the face of the deity, "God's face" is one of the most popular theological terms. This discrepancy makes sense. One veil can be removed if another one has already moved in to take its place. Thus as long as no character is described as looking at God, the reference to the deity's face is not likely to conjure up an image and questions such as whether this face is bearded or not do not arise. The metaphor of the divine face thus does not threaten to raise the issue of God's sex. But in contexts in which a character is said to see God, as when Moses asks to see God (Exodus 33), if the face were to be described, the presence or absence of a beard would have to be confronted. Deuteronomy explains that the prohibition on images reminds Israel that they did not see God but only heard the deity's voice. The voice is one step removed from a face. It signifies presence without evoking an image.

It is not because the head is the most spiritual part of the body that so many theological terms focus on God's face. Indeed, the heart and liver were generally thought to be the seat of higher intellectual functions. But by focusing on the head, the other parts of the body are kept out of focus, in the margin of the field of vision. What is emerging here, then, is a split of the upper and lower body. Because the lower body cannot be thought, the upper body (the face and voice) take on assumed importance. This upper and lower body displacement has some similarities to that described by Freud. Freud argued that this sort of symbolic displacement occurred with some of his clients. In the case of Dora, for example, Freud argued that because Dora could not acknowledge her erotic feelings, they were displaced into her mouth and exhibited there in various symptoms (Freud 1905a, 30, 83).[22] As

Freud would later work out, patients displaced feelings and struggles that they could not admit to themselves.

A similar process is at work in the later biblical sources, whose restricted symbolism of the deity had its origins in a variety of cultural motivations. Because the phallus of God had to remain unthought, the symbolic concerns that might normally be associated with the phallus were deflected onto the "Godhead." Recall, for example, how in Ezekiel, at the moment of union between God and Israel, an oral act (an oath) substitutes for a genital one. Moreover, as other interpreters have noted, in one version of the creation story, God creates the world by speaking. This theory of upper body displacement may suggest the origin of the Memra theology of the Aramaic translations of the Hebrew Bible. In these translations, references to God or God's presence are translated as "God's Memra" [Word, Speech]. The circumlocution has typically been explained as reflecting a wish to avoid anthropomorphism, and interpreters have also debated whether the Memra is a part of God or a split-off hypostatized entity.[23] In any case, divine speech, like the divine voice, becomes a metonym for God. It replaces a fuller image of what the deity is. I am *not* suggesting that the divine speech is a veiled reference to God's phallus, but that because God's phallus could not be conceptualized or imagined, divine speech absorbed the symbolic concerns that otherwise would have been invested in the divine phallus.

A similar kind of displacement motivates the "Name theology" that is particularly concentrated in the book of Deuteronomy. This book routinely describes God's "causing his name to dwell" (Deut. 12:5, 11, 21; 14:23ff.; 16:2; 26:2) in Jerusalem, the place he has chosen. Because it eliminates all anthropomorphism, Name theology is often cited as the culmination of the process of spiritualization or as evidence of the growing insistence on God's transcendence and the fact that God no longer dwells in the Temple but in heaven (Eichrodt 1967; Mettinger 1982; Weinfeld 1972).

What does it mean that God causes his name to dwell in the Temple? There is, of course, an understanding of name as the essence of something. Putting God's name in the Temple may even signify an act of ownership. But the importance of the divine name shares other meanings and functions with the human name, particularly the Name of the Father as defined by both Freud and Lacan.[24] Early in the book of Deuteronomy (3:14), in a list of the tribes of Israel and their allotment in the land, there is a reference to Jair, the son of Manasseh, a leader who names a geographical area after himself. This act is similar to God's putting his name in Jerusalem, as if God's allotment in the land is the Temple. We must remember that there was a close link in Israelite imagination between lineage and land: tribal designations were both genealogical and geographical (Prewitt 1990; see, e.g., Deut. 3:14). To name a geographical area was like naming one's descendants, who were to live in that area, after oneself. The genealogical importance of a father's name is also evident in the levirate marriage law found in Deuteronomy. When a man died and left no male descendants, his brother was expected to go into his wife and raise up children in the deceased's name (Deut. 25:6). It was critical to preserve the name—the line—of the dead man. Indeed, one of the most severe punishments was to have one's name blotted out from under heaven (Deut. 29:19).[25] The father who withdraws into heaven is not completely different from the father who dies, for it is through their names that the connection with those who are left behind is maintained. In the human realm, of course, being of the name of the father means being of his seed and blotting out his name means wiping out his descendants. Thus the name of the human father is linked to physical procreation, that is, to the penis. The name of the father in heaven, by contrast, is the only thing that connects him with his children on earth. The development of a Name theology may indeed refer to God's transcendence, but that transcendence itself is a gendered absence that is imagined as a father whose body is veiled.

The receding of the divine body in Deuteronomy is consistent with the fact that this book, in contrast to other Israelite texts, almost never feminizes Israel. Although the Deuteronomist outdoes even Hosea's emphasis on love between God and Israel (Deut. 4:37; 7:7; 10:15; 11:1; 19:9; 23:6; 30:16, 20) and repeatedly enjoins Israel to love God with a whole heart and soul (4:29; 10:12; 11:13, 18; 13:4; 30:2, 6), Israel is only once personified as a woman. The preferred metaphor is the relationship of father and son (Deut. 1:31, 8:5, 14:1).[26] "It was to your fathers that the Lord was drawn in His love for them. . . . Cut away therefore the thickening around your hearts and stiffen [your necks] no more" (Deut. 10:15).[27] It is significant, too, that although Deuteronomy is replete with warnings against worshiping foreign gods (6:13, 8:19, 11:16, 12:30, 17:3, 30:17), Israel is never portrayed as an adulteress. The word znh, "whoring," which is so commonly used to describe Israel's relationship to foreign cults and nations in the prophets, is used only once (Deut. 31:16). Deuteronomy prefers the term "lured" (11:16, 12:30, 30:17) or "turning" (17:3) or "following" (6:13, 8:19) to describe Israel's desires for other cults. Yet God is still described as a passionately jealous deity (Deut. 4:24; 5:9; 6:15; 32:16, 21), in language reminiscent of a zealous husband.[28]

The term love was used to describe the relationship of vassal to lord in ancient Near Eastern treaties and thus does not necessarily convey erotic overtones.[29] Still, the terms used for the love of God in Deuteronomy are the same used to describe the love between man and wife (Gen. 24:67, 29:20, 30; Deut. 21:15), as well as carnal desire (Gen. 34:3; Judg. 16:4, 15; 2 Sam. 13:1, 4, 15) and the adultery of Israel (Jer. 2:25; Ezek. 16:37; Isa. 57:8). Israel's desire for God is described with the same word used about the desire that men have for women captured in war. In Deuteronomy, the (male) Israelite is admonished to love God with all his heart, soul, and might, and to hold fast (*dbq*) to him (10:20, 11:22, 13:5, 30:20). What does this mean? The term *dbq* refers to the most intimate type of contact, often of things joined physically, as a tongue to the cleft of the mouth or gums (Ps. 22:16; Ezek. 3:26), a hand to the sword (2 Sam. 23:10), the bone to the skin (Job 19:20), Israel the girdle to the loins of God (Jer. 13:11), or crocodile scales joined together (Job 41:9). It is used figuratively to speak of loyalty and affection, retaining the idea of physical closeness. "A man leaves his father and mother and clings to his wife, so that they become one flesh" (Gen. 2:24). The reference to holding God fast occurs in three contexts in Deuteronomy: in following his commandments, in worshiping him, and in swearing by his name. In these contexts, the term is clearly associated with and intensifies the exclusive loving relationship Israel has with God. Swearing by God's name is one of the ways that one is able to grasp God in a loving way (10:20). In Ezekiel 16, as we have seen, God's oath of fidelity to Israel took the place of sexual intercourse. And like the underling who grasps the penis of the patriarch when swearing an oath, one grasps God's name as a sign of faithfulness to him.

The analogies are clear, and it thus makes sense that in Deuteronomy the father's body is so far removed from earth. Imagining only God's name in Jerusalem, and only his voice emanating from fire at Horeb, masks the potential desire that might arise between a divine father and a human son who love each other and who cling to one another like husband and wife.

A different solution to this problem is hinted at in Malachi. In the three short chapters that compose this book, the prophet several times uses the metaphor of father and son to describe Israel and God's relationship (1:6, 2:10, 3:18). In contrast to Deuteronomy, however, the prophet restores erotic imagery to the description of Israel's turning away from God. But here it is a male Israel who "has profaned what is holy to the Lord—what He desires—and espoused daughters of alien gods" (Mal. 2:11).[30] Israel's sacrifices are no longer acceptable to God because Israel has broken faith with the wife of his youth: "The Lord is a witness between you and the wife of your youth with whom you have broken faith, though she is your partner and covenanted spouse" (2:14). "'Let no one break faith with the wife of his youth. For I detest divorce'—says the Lord, the God of Israel" (2:15–16). Who is this covenanted spouse, this wife of youth, that Israel first married? It may well be that these passages refer to a social situation in which Judean men were marrying foreign women, as Camp (1991) suggests. But in following out the metaphor on the theological level, God appears as the covenanted spouse with whom Israel broke faith, for it is God's ways that Israel has abandoned (1:12, 2:8). The images thus parallel those of Hosea and Ezekiel, but now God takes the feminine position.

The genders have been reversed in the process of allowing for Israel's masculinity to assert itself. To allow Israel to be male, God is feminized.

Still another solution to the homoerotic dilemma occurs in the book of Proverbs, where the relationship of the father and son is dominant. Many of the proverbs are addressed to "my son" (4:20, 5:1, 6:1–2, 23:19). Much advice is given about the appropriate role of discipline and corporal punishment in the father-son relationship, and the way in which a son honors or dishonors his parents, particularly his father (10:1; 13:24; 15:5, 20; 17:2, 25; 19:13, 18, 26, 22; 20:11, 19; 22:6; 23:13; 28:5; 29:3, 17). Proverbs was probably written in the postexilic period and may reflect the need for family stability. The advice is addressed at least in part to actual father-son relationships.

Yet it is clear that the relationship of the father and son is sometimes also regarded as parallel to that between God and Israel (3:12). "The eyes of the Lord are everywhere observing the bad and the good. . . . A fool spurns the discipline of his father" (Prov. 15:33–35). Noting this shift from human to divine father, Newsom writes, "It is not enough to ground the authority structure of Proverbs 1–9 in the patriarchal father. The authority of the transcendent Father of fathers is needed" (1989, 150). Many of the proverbs move from advice about proper discipline of the son to the nature of the proper relationship between a man and God. In some cases, it is unclear which father is speaking or being spoken about: "My son, heed my words; and store up my commandments with you. Keep my commandments and live, My teaching, as the apple of your eye. Bind them on your fingers; write them on the tablet of your mind" (7:1–3). "My son, if you accept my words and treasure up my commandments; If you make your ear attentive to wisdom and your mind open to discernment; if you call to understanding and cry aloud to discernment . . . then you will understand the fear of the Lord and attain knowledge of God" (2:1–5). "My son, keep your father's commandment. Do not forsake your mother's teaching. Tie them over your heart always; bind them around your throat. When you walk it will lead you; when you lie down it will watch over you" (Prov. 6:20). In these passages, particularly the last, we find a variation of the command in Deuteronomy to bind God's word on the arm and between the eyes and to speak of it when you lie down and rise up.

The father's advice is personified as Wisdom, a female figure (e.g., Proverbs 8 and 9). Wisdom is to some extent a motherly image. She is the wife who "has built her house, prepared the feast, mixed the wine and also set the table" (Prov. 9:1–2). The son is constantly imagined as having to choose between faithfulness to the father's words, to Wisdom, or to the words of the sexually provocative and inappropriate woman whose mouth is a deep pit (22:14) with a smooth tongue (6:23) and whose lips drip honey (5:3). Who this alien woman represents is subject to dispute. Until recently she was thought to stand for ethnically foreign women who threatened Israel's social and religious purity, but more recent writings have pointed to the fact that she may be Israelite and hence indicative of the beginning of an ideology that condemned all women as a threat to the attainment of Wisdom, the Father's word (Camp 1991). Although Wisdom is herself imagined erotically on occasion (4:6–8, 5:7), sexuality is not depicted as central to the relationship with her, belonging instead to the realm of real women (Newsom 1989).[31]

Wisdom is not conceptualized totally independently of God. There is a slippage between the father's words and the words of female Wisdom. Indeed, the proverbs addressed to "my son" can sometimes be read in three different voices, the human father, God, or Wisdom herself: "My son, listen to my wisdom . . . sons pay heed to me, and do not swerve from the words of my mouth" (5:1–7). There is a similar slippage between Wisdom and God: "Keep my commandments and you will live. Acquire wisdom, acquire discernment; Do not forget and do not swerve from my words. Do not forsake her and she will guard you; Sons do not swerve from the words of my mouth" (5:7). Not forsaking Wisdom means attending to the words of the human or divine father. As Newsom puts it, "Her voice, of course, is the cultural voice that speaks through the father, the voice that grounds the social fathers. Hers is the voice that mediates between the transcendent father and his earthly sons" (1989, 156).

Newsom suggests that the alignment of the human male and the divine father is a way to stop the threatening identification of the female Wisdom with divine authority, which undergirds but also threatens to undermine the authority of the patriarchal father. But there is another way of viewing the matter: the female Wisdom interposes herself in the relationship of God the father and Israel the son. Hence, for those who remember Ezekiel and Hosea's descriptions of the lovemaking of God and Israel, the interruption of a female figure restores heterosexual imagery. This essentially nonsexual female image allows sons to love God's words while keeping homoerotic associations at bay.

We have seen how the dilemma of homoeroticism is dealt with in different ways in different biblical contexts: Ezekiel narrates the act of God's intercourse from God's perspective, Deuteronomy does away with the divine body and imagines God as a voice and name, Malachi seems to feminize the deity, and Proverbs imposes female Wisdom between the son and father. The transsexual nature of Israel in ancient Judaic literature—sometimes as woman to the male God or to other gods and nations, sometimes as male sons to God and as male lovers of other nations and religions—is evidence of the struggle of the tradition to preserve its heterosexual imagery. To some extent this shifting of metaphors worked. It obscured the implied homoeroticism between the loving father and the loving son. But Israelite thought—as is true of any cultural system—could not be wholly compartmentalized. There was always seepage from one metaphorical domain to the other. The reversal of Israel's and God's sexes, the disappearance and veiling of God's body reveal the discomfort with the loving relationship of Israel and God.

The Disappearing Body

If monotheism created a tension around the representation of the deity's sex, then it is not very surprising that many Jews found the Greek idea of a disembodied and incorporeal God so plausible and satisfying. This conception of God disposes once and for all of the problem of the divine genitals. I do not mean to imply that the tradition of denying God a body developed exclusively or even primarily as an effort to avoid the question of God's sex. I am suggesting that the idea of an incorporeal God spoke to profound concerns in Judaism that help to explain why it penetrated so deeply into Jewish imagination. Modern interpreters who say the Jews believed in an incorporeal God from the first are not simply engaging in an anachronistic reading of monotheism. They are inadvertently participating in the very process they are trying to understand. By importing questionable assumptions into those texts that depict God's body, they render incomprehensible any questions about God's genitals specifically, and about the divine sex generally. The hiding of God's body, however, was only one solution to the dilemma of homoeroticism, as we shall now see. Another solution was to feminize Israelite males so they could assume the role of God's wife.

PART III

*For
the Love
of God*

Moses by Michelangelo. St. Pietro in Vincoli, Rome.
Photograph from Alinari/Art Resource, New York.

Chapter Six

Unmanning Israel

Annul me in my manhood, Lord, and make
Me women-sexed and weak,
If by that total transformation
I might know Thee more.
What is the worth of my own sex
That the bold possessive instinct
Should but shoulder Thee aside?
What uselessness is housed in my loins,
To drive, drive, the rampant pride of life,
When what is needful is a hushed quiescence?
"The soul is feminine to God."

BROTHER ANTONINUS (WILLIAM O.
EVERSON), The Crooked Lines of God

I WANT TO RECALL for a moment Freud's analysis of Schreber's case, which provided the foundation for Freud's thoughts about the homoerotic and religion.[1] Whatever the causes of Schreber's fantasies of being unmanned and sexually desired by God, his writings took him to the heart of what I have called the dilemma of monotheism. Schreber's "caricature of God" is not in fact a caricature at all.[2] He was able to think the unthinkable and thus express what traditional theology has always been afraid to face.

When a man confronts a male God, he is put into the female position so as to be intimate with God.[3] The masculinity of Israelite men was thus most secure when God turned his back, hid his face, or kept himself covered in a cloud or in the heavens. But when Israelite men had to face God, their masculinity was made uncertain. The defining traits of what it meant to be a man were called into question. In the literature of ancient Judaism, this threat to masculinity proceeds in ways parallel to Schreber's: sometimes through violence that threatens castration, even death, at other times in more subtle forms of gender reversal.

The threat to Israelite masculinity was part of a complicated process in which a complementary model of two genders or sexes (male/female) was imposed on a *ménage à trois*: God/Israelite man/Israelite woman. Because the desire of heaven was nearly always imagined as male and heterosexual, Israelite women theoretically should have been the appropriate objects of divine desire. The insertion of Israelite men into this equation required their unmanning. This chapter explores threatened masculinity in various intimate contexts of ancient Judaism: in the relationship between God and certain Israelite men, in the intrusion of God into the relations between husband and wife, and in the stories of divine attacks upon Israelite men.

Odd Men Out

Let us return for a moment to Genesis 6:1–4, the myth about the sons of God who have intercourse with the daughters of man. Whatever else this myth might say, it offers a paradigm for the imposition of heterosexual imagery on heaven and earth. The divine realm, because it is imagined as more powerful and hierarchically superior, is assimilated to the male; the human realm, because it is seen as inferior, is assimilated to the female. There is no "natural" place for human men in this divine-human paradigm.[4] They are odd men out, for they can occupy neither the male nor the female position. The imbalance can only be rectified if female angels are posited, as they are later in one Gnostic text.[5]

The implied superfluousness of human males in this myth is more explicit in subsequent retellings. The sons of God are later described as fallen angels, or Watchers, who are responsible for the fall of humankind. God brings the flood to wipe the slate clean. But these myths reflect more than fears about human corruption, for the male angels generate specific anxieties in human men. In the Genesis Apocryphon, for example, Lamech wonders whether he is actually the father of his son Noah, because he suspects his wife of having consorted with the Watchers.[6] Husbands must fear their wives' adultery with divine as well as human men. The Testament of Reuben (5:4–6) also tells how the Watchers desired human women and assumed the form of men while the women were having intercourse with their husbands. The women conceive giants because they have gazed with lust at these apparitions. These reflections on the divine impregnation of women anticipate the stories of Jesus' conception, to which we return in chapter 9, and illustrate how divine intervention in pregnancy undermines human masculinity.[7]

Thus, although the rivals described in the sons of God myth and its later expansions are destroyed in the flood, the threat of the divine masculine remains. To be sure, unlike the fallen angels, God is not imagined as having physical intercourse with specific Israelite women, but he is the ultimate dispenser of fertility throughout the narratives of the Hebrew Bible.[8] Particularly in Genesis, barren matriarchs cannot conceive until God intervenes and opens their wombs. Even though they are potent with other women, the patriarchs are powerless to impregnate their wives. Sarah is described as barren (Gen. 11:30) and as being restrained or shut up by God (16:1–2).[9] To get Abraham a child, she has him go into Hagar, who conceives easily (16:1–6). God subsequently informs Abraham that Sarah will be visited the following year and will have a son (18:9–17). Sarah finds this promise highly amusing since she has reached menopause and since Abraham is old. God is annoyed, because "nothing is too wondrous for the Lord" (18:14). This seems to be the theological point of these stories of childless women. It is God who oversees fertility. "The Lord took note (*paqad*) of Sarah as He had promised and the Lord did for Sarah as He had spoken" (21:1–2).[10] Isaac's wife, Rebekkah, is also described as barren (Gen. 25:21), and when Isaac entreats God on her behalf, she becomes pregnant with twins. God is also responsible for opening the wombs of Jacob's wives, Leah and Rachel. God opens Leah's womb first to compensate her for not being Jacob's true love (Gen. 29:31). Rachel, who remains barren, demands that Jacob give her a child. But Jacob gets angry and retorts, "Can I take the place of God, who has denied you fruit of the womb?" (30:2). God does eventually remember Rachel and allows her to conceive (30:22).

The role of God in conception is repeatedly recognized by mothers who name their children after the divine and not the human father. Eve, for example, gives one of her sons the name Cain (*qayin*) because "I have gained a male child (*qānîtî*) with the help of the Lord" (Gen. 4:1). As Pardes has noted, this statement by Eve reflects her claim to be co-creator with God and underscores the lack of Adam's participation in the conception.[11] And Leah refers to God's role in the names of her sons: Reuben ("The Lord has seen my affliction"), Simeon ("This is because the Lord heard"), and Judah ("This time I will praise the Lord") (Gen. 29:32–33). Raising a child in one's own name is one of the central expectations of manhood. As we have seen, if a man died childless, his wife was expected to marry his brother in order to raise up a child in his name (Deut. 25:6). In the stories of the patriarchs' wives, however, the male children are named after their father in heaven.

It is true that in the culture of ancient Israel a masculine God does authorize male domination in the social order and the association of masculinity with creativity (Delaney 1991; Adler 1977). But if we do not conflate human and divine masculinities, if we examine them as two separate and sometimes conflicting symbols, another story emerges. The divine male can be seen to compete with and threaten the role of human males. This is not to argue that God's participation in conception negates the manhood of Abraham or Isaac or Jacob in some ultimate sense. These stories do not tell of virgin births and the human fathers are not dispensable. But God must open the woman's womb (Gen. 29:31, 30:22) before she is receptive to the man's seed. Try as he might, the man cannot impregnate his wife without the blessing of God. Like Jacob, the men can only throw up their hands when their barren wives ask them for children. The human male, therefore, can never really control the womb of his wife. Virginity may be proof that he has been the first to possess her (Deut. 22:13), but only the father God possesses her womb.

This tension over conception and reproduction in the Genesis stories differs in significant respects from the Oedipus struggle that Freud describes in *Totem and Taboo* and that he later imagines to take place between the symbolic father God and the human male. For Freud, the sons and father are in competition for the sexual rights to the mother and her offspring. The father either banishes his sons or castrates them to preserve his exclusive claims to reproduction. In the ancient narratives of Israel, by contrast, the father God and son jointly participate in procreation. The Father must open the womb and the son must plant the seed. Still, the son's virility is very much threatened by the Father's control. It is the Father who dispenses the rights of reproduction to the son. This control over the son's reproductive success is one of the reasons why the male genital organ is marked with the sign of circumcision. It signifies the Father's blessing of the son's reproduction (Eilberg-Schwartz 1990, 141–73).

Unmanning Israel

The dilemma of intimacy between the father God and the human male offers us a new way to account for the denigration of women in Israel's religious system. According to the conventional argument, God is male because the male is the norm. Women are by definition different. The otherness of women is recognized and reinforced through rituals that associate impurity with menstruation and childbirth and that bar women from contact with the sacred. Men alone have access to the sacred and to God and find in the Temple and its cultic activity a mirror that validates the male self. This explanation of women's place in the Israelite religious system presupposes that the primary function of religious symbols is to reflect and legitimate the social order. But religious symbols are born through complex processes whose origins are often lost. Once established, they have lives of their own with unpredictable effects on the moral, imaginative, and intellectual lives of religious actors. Symbolic processes, in other words, cannot be reduced to social functions.

Thus, once God was imagined as male, he assumed male qualities, including sexual qualities. In ancient Judaic culture, as we have seen, this implied heterosexual desire, which seemed to deny men a place as God's intimates. The maleness of God therefore had two simultaneous effects: On the one hand, it established male authority. On the other, it threatened to make human masculinity redundant.

The religious system of ancient Israel dealt with this dilemma of men's potential exclusion and partial redundancy by shifting it onto women. The insistence on female impurity excluded women from competition with men for divine affections. Women's impurity, in other words, arose in part from attempts to shore up men's access to the sacred. If the conventional theory explains women's cultic impurity as a result of her otherness from God, we can also see it as motivated in part by her natural complementarity to a male deity and her symbolic threat to men's place in the religious system. Women's otherness from God is precisely what made them his expected partners. They had to be excluded from the cult because they challenged the male connection with God.

Moses, Masculinity, and Monotheism

The story of Moses and God is in many ways a description of the closest male-male relationship in Israelite religion. Although it is difficult to completely disentangle the earliest mythic accounts of Moses' encounters with God, as we saw in chapter 3, they depict a relationship of deepening intimacy. Because of his intimacy with God, Moses' masculinity is called into question. The feminization of Moses is only partially articulate, but various details in the myths suggest that a gender reversal is in process. [12]

Moses, indeed, is described on one occasion as having to deny his femininity (Num. 11:4–15 E). This denial occurs when the Israelites complain that mana does not satisfy their craving for meat, a complaint that angers God and distresses Moses. "And Moses said to the

Lord, 'Why have You dealt ill with Your servant, and why have I not enjoyed Your favor, that You have laid the burden of all this people upon me? Did I conceive all this people, did I bear them, that You should say to me, "Carry them in your bosom as a nurse carries an infant," to the land that You have promised on oath to their fathers?' "[13] The use of maternal imagery here is important. Moses is denying that he conceived and bore Israel and by implication is saying, "You, God, are the one who mothered Israel and hence you should nurse Your child." This passage is sometimes cited to illustrate how feminine or female imagery is used to describe God (Trible 1983, 69; Mollenkott 1986, 20–21). But Moses' protest may actually reveal more about how the narrator imagines Moses than God. Moses has to deny his femininity because his masculinity is at risk. As God's intimate, he is in the position of God's wife and consequently is supposed to mother God's children. Like Hagar, banished to the wilderness with her child, he fears for the survival of the children of Israel (Gen. 21:14–15).[14] Moses' protest is to the point. God has in effect made him a mother of Israel.

A second suggestion of Moses' feminization can be found in the story of his encounter with God on the mountain. When Moses comes down off the mountain, the skin of his face has been transfigured and frightens the people (Exod. 34:29–35). This story has priestly elements in it, but it may also reflect a much earlier myth. The precise meaning of the transfiguration is unclear because of the use of an unusual Hebrew verb, qāran.[15] This verb appears to be related to the noun for horns (qeren). It is for this reason that the tradition of ascribing horns to Moses developed, a tradition that lies behind Michelangelo's sculpture and other artistic depictions of Moses (Mellinkoff 1970). Some modern interpreters see here allusions to a mask that priests wore, perhaps even a mask with horns, even though there is no evidence for the existence of such masks in ancient Israel. Another longstanding tradition understands qāran as referring to beams of light.[16] A recent philological study based on Semitic etymologies suggests that qrn refers to a disfiguration of Moses' skin (Propp 1987, 384–86). In any case, something is frighteningly different about Moses that requires him to veil his face. But the purpose of the veil cannot simply be to hide what is fearful, for Moses removes it when he is communicating with the people.[17]

Veils do carry associations of femininity. Although the veil was not standard attire of women in ancient Israel, it is viewed as feminine attire. Out of modesty, Rebekkah veils her face when she first sets eyes on Isaac (Gen. 24:65 J). And Tamar veils her face so that Judah will not recognize her, enabling her to seduce him (Gen. 38:14). Moses is the only Israelite male to be described as covering his face. It is true that the term for this covering (*maseweh*) is never used to describe the veils of women.[18] Still, it is likely that a covering of the face would evoke associations of feminine veiling. Cassuto intuitively makes this connection but does not see the implications for gender imagery. He writes that Moses "put over his face, out of a sense of humility and modesty, a kind of veil, like the veil or head-scarf that women in Israel usually wear over their faces during summer to protect themselves from the sun's glare" (1967, 450). In addition to hiding his transfiguration, the veiling of Moses partially feminizes him. It points to his transformation into the intimate of God.

We may be in a position now to understand why the narrator of this story chose *qāran* to describe Moses' transfiguration. The verb's association with "horns" could have been present even if etymologically it originally meant "to disfigure the skin." The mistake of understanding a word exclusively in terms of its etymological origins still tends to dominate biblical scholarship. The etymological origins of a word are forgotten by language users. And even when the original meanings of a word are still in currency, words convey additional meanings based on the synchronic relations of the linguistic system, what linguists call "syntagmatic" similarities.[19] For example, etymologically the word "whole" and "hole" have no relationship. But one can imagine a context in which one of the terms draws on meanings from the other: "There is a huge emptiness, a bottomless pit in my heart. I shall never be whole." Puns, jokes, advertisements, dreams, and good literature depend on such linguistic associations. The same process is at work in myth. Associations to words that are etymologically unrelated convey meaning. This process need not have been conscious. The choice of words in a myth or story is perceived as just right because they build up layers of meaning that speak to people on many levels.

It therefore may have been no accident that Moses' disfiguration is described with a word that also conjures up the image of horns. The hint of a horned Moses may have partly inspired the narrator to choose this odd word. Horns, after all, are important symbols in Israel. The metaphor of Israel standing with horns held high presupposes the metaphor of Israel as bull or ram.[20] The Psalmists pray that God lift the horn of his people (Ps. 148:14) and not the horns of the wicked (Ps. 75:5). Joseph is described in Moses' final blessing in Deuteronomy as "like a firstling bull in his majesty. He has horns like the horns of the wild-ox; with them he gores the peoples" (33:17). Interestingly, the Blessing of Joseph alludes to "the favor of the Presence in the Bush," the only biblical reference to the story of Moses' encounter with God at the burning bush. Here, then, is another representation of an Israelite leader who has been metaphorically horned as a result of contact with God.

Whether or not the horned Moses and Joseph are related, the metaphor is clearly masculine; it calls to mind the prowess and might of bulls and rams, as well as an image of virility. At the very moment of Moses' feminization, then, a word is chosen that reasserts his masculinity. Moses is imagined with his face covered like a woman, but with horns like a proud bull. He is caught between genders—a man as a leader of Israel, a woman as the wife of God.

The need to reestablish Moses' masculinity may explain two other perplexing statements about him. First, the priestly material which refers to Moses' "horns" also describes him as having "uncircumcised lips" (Exod. 6:12, 30), a curious way of explaining his speech impediment. This impediment had been described in an earlier myth as a "heaviness of lips" (Exod. 3:10 J). Why did the priestly narrator feel compelled to find another metaphor? The allusion to circumcision has a very powerful association with the domain of masculinity. Moses' mouth is linked via the metaphor of circumcision to the penis. Through this "phallicization" of Moses' mouth, his masculinity is reasserted.

Second, just after learning that Moses dies in the land of Moab before he can enter the promised land, we are told that "Moses was a hundred and twenty years old when he died; his eyes were undimmed and his freshness unabated" (Deut. 34:7). It is not entirely certain to what this "freshness" (leh) refers, but it may be a reference to his virility (Albright 1944, 32–35). Why should it be necessary to assert his virility at the time of his death? In part, the narrator is indicating that Moses died in his prime. Despite his age, he was not an old man, and his eyes had not dimmed. But why should Moses' freshness be mentioned? Perhaps Moses' intimacy with God and his subsequent feminization raised the question of his masculinity, and it was only with his death that his manhood could be reasserted. The story suggests that one cannot be both a man and a lover of God. This line of analysis is confirmed in the story of God's attack on Moses discussed below.

As we have discussed, on a heterosexual model of desire, an intimate of a male God should be female, so Moses can only insert himself into this equation through his own partial feminization and the exclusion of women. A hint of these tensions is evident in the myth of the Sinai revelation, the first revelation to the children of Israel after their departure from Egypt. This is the first time the impurity of women is referred to in the Hebrew Bible, and this myth may be one of the oldest sources of Israelite religion to refer to women's impurity.

God says to Moses, "Go to the people and warn them to stay pure today and tomorrow. Let them wash their clothes. Let them be ready for the third day; for on the third day the Lord will come down in the sight of all the people, on Mount Sinai" (Exod. 19:10–13 J).[21] Note, however, what happens when Moses carries out God's instruction. Moses "warned the people to stay pure, and they washed their clothes. And he said to the people, 'Be ready for the third day: do not go near a woman'" (Exod. 19:15). There is a significant discrepancy between God's instruction to Moses and Moses' charge to the people. It is Moses and not God who insists that men stay clear of women. Most interpreters ignore or minimize the significance of this discrepancy. It seems self-evident to them that women must be avoided before an impending encounter with the sacred. But Moses' elaboration of God's instruction is ambiguous. Does the narrator wish the reader or listener to assume that Moses interpreted God's words properly? Or are we to understand that Moses' words reflect his own understanding of what it means to stay pure? Moreover, precisely why women should be avoided is not spelled out. Is it because men will spill semen and become impure? Is it because of potential contamination of menstrual blood? Or is sexual intercourse itself treated here as antithetical to the encounter with the divine?

Most interpreters sidestep these issues. They generally presume that Moses is simply making explicit what God intended. Cassuto writes that "in the account of the implementation of the command, the words of the injunction are reiterated as usual. But Moses further adds, not as a thematic supplement of his own, but as a detailed instruction in elucidation of the concept of sanctification: *do not go near a woman*" (1967, 230). Similarly, Childs writes that Moses "initiates the required sanctification, summarizing the commands with a specific, concrete injunction. 'Do not go near a woman!'" Childs continues: "The holy God of the covenant demands as preparation a separation from those things which are normally permitted and good in themselves. The giving of the covenant is different from an ordinary event of everyday life. Israel is, therefore, to be prepared by a special act of separation" (1974, 268–69). Why the special act of separation is the avoidance of women, neither Cassuto nor Childs speculates. None of these interpreters see any need to explain women's impurity in this context. They assume it makes sense and hence does not call for any explanation.[22]

These interpretations miss the significant fact that the avoidance of women is ascribed to Moses and not God. It seems plausible to assume that the narrator on some level wishes the reader to view this as Moses' interpretation of God's word. It is striking that when Eve adds something to God's command in the garden (Gen. 3:3), interpreters routinely assume that the narrator wishes to indicate something about her state of mind, but they have nothing to say about Moses adding to God's words in Exodus 19:15.[23] The narrator may very well have wanted to ascribe to Moses this prohibition against coming near women. After all, God's instruction seems addressed to the Israelite people as a whole, including the women; Moses is obviously directing his comments to the men alone. In this myth, the notion of women's impurity thus originates with human men and not with God, and it originates at the very moment when God calls men to face him. It is through Moses that the narrator expresses male anxieties about the promise of a God sighting. If Moses does not hide his face (Exod. 3:6), or if God does not turn his back (Exod. 33:20–23), then Moses will have to confront the full significance of a male God. To come face to face with God is to see oneself in the position of wife. "Do not come near a woman" addresses the problem. When God approaches, men avoid women and cease temporarily to act as husbands. In this way, men collectively prepare themselves to be a feminine Israel. And by linking women and impurity, the natural complementarity between God and women is broken.

The same tensions may explain why Miriam is punished with leprosy after her attack on Moses' authority (Numbers 12), a story we considered earlier.[24] This is the story in which Miriam and Aaron protest Moses' role as God's only spokesman. God answers by telling them that Moses alone sees God's form and speaks to God "mouth to mouth." Although the challenge comes from both Miriam and Aaron, Miriam alone is stricken with snow-white scales. It may be that the author of this source was a priest who viewed himself as a descendant of Moses and wished to glorify Moses and belittle Aaron (Friedman 1987, 78). But this explanation does not exhaust the meanings of the story. In particular, it does not explain why Aaron, who is equally involved in the challenge to Moses' authority, is not punished. The imbalance is intriguing. It is as if Miriam has committed a sin that Aaron has not. The emphasis on Miriam's role makes sense given the threat posed by her gender. As a woman, Miriam is a more "natural" intimate of God than Moses. Her challenge to Moses is thus more of a threat than Aaron's. Miriam's affliction with leprosy thus shores up Moses' relationship with God. Indeed, in the previous chapter of Numbers, the same narrator recounts the story of how the spirit of God comes upon two lads, Eldad and Medad. In this case, Moses receives the news joyfully (Num. 11:26–29). The narrator does not imagine the boys as a threat to Moses. Not so with Miriam.

There may be other indications of the competing expectations of Moses as both husband and wife of God. The narrative of Miriam and Aaron's protest begins with what seems to be an irrelevant complaint: "Miriam and Aaron spoke against Moses on account of the Cushite woman he had married, 'He married a Cushite woman!'" (Num. 12:1). The reference is odd. Some take it to mean that Moses has married a black woman, since Cush refers in the Bible to Ethiopia. But there is no report of Moses having married anyone other than Zipporah, who is a Midianite.[25] The protest against the mysterious Cushite woman is never developed and therefore is often taken to be a pretext for the real complaint about Moses' claims to an exclusive relationship with God. Although substantively the two protests seem unconnected, they may be more closely related than initially appears. Just as Moses' relationship with the Cushite woman is called into question, God's relationship with Moses is challenged. The first protest, which otherwise seems to have no relevance to the story that follows, allows the parallelism to emerge and puts Moses in the structural position of wife. Moses' feminine positioning is underscored by an abrupt aside in the narrative. After Miriam and Aaron's protest, the narrator suddenly reminds us that "Moses was a very humble (ʿānāw) man, more so than any other man on earth." The word "humble" is used in this singular form in no other context. Why would the narrator want to mention Moses' humility at this point? Perhaps to reiterate his uniqueness among the prophets. But it is interesting to note that the word the narrator chooses is derived from a verb that is used to refer to rape, that is, to the humbling of a woman through forced intercourse (Gen. 34:2; Deut. 21:14, 22:24, 29; Judg. 19:24, 20:5; 2 Sam. 13:12, 14, 22, 32; Ezek. 22:10, 11; Lam. 5:11) (Brown, Driver, and Briggs 1975, 776). Moses is the humblest of all men because he submits completely to God.

This understanding of Moses as occupying a feminine position with respect to God suggests another way of viewing the complaint regarding the Cushite woman. There is actually an ambiguity in the Hebrew text that is glossed over in most translations. Miriam and Aaron speak against Moses "on account of the Cushite woman he had married." The word ʾôdōt, like the English "on account of," has two meanings: "because" or "on behalf of," as rabbinic commentators to this passage realize.[26] Miriam and Aaron thus can also be seen as speaking against Moses "*on behalf of* the Cushite woman he had married." That is, they are concerned that Moses' intimacy with God competes with his obligations to his Cushite wife. "He married a Cushite woman and not you, God!" They are protesting on her behalf. And they do so by pointing out that God has spoken through other people and therefore need not retain the exclusive relationship with Moses. But God refuses their claim. While he does speak through other prophets, he is intimate with Moses alone. Moses alone sees his form and speaks to him "mouth to mouth."

The narrator of the myth was probably not conscious of these associations. But on some intuitive level, these two protests must have seemed just right. And part of what made them "just right" was the structural parallel they established and the recognition they made of Moses' role as wife of God. Moses is cast here as having conflicting obligations, as husband to his wife, and as wife to God.

One need not fully accept this deep reading to agree with the overall point. It is significant that two of the earliest Israelite myths to reflect on women's impurity both involve contexts in which the subject is men's relationship with God. The fear here was not of woman's natural otherness, nor of her menstrual pollution. She was feared because she posed a threat to men's intimacy with the divine. Her punishment and removal opened a position for men to occupy. This explanation, of course, cannot account for the Israelite rules of impurity as a whole. Men were also deemed impure under certain conditions, and a variety of other symbolisms entered into the meaning of impurity (Eilberg-Schwartz 1990, 141–76). But this analysis suggests an additional reason for the development of laws regarding women's impurity. By removing women, Israelite men were able to come closer to God. But that intimacy involved risks: feminization, loss of manhood, and perhaps even death.

Death, Emasculation, and Circumcision

Israelite religion imagined contact with the deity as a terrifying experience. The incursion of the sacred into the realm of the profane was perceived to be devastating, resulting in death and disorder. This explains why boundaries are set around the mountain for God's appearance, why God hides in a cloud, is protected in a Temple behind veils, and why Moses is permitted to see only the divine back. The sacred operates in similar ways in other religious traditions. Indeed, the word "sacred" is used precisely because it attempts to designate a phenomenon that occurs in many religious traditions. But this vague appeal to the dangers of the sacred ignores the fact that in this case, the sacred was a male God. The danger of contact with "the sacred" was a particular one. It was the danger of intimacy with a male God, a threat that could be diminished only by a partial unmanning of the Israelite man.

This way of looking at Israel's conception of the sacred helps explain two early Israelite myths which have proved somewhat mysterious. The first involves Jacob's struggle with the angel as he journeys back to his homeland and prepares to face his brother Esau (Gen. 32:23–33); the second tells of God's attempt on Moses' life, as Moses and his family journey back to Egypt to help free the Israelites. These two narratives bear remarkable similarities to each other (Westermann 1984, 517). Each involves an attack by a superhuman being during the night as the hero returns to the land of his birth and prepares to face his destiny. Each attack, as we shall see, ends with a mark on the male genitals: in the first case those of Jacob, in the second, those of Moses' son.

Not surprisingly many interpreters see in these perplexing stories vestiges of older myths that were incorporated into Israelite narratives. It is a river demon, according to many interpreters, whom Jacob encounters and wrestles with on the banks of the Jabbok. This demon is only identified as a superhuman being in later accretions of the myth. For similar reasons interpreters believe the story of God's attack on Moses is a transformed story of a local demon.[27]

It is no longer tenable to assume that these myths originated in non-Israelite contexts and reflect primitive religious notions simply because they do not fit preconceived images of monotheism (Eilberg-Schwartz 1990, 1991b). Moreover, even if these stories could have derived from pre-Israelite traditions, it is striking that two such similar stories have been preserved and that the attack in question was ascribed to God or to a divine being. Something about these stories struck a chord in the religious culture of Israel and led Israelite narrators to attribute the attacks to God.

Israel's Unmanning

Recall the story of Jacob wrestling with the divine being on his return to Canaan (Gen. 34:23–33). When dawn began to break and the being "saw that he had not prevailed against him, he wrenched Jacob's hip at the socket (*kap-yĕrēkô*), so that the socket of his hip was strained as he wrestled with him." The narrator tells us that this is why the children of Israel do not eat the "thigh muscle (*gîd hannāšeh*) that is on the socket of the hip (*kap yĕrēkô*)."

It is confusing as to who prevails in this contest.[28] The struggle obviously goes on all night. While the angel is able to injure Jacob, Jacob is still able to wrest a blessing from his opponent. Moreover, the angel recognizes Jacob's success in the name Israel, which is interpreted in this narrative at least to mean "He has prevailed against beings divine and human." But Jacob leaves the struggle with a limp and is unable to discover the being's name, and he himself does not say he prevailed, but that his life was preserved, describing it as a stand-off rather than a victory. In fact, the name Israel may originally have meant "and God prevailed" (Sarna 1989).

Most interpreters understand the injury to Jacob to refer to some part of his leg, the thigh muscle or sciatic nerve. But there are several indications that Jacob was actually struck on the genitals, as S. H. Smith (1990) has now argued quite convincingly.[29] The divine being touched "the hollow of the loins" (*kap yĕrēkô*). The thigh or loins is frequently a euphemism for the penis. Jacob's offspring, for example, are said to spring from his thigh (Gen. 46:26; Exod. 1:5). Recall also the oaths taken by placing the hand "under the loins" (Gen. 24:2, 9; 47:29). The reference to the thigh muscle (*gid hannaseh*) in the Jacob story may be a reference to the penis. Smith also suggests that the word "heel" with which Jacob's name is associated is sometimes a euphemism for the genitals, as it is in Jeremiah 13:22: "It is because of your great iniquity that your skirts are lifted up, your heels exposed." Here "heels" is an obvious reference to genitals, consistent with the use of the foot more generally as a euphemism (Judg. 3:24; 1 Sam. 24:4; Isa. 6:2, 7:20, 47:2). Smith suggests that when Jacob is imagined as grabbing the heel of Esau in the womb, a pun may be involved. In grabbing Esau's genitals, the story signals Jacob's future usurpation of Esau's birthright, that is, the right to be the genealogical father of Israel.

What could be the significance of this genital injury? Smith argues that "by striking Jacob on the *kap hyerek* [inside of the thigh] God was asserting his sovereign power over Jezreel's [Israel's] procreative power. But once Jacob had acknowledged God's strength as supreme, God allowed him to inherit the Abrahamic promise, so that children sprang freely from the very loins over which God had asserted his dominance" (1990, 469).[30] Smith also notes that this injury to Jacob's genitals occurs just as he sets off to claim what by rights belongs to Esau. "It is only by recognizing the carnal limitation of his own procreative power that Jacob, as heir apparent to the covenantal promise, is allowed to inherit the promise in reality. By striking Jacob, symbolically, upon his genitals God demonstrates that only he has the power to bring Jacob's aspiration to fruition" (ibid., 472).

Smith's analysis is compelling, but there is more to be said about the symbolism of Jacob's injury. It is important to realize that Jacob has already fathered eleven of his twelve children before he is struck on the genitals. The mark on the genitals therefore cannot refer to his future virility. If it symbolizes potency at all, it is an acknowledgment that God was responsible for Jacob's past fatherhood, that he controls the continuation of Jacob's line. More significant, then, is the submission marked by this genital injury.

It is critical to note that the injury coincides with Jacob's assertion of his masculinity. Jacob begins his life as a "mama's boy." Unlike his brother Esau, who is born hairy and who is a hunter of game, Jacob is smooth skinned and stays at home (Gen. 25:27). Indeed, Jacob's femininity is underscored by his fleeing to Haran and marrying his matrilineal cousins, Leah and Rachel, the daughters of his mother's brother. Actually, Rachel and Leah are not only Jacob's maternal cousins but also distantly related patrilineal cousins, a point of significance, as we shall see. Initially, however, the narrative mentions only his maternal connection to these women, underscoring his association with his mother. Eventually, Jacob realizes that his uncle is taking advantage of him and he decides to return to his homeland. Jacob's break with Laban is the beginning of his self-assertion and reclamation of his own identity. Laban overtakes him. They build a mound and pillar to mark their treaty with one another. Laban swears that if either of them violates the treaty "may the God of Abraham and the God of Nahor . . . judge between us" (Gen. 31:53). Nahor was the brother of Abraham, Jacob's paternal grandfather, so when Laban swears in the name of Abraham and Nahor, he is singling out the two men who link him to his nephew patrilineally (Jay 1988; 1992, 94–111). In this way, he marks his male connection with Jacob and ceases to consider him merely as his sister's son. Thus, as Jacob starts to reclaim his masculinity, as he takes control of his future and heads back to face Esau, perhaps risking his life, his matrilineal connection is abandoned and his patrilineal descent recognized. He is ready to become father of Israel.

Jacob for his part swears an oath by "The Pahad of Isaac." This cryptic expression is generally interpreted to be a name for God, and *pahad* is normally translated as "fear." But there is evidence that *pahad* may very well be an Aramaic word meaning "thigh, hip, and loins." Jacob thus swears by the "Thigh of Isaac." As several interpreters have suggested, this represents another allusion to the oaths which are taken by grabbing a patriarch's genitals.[31] Although Jacob cannot literally grab

Isaac's genitals, since his father is not present, he swears by them, indicating his own willingness to assume the obligations of the patrilineage (Eilberg-Schwartz 1990, 169–70). Jacob will later ask his son Joseph to take an oath in the same way (Gen. 47:29). By figuratively grabbing the genitals of the father, the son takes on the responsibility of the father's genealogy.

In short, Jacob has become an independent young man, no longer controlled by his uncle or afraid of his brother. He is ready to take up the obligations of manhood, and it is only after this decision that he is attacked by the angel. Significantly, he has already had one encounter with the divine that has left him unscathed. In the story of Jacob's dream, Jacob simply sees God at the top of the ladder with angels ascending and descending. But as soon as he is recognized as a man, he must be marked on the genitals, signifying his submission to God. Jacob only becomes Israel through an act of partial emasculation. Or to put it another way, the entity "Israel" only comes into being at the moment of emasculation. The story of Jacob's wrestling match thus contains within it an inchoate representation of Israel, the collective entity who is to be imagined as God's wife. The narrative ends with the observation that this collective Israel does not eat the "thigh muscle."[32]

The thrust of this analysis is confirmed by the retelling of the wrestling incident between Jacob and the divine being in Hosea (12:3–5). There are a number of intriguing differences between the Hosea and Genesis versions of this story, and there has been much discussion whether Hosea refers to the Genesis narrative or is relying on an independent tradition about Jacob. What is most striking for our purposes is how the version in Hosea underscores the issue of masculinity:

> The Lord once indicted Judah
> and punished Jacob for his conduct,
> requited him for his deeds.
> In the womb he tried to supplant his brother
> grown to manhood ('ônô), he strove with a divine being.

He strove with an angel and prevailed—
he had to weep and implore him. . . .

Hosea's retelling emphasizes that Jacob's struggle with God occurred in his manhood ('ônô).[33] Furthermore, it makes Jacob's supplanting of Esau parallel Jacob's struggle with God. Hosea views the struggle with God as part of Jacob's (Israel's) hubris. He is so defiant that he is willing to stand against God. As commentators have noted, it is not at all clear who ends up crying.[34] Is the angel crying and begging Jacob to release him? That would make sense given that Jacob is described as prevailing. But the overall thrust of Hosea's version is to condemn Jacob, who is described as being arrogant from birth. In the context of God's punishment of Jacob, it makes better sense for Jacob to "weep and implore." "It is certainly Jacob who weeps and entreats favour, not the angel. . . . In any case the Jacob whom Israel proudly claims as its representative ancestor was overcome by God and brought to tears and dependence" (Mays 1963, 164). Perhaps Hosea is speaking ironically in saying that Jacob prevailed. "Israel, you think Jacob prevailed—he was so victorious he had to cry." In other words, Hosea is playing on the expectations of his audience that Israel means "He struggled with God and prevailed." This expectation is then undercut by the ambiguity in the passage. Although Hosea does not explicitly allude to Jacob's injury, Jacob's weeping may be an oblique reference to that event. In his manhood, he has been made to cry.

The idea that a man's inability to protect his genitals is a sign of his domination is not limited to the myth of Jacob's wrestling. As we have seen, this is one of the reasons that sons should not see their fathers naked. It is one thing when the father chooses to expose himself for the purpose of making his sons take an oath, quite another when he does not choose. His unwilling exposure is shameful and humbling. The prophets speak metaphorically as well of God exposing Israel's nakedness, which shames "her" and signifies her domination by other nations (Ezek. 16:37; Hos. 3:11–12; Isa. 3:17). If exposure of the genitals is shameful, the touching or injury of the genitals is that much more humiliating. This explains why a woman is expressly forbidden to grab the genitals of a man who is wrestling with her husband (Deut. 25:11–12). To do so puts her in a position of dominance over her husband's opponent. Even at the moment when her husband may need help, she may not grab the manhood of his opponent. Her husband's safety is less important than his opponent's honor. Significantly, the law does not prohibit her from assisting in some other fashion. If she bangs him over the head, he is not considered dishonored in the same way. The association of domination and circumcision is also present in the story of David's bringing back foreskins of two hundred Philistine warriors as payment of a bride price for King Saul's daughter Michal (1 Sam. 18:17–29; 2 Sam. 3, 14). David's military prowess alone is not sufficient. He must bring back a piece of his opponents' genitals, signifying their emasculation.

Circumcision itself conveys similar meanings.[35] It is ideally an injury inflicted by the father on the son to signify their submission to God. That circumcision carries such associations is assumed in the story of Dinah's rape in Genesis 34, which follows shortly after the story of Jacob's struggle with the angel.[36] Dinah, the daughter of Leah and Jacob, is raped by Shechem the son of Hamor, the Hivite. Shechem asks Jacob to give Dinah to Hamor in marriage. He suggests that the Hivites and the "sons of Israel" become one people. But Jacob's sons reply that they cannot do so unless the Hivites circumcise themselves. The Hivites acquiesce to the request, and while they are incapacitated from the operation, Simon and Levi kill them. Interpreters have generally emphasized the ethnic significance of circumcision in this story. The narrative presupposes that belonging to Israel requires circumcision. While that may be true, much more is going on here. Circumcision is also part of the Israelite stratagem here. It is a vehicle for the domination of the Hivites and serves as revenge for the rape and humiliation of Dinah. Where Hamor did violence to Dinah's genitals, Jacob's sons do violence to the Hivites by getting them to injure their own genitals. The rape has been reversed.[37] In other words, circumcision is an eminently appropriate way of unmanning the Hivites and preparing to murder them. What Jacob's sons do to the Hivites, God has done in part to their father, Jacob. Indeed, read as a narrative, one could infer that Jacob's sons got the idea from their father's own injury.

Unmanning Moses

The understanding of circumcision and genital injury prepares us for the story of God's attack on Moses.

> And the Lord said to Moses, "When you return to Egypt, see that you perform before Pharaoh all the marvels that I have put within your power. . . . Then you shall say to Pharaoh, 'Thus says the Lord: Israel is My first-born son. I have said to you, "Let My son go, that he may worship Me," yet you refuse to let him go. Now I will slay your first-born sons.' "
>
> At a night encampment on the way, the Lord encountered him and sought to kill him. So Zipporah took a flint and cut off her son's foreskin, and touched his feet with it, saying, "You are truly a bridegroom of blood to me!" And when he let him alone, she added, "A bridegroom of blood because of the circumcision." (Exod. 4:21–26)[38]

There are dozens of ambiguities in this story. Whom precisely is God attacking? Whose feet does Zipporah touch with the foreskin? Is Zipporah touching the feet or the genitals? And what does "bridegroom of blood" mean?

When this story is read in context, it seems that Moses must be the object of the attack.[39] Moses, after all, is being addressed by God in the preceding verses. There is also an implied parallel between God's threat to slay Pharaoh's firstborn and God's attack on Moses. Interpreters have been perplexed as to why God should want to kill the messenger he has just commissioned. And why does circumcision stay God's hand? Childs (1974, 101), following rabbinic readings, believes the circumcision corrects the fact that Moses never circumcised his son. It was this failure for which Moses was attacked. Robinson (1986, 456) assumes that Moses himself was uncircumcised and what takes place here is his vicarious circumcision. Propp (forthcoming) sees God's attack as an act of retribution against Moses for the manslaughter of the Egyptian taskmaster. The circumcision is an act of propitiation that saves his life.

But another solution to some of these questions emerges by taking seriously the similarity of this story to the attack on Jacob as he is homeward bound.[40] That story involved a threat to the man for whom all Israel would be named. Moses, too, is returning to his homeland to take up his obligations to God's people. He is reluctant to do so, protesting that he has a heaviness of lips that makes him an inappropriate spokesman. Rhetorically, the threat to Moses' life serves the same function as Jacob's wrestling with the divine being. It establishes Moses' submission to the deity, that Moses is now at the deity's mercy. God "sets about showing Moses that although he is safe from other men (Ex. iv 19) he faces a much greater danger to his life in the wrath of the God whom he is so reluctant to serve (iv 14). Like Jacob before him, Moses must undergo a night struggle with his mysterious God before he can become a worthy instrument of YHWH" (Robinson 1986, 459–60).

A genital injury occurs at the end of each of these divine attacks. Jacob's genital injury establishes his submission to God and occurs at dawn just before the struggle is over. In the case of Moses, it is the genital disfigurement of his son that saves his life. Moreover, it is a woman and not a divine being who is the agent of the injury. Moses' wife Zipporah somehow knows that this is the way to ward off the attack on her husband. Indeed, according to one probable reading of this story, Zipporah takes the foreskin of her son and touches Moses either on the feet or, if feet is a euphemism, on the genitals.[41] Some interpreters see evidence here that Zipporah is performing a Midianite magical practice. Others see the remnant of an Egyptian myth in which the goddess Osiris hovers protectively over the genitals of her dead husband.[42] But what is this story saying about Israel's religious imagination? Certainly, as Robinson suggests (1986, 453), Zipporah's act anticipates the blood that Israelites will later put on the lintels of their house so God will not slay the Israelite firstborn (Exodus 12:23). But it also shows what is symbolically at stake in this attack. If it is Moses' genitals that she touches, then Moses' manhood must already be exposed. God's attack on Moses is in part an attack on his masculinity. This is why circumcision appeases God. The blood of circumcision is a symbolic acknowledgment that a man's masculinity belongs to God. Submitting to God and surrendering one's masculinity amounts to the same thing. The blood of circumcision, like the blood on the doorposts, is a sign to God that he should pass over Israelite men and not take their lives. In turn, it is a reminder to Israelite men that as men of God they belong to their father in heaven.[43]

Zipporah's prominence in performing the act of circumcision is striking, especially when viewed against the backdrop of ethnographic studies of circumcision. Typically, circumcision is a male bonding ceremony in which fathers or uncles are responsible for initiating men into adulthood. Furthermore, circumcision is often a rite that symbolically rips a boy out of the world of the mother and brings him into the world of men. The same themes are present in the practice of Israelite circumcision as it is articulated in later sources in the Hebrew Bible (Eilberg-Schwartz 1990, 141–76). One need not see Zipporah's centrality here as a survival of a goddess myth from Egypt. Her importance underscores the way in which women's power always potentially threatens to erupt when men encounter a male God. If that encounter is not handled properly, through a sacrifice of human masculinity and a symbolic submission to a dominating male God, then the human male is eliminated. Into the space vacated by her husband, the wife steps to assert her role as a legitimate ritual actor. If men do not submit to God, if they do not take their proper role as God's wives, then the human women are always ready to assume that role.

Zipporah's words underscore the issue of masculinity. "You are a bridegroom (ḥātān) of blood to me." The term ḥātān is sometimes used to mean "father-in-law," "bridegroom," and "son-in-law." In other words, it refers to a relationship that is created through marriage. It is not a genealogical bond. These words have been subject to differing interpretations. Some suggest that circumcision was originally a marriage rite that protected the bridegroom from an attack by a demonical being. Indeed some argue that this story symbolizes the shift from circumcision as a rite of marriage to a birth ritual. But these historical speculations have no evidence to support them.[44] One thing, however, is certain. In the attack, Zipporah is in danger of losing Moses to God. "You are a bridegroom of blood *to me*!" she says. You belong to me, not God. The threat to his life and masculinity is associated with Moses' becoming a man of God. You are not God's wife, you are my bridegroom. This story thus anticipates the tensions that later develop. For Moses does become the wife of God, and his siblings end up protesting "on behalf of the Cushite woman."

The ambiguities of this story permit still another reading that has relevance to our analysis. When the myth says that Zipporah touched "his feet/genitals," it is possible that this refers to the deity. Touching God with the circumcised flesh of her son's foreskin, she declares, "You are a bridegroom of blood to me." On this interpretation, she is telling him to lay off Moses. He is not your wife. I am.[45] And by touching her son's foreskin to God's "feet," she identifies God as the father. This myth of God's attack on Moses is thus not altogether dissimilar to the story of the sons of God who have intercourse with the daughters of man. Here, too, the redundancy of the human male is implied and the natural complementarity between divine male and human female is asserted.

The image of Zipporah thus serves two contradictory functions. It indicates the threat men perceive of women stepping into the place they have vacated. But at the same time, it is an ideal image of an Israelite woman. Israelite women are in danger of losing their men to God. But God will leave their husbands intact if as mothers they condone the genital disfiguration of their sons and acknowledge that Israelite masculinity has been sacrificed to God.

What this analysis suggests is that circumcision was for the ancient Israelites a symbol of male submission. Because it is partially emasculating, it was a recognition of a power greater than man. The symbolism of submission to God is obviously related to the images of the feminization of Israelite men in the Hebrew Bible. Both were symptoms of the same phenomenon. God was acknowledged as the ultimate male and in his presence human masculinity was seen to be compromised and put at risk.

These symbolic associations were never fully articulated in the ancient texts. But what was not fully comprehended in the ancient Israelite religion would become explicit in certain forms of late antique Judaism, as we shall now see.

Chapter Seven

Women Rabbis and the Orchard of Heavenly Delights

*A completely refined soul . . . has but a single
and perfect desire, to be introduced by the king into
his chamber, to be united with him, to enjoy him.*
ST. BERNARD, Sermones de diversis

To be a man of God involves imagining oneself as a woman, at least when the divine human relationship is considered analogous to a marriage, as it was in ancient Israel and as it continued to be in late antique Judaism. This process of feminization, which is partial and undeveloped in Scripture, was given greater articulation by the rabbis, the late antique interpreters of Judaism. The rabbis understood full well the fact that in the relationship with God, men must assume the position of wives. Consequently, their readings of Scripture emphasized the ways in which the patriarchs were portrayed as women with respect to God. But the sages also saw the implication of this feminizing for themselves. They, too, were wives of God. At times they read Scripture as if they imagined themselves as women, looking to female models for how they should behave. And we shall see that for the sages, as for their predecessors, the thought of seeing God was a decidedly erotic experience.[1]

The rabbis' tendency to feminize men is nowhere clearer than in the rabbinic handling of the Song of Songs, the erotic biblical love poem recounting the love between a man and a woman. By the time of late antique Judaism, if not earlier, the Song of Songs was widely interpreted as an allegory of God's love of Israel. [2] This allegorical reading of the Song was in many ways a natural extension of metaphors already common in Israelite religion. Marriage and adultery, after all, were favorite metaphors of biblical writers for the relationship of God and Israel. At one level, then, the allegorization of the Song supplants the poem's erotic meanings with spiritual ones, but it also has the reverse effect of eroticizing the relationship between God and Israel. God and Israel's relationship is described in highly evocative language. All of Israel's history and all the expectations of God toward Israel are imagined as part of a sensual and loving relationship between a man and a woman.

The allegorization of the Song of Songs, like the biblical metaphors which preceded it, puts men in the position of the woman. The male lover of the poem is identified as God, and the female lover as Israel. This time, however, it is not simply Israel as a collectivity who is imagined as God's lover. Specific Israelite men are identified as the female lover of God. Israel is Abraham, Isaac, Jacob, and David, among other men. And her erotic experience with her lover defines each man's relationship with God. In the Song of Songs, the male-male relationships implicit in the biblical image of a feminized Israel and a husband God are brought out into the open. Israelite men are feminized so that they can be understood as God's lovers.

Consider, for example, the sages' reading of the lover's praise for his love above all women: "There are sixty queens, and eighty concubines, and damsels without number. Only one is my dove, My perfect one, the only one of her mother, the delight of her who bore her. Maidens see and acclaim her; queens and concubines, and praise her" (Song 6:8–9). The rabbis interpret this as referring to the patriarchs:

"*Only one is my dove, my perfect one* alludes to Abraham as it says, *Abraham was one . . .* (Ezek. 33:24). *The only one of her mother* refers to Isaac who was his mother's only son. *The delight of her who bore her* refers to Jacob who was choice to his mother. *Maidens see and acclaim her* alludes to the tribal ancestors. *Queens and concubines and praise her* [refers to the sons of Jacob for] The *news reached Pharaoh's palace* [*Joseph's brothers have come*] (Gen. 45:16)" (GenRab 94:1).[3]

In classic rabbinic style, the sages see the redundancy of Scripture's language as highly significant. Each phrase must have its own allusion. God has several female lovers or wives in mind, and they are the patriarchs. God's relationship with Israel, at this level of specificity, is polygamous. There are many Israelite men who make up the feminine Israel he loves.

A similar feminization of the patriarchs occurs in the sages' interpretation of Songs 2:10: "*My beloved spoke thus to me, 'Get yourself up,*[4] *my darling; My fair one, come away!'* (Song 2:10). *Get yourself up*—O daughter of Abraham to whom were addressed the words, *Remove yourself from your native land* (Gen. 12:1). *My darling, my fair one*—O daughter of Isaac who drew close to me and glorified me on the altar. *Come away*—O daughter of Jacob who listened to his father and mother, as it says *Jacob obeyed his father and mother and went to Paddan-aram* (Gen. 28:7)" (SongRab 2:9, 5).

This reading also construes references to the female lover as allusions to the patriarchs. But note here the roundabout way the allusion is made. "O daughter of" precedes the references to Abraham, Isaac, and Jacob, as if a woman is being addressed. But it is obvious that in none of the cases is it a daughter to whom God speaks. The references are to Abraham, Isaac, and Jacob themselves, identified by key words in each of their stories. Abraham was the one who left his native land, when God commanded him to "take himself" (*lēk lĕkā*) from his birthplace (Gen. 12:1). Thus Abraham is being referred to as "O daughter of Abraham." It was Isaac, not a daughter of Isaac, who "glorified God on the altar," a reference to Abraham's near sacrifice of Isaac as a boy (Genesis 22). And it was Jacob, not his daughter, who listened "to *his* father and mother," presumably a reference to Rebekkah's urgent command that Jacob "get up and flee for his life" (*qûm běraḥ lěkā*) (Gen. 27:43) and Isaac's wish that Jacob "get up and go" (*qûm lek*) (Gen. 28:2) to Paddan-aram to live with Laban and marry among his own kin.

In addition to the patriarchs, the sages also feminize Moses. Moses is described as like "a king's wife who being about to depart from the world said to her husband, 'My Lord the King I commend my children to you.' He said, 'Instead of bidding me look after my children bid them look after me'" (SongRab 1:10, 3). Moses is also identified as the female lover who says to God, "Tell me, you whom I love so well" (Song 1:7), and God is the male lover who responds, "If you do not know, O fairest among women" (Song 1:8). In this reading, the sages reflect on why the prophets are feminized: "Rabbi Yose ben Jeremiah said: Why are the prophets compared to women? To show that just as a woman is not ashamed to demand from her husband the requirements of her household, so prophets were not ashamed to demand the requirements of Israel from their Father in Heaven" (SongRab 1:7, 2). But this is less an explanation than another example of the phenomenon that needs to be explained. The sages were aware of the feminization process without fully comprehending its significance.

Even the body of the female lover in the Song of Songs is taken as referring to Israelite men. Thus, where the poem says, "Every part of you is fair, my darling; there is no blemish in you" (Song 4:7), the sages explain, "This refers to our ancestor Jacob for his bed was blameless before Him and no flaw was found in it" (SongRab 4:7, 1). The sages read the lack of a blemish in the female lover as referring to Jacob's unblemished sexual past. They give an even more startling interpretation to "Your breasts are like two fawns, twins of a gazelle" (Song 4:5):

> These are Moses and Aaron. Just as the breasts are the pride and beauty of a woman, so Moses and Aaron are the pride and beauty of Israel. Just as the breasts are the ornament of a woman, so Moses and Aaron are the ornament of Israel. Just as the breasts

are the honor and praise of a woman, so Moses and Aaron are the honor and praise of Israel. Just as the breasts are full of milk, so Moses and Aaron filled Israel with Torah. Just as whatever a woman eats ends up nourishing and nursing the suckling, so all the Torah that Moses our master learned he taught to Aaron, as it is written *And Moses told Aaron all the words of the Lord* (Exod. 4:28). . . . Just as one breast is not greater than the other, so it was with Moses and Aaron; for it is written, *These are the same Moses and Aaron* (Exod. 6:27). (SongRab 4:5, 1)

This identification of Moses and Aaron is a variation on the process of feminization discussed earlier. In this case, Moses and Aaron are the two breasts of a collective female Israel. To belong to this Israel, men either have to be feminized and represent her metaphorically or be thought of metonymically as part of her body, in images not unlike Paul's description of the church as the body of Christ.

But it was not just the great heroes of old that the rabbis imagined as women. They regarded all observant Jews as women with respect to God. The commandments that Jews obey are thus like ornaments or jewelry that women wear. "Ah, you are fair, my darling" (Song 1:15) is said to refer to the performance of religious duties, including tithing, not making mixtures (*kilayim*), praying, and circumcision, among other things (SongRab 1:15, 1). Israel is described as wearing the Ten Commandments like the ornaments of a bride (SongRab 4:10, 1). And according to the sages, "you have captured my heart with one [glance] of your eyes" (Song 4:9) means, "with the blood of the Passover and the blood of circumcision" (SongRab 4:9, 1). Although it is not clear why the rabbis linked these rituals to the eye, possibly a phallic symbol, their point is that Israel's performance of the commandments ravishes God's heart.[5] When the female lover says, "I am dark but comely" (Song 1:5), the sages understand Israel as saying, "I was comely in Egypt, with the blood of Passover and the blood of circumcision" (SongRab 1:5, 1). We shall return again to this striking image of circumcision making Israel comely in God's sight.

The eroticism between God and individual Israelite men suggested by these images becomes more explicit in other rabbinic glosses. For example, the sages interpret "His left hand was under my head, his right arm embraced me" (Song 2:6) as referring to many of the commandments. God's left hand refers to the first tablets of the Ten Commandments, the fringes on the corner of garments, the Shema prayer, the sukkah, and the mezuzah. The right hand refers to the phylacteries, the Amidah prayer, the cloud of divine presence in the time to come (SongRab 2:6, 1). So when men perform the commandments, they have God's left hand under their heads and his right arm around them. "Let him kiss me with the kisses of his mouth" (Song 1:2). The sages offer a number of interpretations of these kisses. But they include among other things the precepts that issued from God's mouth. According to one view, of the six hundred and thirteen commandments, two came to Israel directly from God's mouth. That is why the numerical value of Torah is 611, two short of the 613 total. Moses gave the Torah (611) to Israel. The missing two commandments, the kisses, came directly from God's mouth. The two commandments are "I am the Lord your God who brought you out of the land of Egypt, the house of bondage" and "You shall have no other gods besides Me" (Exod. 20:2–3). Significantly, these kisses remind Israel of the fidelity "she" is expected to have to God. According to another view, however, all the commandments from God are divine kisses (SongRab 1:2, 2).[6]

The eroticism and gender reversal evident in the rabbis' reading of the Song of Songs reflects a broader tendency to see women's experience as useful for understanding the relationship of God and men. This is particularly evident in the parables that the sages offered in interpretations of scriptural verses. These parables, which typically describe God as a king, often cast human men as women.[7] Consider, for example, the parable used to explain the story of Adam's sin:

> Rabbi Levi said: Imagine a woman borrowing vinegar, who went to the wife of a snake-charmer and asked her, "How does your husband treat you?" "He treats me with every kindness," she replied, "except that he does not permit me to approach this cask which is full of serpents and scorpions." "It contains all his fin-

ery," said the other; "he wishes to marry another woman and give it to her." What did she do? She inserted her hand into it, and they began biting her. When her husband came he heard her crying out. "Have you touched that cask?" he demanded. Similarly, [God said to Adam] *Did you eat of the tree from which I had forbidden you to eat?* (GenRab 19:10)[8]

In casting God as a snake charmer, this parable partially blames him for the presence of the snake in the garden. Moreover, since Adam is cast as the snake charmer's wife, Eve cannot be Adam's wife. She becomes a neighbor who needs to borrow a proverbial "cup of sugar." Here is another example of how the feminization of the male character displaces the female character. Eve convinces Adam to open the cask which "her" (Adam's) husband has said is dangerous. It is interesting just what pretext Eve uses to get "God's wife" to open the box. She tells her that God is saving the finery for another woman. In other words, Eve plays on the man's fears that his position as God's wife is insecure. In short, this retelling of the story shifts the blame back to Adam, but in doing so, it feminizes him as the wife of God.

The feminization of Adam continues in the retelling of the expulsion from the garden. Commenting on the relevant verse "He drove the man out" (Gen. 3:24), R. Yohanan says, "Like the daughter of a priest who has been divorced and cannot return to her husband." R. Simeon b. Lakish says, "Like the daughter of an Israelite who has been divorced and is able to return" (GenRab 21:8). The rabbis thus disagree as to whether the expulsion is an irreparable divorce. If God is imagined as a priest, then God cannot remarry Adam because priests do not marry divorced women (Lev. 21:13). But God may be like an ordinary Israelite who is permitted to marry a divorced woman. These interpretations pick up on the fact that the word for expulsion also means divorce. But this is merely linguistic grounds for the rabbinic tendency to feminize male characters in their relationship with God.

To explain why God created Adam before Abraham, since Abraham is regarded as more virtuous, Rabbi Levi explains, "You bring a virtuous woman into the house of a corrupt one, but not vice versa" (GenRab 14:6). Similarly, in an explanation of the ten trials of Abraham, Abraham is cast as a long-suffering wife. At the end of the last trial, as Abraham is about to sacrifice Isaac to God, an angel stays his hand and cryptically says, "By myself I swear" (Gen. 22:15). The rabbis account for the angel's oath this way:

> A king. . . was married to a noble lady. She gave birth to her first son by him, and he divorced her; a second, and he divorced her; a third, and he divorced her. When she had given birth to a tenth son by him, they all assembled and demanded of him, "Swear to us not to divorce our mother again." Similarly when Abraham had been tried for the tenth time, he said to Him, "Swear to me not to test me again." (GenRab 56:11)

In testing Abraham, God is said to be like a king who repeatedly divorces his wife, despite the fact that she keeps giving him sons. Abraham's good deeds and faithfulness are thus the sons that he gives to God in their marriage.

The feminization of Abraham continues after the ordeal with Isaac. When Abraham returns to the young men who had earlier accompanied him, Isaac is not mentioned (Gen. 22:19). The text's silence regarding Isaac leads the rabbis to speculate that Abraham sent him to study Torah with Shem: "This may be compared to a woman who became wealthy through her spinning. Said she, 'Since I have become wealthy through this spinning, it will never leave my hand.' [Thus said Abraham: 'All that has come to me is only because I engaged in Torah and good deeds; therefore I am unwilling that it should ever depart from my seed']" (GenRab 56:19).[9] Like a woman who conserves the wealth she has earned, Abraham ensures that the knowledge of Torah will be passed on to his son.

We have already seen the association between circumcision and femininity in the biblical myths of divine attacks on Jacob and Moses, as well as in the story of Dinah's rape (chapter 6). This association figures even more prominently in rabbinic reflections:

> Precious are Israel for Scripture has surrounded them with commandments; phylacteries on their heads, phylacteries on their

arms, mezuzahs on their doors, ritual fringes on their garments. Concerning these [precepts] David said, *I praise You seven times each day for Your just rules* (Ps. 119:164). When he went into the bathhouse and saw himself naked, he said "Woe to me, I am naked of commandments," but then he saw his mark of circumcision and began to praise it saying, *For the Leader on the eighth (sheminith) a psalm of David* (Ps. 12:1).

A parable: a king of flesh and blood said to his wife "Deck yourself out with all your jewelry so that you look desirable to me." This also the Holy One said to Israel, "My children be decked by my commandments so you look desirable to me: Hence Scripture says, *You are beautiful, My darling* (Song 6:4)." (Sifre Deut. 36; Tos. Ber. 7:25)[10]

The religious precepts are regarded as a kind of clothing in which a man covers himself. Circumcision has the distinction of making sure that a man is never naked of God's commandments. David is even imagined to have dedicated a psalm in praise of circumcision. He dedicates it to "the eighth," which the rabbis interpret as referring to the eighth day, the day on which a boy is circumcised after birth. But if circumcision keeps a man from being naked, it also makes him desirable to God. Note how the parable makes this point about desirability only after the man is first represented as the wife of God. The feminization enables the eroticism to be expressed. And the reference to the Song leaves no doubt that a heavy dose of eroticism is intended. Circumcision is part of what beautifies men in God's eyes.

In an analogous reading, Abraham's circumcision is imagined as a detail of proper female adornment. Just before giving Abraham the commandment of circumcision God says, "Walk before me and be whole" (Gen. 17:1):

Rabbi Levi said: This may be illustrated by a noble lady whom the king commanded, "Walk before me." She walked before him and her face became ashen, for she thought, perhaps some defect may have been found in me? Said the king to her, "You have no defect except that the nail of your little finger is slightly too long; pare it and the defect will be gone." So said God to Abraham, "You have no blemish except this foreskin. Remove it and the defect will be gone. Hence *Walk before me and be whole.*" (GenRab 46:4)

In this case, circumcision is viewed as perfecting the male body. "Be whole" is taken as a reference to the purity of the body. This fits the sages' general conception of creation as being incomplete and requiring human action to perfect it. Mustard and vetches need sweetening, wheat needs grinding, and man, too, needs to be completed (GenRab 55:4, 42:3). It is for this reason that the sages say various virtuous men were born already circumcised, including Shem (GenRab 26:3), the king of Salem (GenRab 43:6), Jacob and Joseph (GenRab 63:7, 84:6), and Moses (LevRab 20:1). But this text superimposes another symbolism on the idea of perfection. It depicts circumcision as the final touches in an elegant woman's toilette. The foreskin is a small, almost undetectable, imperfection on her little finger. In another context, a woman's little finger is also treated erotically. "Whoever gazes intentionally at a woman it is as though he had intercourse with her. Hence the rabbis declared: Whoever touches a woman's little finger, it is as though he touched that place [her vagina]" (BT Ber. 24a).

What makes the woman of the Song of Songs beautiful is her paring of her little fingernail. Or to put it another way, what makes an Israelite man into God's beautiful female lover is his circumcision. Says the lover to his love in the Song of Songs,

> *The head upon you is like the Carmel [= crimson wool], the hair on your head is like purple* (Song 7:6). The Holy One, blessed be He, said to Israel: "The poorest among you are as dear to Me as Elijah who ascended Carmel." As it is written, *Elijah meanwhile climbed to the top of Mount Carmel, crouched on the ground, and put his face between his knees* (1 Kings 18:42). Why did he put his face between his knees? He said to the Holy One, blessed be He, "Sovereign of the Universe! if we have no merit, then look to the covenant of circumcision." (LevRab 31:4)

The sages interpret the reference to the female lover's head as a reference to "the poor among you," that is, even the average Israelite. "Is like the Carmel" means like the prophet who climbed the Carmel, namely, Elijah. Although the sages do not give a specific reading of "the hair on your head is like purple," the analogy to Elijah, who puts his head between his legs, suggests that they construe this as a reference to circumcision. The head is the penis, and the purple the blood of circumcision.

The insistence on this link between circumcision and femininity explains why the sages find an allusion to circumcision in Ezekiel 16, where it is completely absent. As previously discussed, Ezekiel 16 recounts how God discovers the infant Israel wallowing in the blood of her birth. God says to her, "By your blood live, by your blood live." But the sages assume it is the blood of circumcision and the blood of the Passover to which God is referring (ExodRab 17:3). What prompts this interpretation must be in part the association of circumcision with femininity. Indeed, we recall that the verses that follow describe the most erotic scene between God and Israel. When this baby girl matures into a woman, God finds her desirable and has intercourse with her. The rabbis make no explicit connection here between circumcision and eroticism. But given the comparison of circumcision with female beauty in other contexts, such associations may be operative here as well.

We do know that the sages regarded circumcision as a prerequisite for God's appearance to men:[11]

> Said Abraham, "Before I was circumcised, slaves and captives came to me; once I am circumcised will they no longer visit me?" God said to him, "Before you were circumcised, uncircumcised men came to you, now I in My glory will appear to you." Hence it is written, *and the Lord appeared unto him* (Gen. 28:1). . . . And then again, *[This after my skin will have been peeled off.] Through my flesh shall I see God* (Job 19:26). Had I not done so God would not have revealed himself to me. (GenRab 47:10, 48:2)

Circumcision, then, completes a man and makes him ready for a theophany. Through the act of circumcision, one may stand in the presence of God. This merit is deserved not only because circumcision is a sign of the covenant, but also because men may meet God only as women. And circumcision makes them desirable women.

The link between circumcision and theophany returns us to the issue of eroticism in God sightings. In rabbinic imagination, as in biblical myths, God sightings are sexually charged and must be approached with caution.

Eroticism in the Orchard of God

This is the story of the four rabbis who entered the orchard of God, only one of whom survives:

> Four entered Pardes [Orchard/Paradise]: Ben Azzai, Ben Zoma, "the Other" [i.e., Elisha Ben Abuya] and Aqiba. One gazed and perished, one gazed and was smitten, one gazed and cut down sprouts, and one went up whole and came down whole.
>
> Ben Azzai[12] gazed and perished. Concerning him Scripture says, *Precious in the sight of the Lord is the death of his saints* (Ps. 116:15).
>
> Ben Zoma gazed and was smitten (*npgʿ*). Concerning him Scripture says, *If you have found honey, eat only enough for you, lest you be sated with it and vomit it* (Prov. 25:16).
>
> Elisha gazed and cut down sprouts. Concerning him Scripture says, *Let not your mouth lead your flesh (bĕśārekā) into sin* (Qoh. 5:5).
>
> R. Aqiba entered[13] without incident and came out without incident. Concerning him Scripture says, *Draw me after you, let us make haste. [The King has brought me to his chambers]* (Song 1:4).
>
> To what is the matter like? To a royal garden with an upper room built over it [to guard it]. What is [the guard's duty]? To look but not to feast his eyes on it. (Tos. Hag. 2:3–5)[14]

Ascensions into heaven are not uncommon in religious texts of the Hellenistic and late antique periods. Jewish apocalyptic literature describes various biblical characters, such as Enoch, Abraham, and Isaiah, ascending into the heavens, where they encounter angels, learn the mysteries of the universe, and see God.[15] Almost all of these visions are dependent in various ways on Ezekiel's vision of God riding the divine chariot. And like Ezekiel, most of them imagine the deity seated on the divine throne. For example, in what is called Ethiopic Enoch (1 Enoch 14), an apocalyptic text written sometime in the mid second century B.C.E., Enoch is described as coming into heaven and entering a series of palacelike structures which are surrounded by fire. He sees a lofty throne:

> Its appearance was like crystal and its wheels like the shining sun . . . and from beneath the throne were issuing streams of flaming fire. It was difficult to look at it. And the Great Glory was sitting upon it—as for his gown, which was shining more brightly than the sun, it was whiter than any snow. None of the angels was able to come in and see the face of the Excellent and Glorious One, and no one of the flesh can see him. (1 Enoch 14:8–25)[16]

Similar visionary experiences may have been part of merkavah (chariot) mysticism, a religious form of the early rabbinic period that took as its focus Ezekiel's chariot vision.

The story of the rabbis entering the garden seems to belong to the same genre, and it thus provides a point of departure for our analysis of late antique visions of God. The story has much to tell us about the rabbinic understanding of visionary experiences. We shall see that the dilemma of male erotic desire for God partially explains why visions of God were problematic and why it was forbidden to study certain parts of Scripture. Focusing on the issue of eroticism illuminates some troubling questions regarding the esotericism of early rabbinic culture.[17]

It is clear that the story of the four sages is a cautionary tale that depicts the dangers involved in a particular kind of religious experience. Three sages enter the garden, gaze inappropriately, and die. Aqiba, who does not gaze, is spared. Following Scholem, some interpreters believe this story describes a visionary experience such as those found in apocalyptic literature, as is suggested by the references to gazing.[18] Indeed, if *pardes* is a reference to Paradise, then the story of the sages is similar to the ascension of Paul, who also claims to have seen Paradise.[19] In several other apocalyptic works, Paradise is also in heaven. These sages, then, have entered the gates of heaven and perhaps seen the chariot vision.

Not all interpreters agree with this reading, however.[20] They argue that *pardes* is not a rabbinic expression for Paradise or the Garden of Eden. Rather, the term is often used in rabbinic literature as a metaphor in parables that are meant to illustrate various religious values. Some interpret the garden as representing other forms of wisdom—gnosticism, for example, which intrigued some rabbis but whose study was banned. According to others the orchard is a metaphor for Scripture itself, and hence the story is a warning about the potential dangers of entering the orchard of Scripture.

The Mishnah, an early compendium of rabbinic law, records a debate about whether it is appropriate to use Ezekiel's chariot vision as a prophetic reading (haftarah) in the synagogue (M. Meg. 4:10).[21] Elsewhere the Mishnah suggests that sages should not "expound upon . . . the work of the Chariot before one, unless he was a sage (and) understands of his own knowledge. . . . And whoever gives no heed to the honor of his creator, it were better that he had not come into the world" (M. Hag. 2:1; Tos. Hag. 2:1). According to this source, and its parallel in the Tosefta, the vision of Ezekiel is an esoteric doctrine that should not be discussed publicly. It is in the context of reflecting on this law that the Tosefta reports the story of the four sages in the orchard, implying a connection between their experiences there and the various subjects being debated. In the same context, the Tosefta (Hag. 2:1–2) reports stories of sages who expounded upon Ezekiel's vision. Thus, even if the story of the four sages did not originally refer to visionary experiences, its placement gave it a new twist and turned it into a story dealing with esoteric doctrinal matters (Halperin 1988, 33; Urbach 1967).

Why Ezekiel's vision should have been seen as an esoteric matter and why visions of God provoked fears has been a central question in the study of apocalypticism and merkavah mysticism. David Halperin frames the question this way:

> Evidently, the rabbis saw something in Ezekiel's vision that was vitally important, yet so fearful that the ordinary person must be warned away from it. . . . But the fear the vision aroused is still mysterious. We understand it no better when we are told that

contemplation of the divine is inherently dangerous, because we do not grasp why this should be so. . . . We must ask precisely what there was about the act of interpreting this Scriptural text, that called forth these responses from the rabbis. Otherwise we miss our chance to understand an important if unconventional aspect of rabbinic Judaism, and perhaps of the phenomenon of the *tremendum* in general. (1988, 5)

One possibility is that the rabbis felt uncomfortable with Ezekiel's vision of the deity in human form riding a chariot.[22] But it is not clear that the avoidance of anthropomorphism can account completely for the rabbis' worries, as Halperin has argued. To begin with, there is increasing evidence that the worries about anthropomorphism in late antique religion have been exaggerated in the study of the Targums and in rabbinic Judaism. The rabbis do not show the aversion to anthropomorphism found in other literatures of the Hellenistic or late antique periods.[23] Indeed, at times the rabbis seem to go out of their way to underscore the human qualities and appearance of the deity. For example, in reflecting upon what Moses might have seen when he saw God from the back (Exod. 33:23), one rabbinic interpretation says that Moses saw the knot of God's phylactery, a religious ornament containing passages of Scripture that Jewish men are commanded to wear on their foreheads and which loops around the head (BT Ber. 7a).[24] This image of God wearing a phylactery strengthens rather than weakens the impression that God is embodied. The human appearance of God is also assumed by a rabbinic reflection on God's putting Adam to sleep (Gen. 2:21). Explaining the need for Adam's sleep, the rabbis suggest that when Adam was originally created, the angels mistook Adam for God and wanted to praise him. The rabbis provide a parable to illustrate: It is like a king and a governor who are riding together in a chariot, and when his subjects become confused as to who is king, the king pushes the governor out of the chariot. So too God causes Adam to fall asleep (GenRab 8:10). The ostensive purpose of this story is to explain Adam's mortality, but it also suggests that God and Adam resemble one another in appearance, an idea that shows up elsewhere in rabbinic reflections on Genesis.[25] The rabbis' ease with anthropomorphic images of God is also reflected in their commentaries on Exodus 15, where the Israelites praise God for their deliverance from the Egyptians. After their crossing of the Red Sea, Moses and the children of Israel sing, "This is my God and I will glorify him" (Exod. 15:2). When singing this verse, the rabbis claim, the Israelites were pointing to God, who had become visible. According to one version of this interpretation, even the maidservant saw more than what Ezekiel and Isaiah would (Mek. Shirah 3). According to another version, it was the young Israelite men who recognized God. When Pharaoh had been killing the male Israelite children, the boys were put into the fields by their mothers. When they were grown and had returned to their families and were asked who had cared for them, they replied, "A certain splendidly handsome young man used to come down and take care of all our needs" (Song 5:10). At the sea, when God appeared, the children said, "This is the one who took care of us" (ExodRab 23:8).[26]

Given the many anthropomorphic descriptions of God in rabbinic literature, Halperin concludes that it was not Ezekiel's vision of God in human form that bothered the rabbis and goes on to suggest an alternative reason that the chariot vision so disturbed them. In a complex argument whose details cannot be repeated here, he argues that it was the presence of the calf in Ezekiel's vision that the rabbis found so unsettling. The calf was one of the creatures transporting the divine chariot, and this calf must have been spotted by the Israelites at the Sinaitic revelation. According to Halperin, the presence of the calf in the vision thus exculpated the Israelites for making the golden calf, for how could they be held responsible for describing part of their vision of God? This conclusion was so radical to the rabbis that it had to be suppressed. Halperin's interpretation may account in part for the rabbis' unwillingness to discuss the Ezekiel passage, but in my view it too readily dismisses their concerns about this vision of God.[27]

I agree with Halperin that there is something disturbing about Ezekiel's vision that did not involve the problem of anthropomorphism generally. "We are looking for a 'something,'" he writes, "that somehow has to do with the visions of Ezekiel, that somehow had the power to stir up fear, excitement, and perhaps even ecstasy" (1988, 11). I suggest that the something for which we are looking is Ezekiel's reference to God's loins. Recall that Ezekiel twice describes God from the loins up and the loins down, as if his gaze is irresistibly drawn there (Ezek. 1:2, 8:2). It is possible that while the general idea of God in human form did not trouble the rabbis greatly, they were upset by the focus of Ezekiel's gaze. This would explain why the rabbis found his vision more problematic than other God sightings. Ezekiel's vision, more than others, raised the possibility of male desire for God, a desire that could cause death if men were unable to act with propriety.

The Targum of Ezekiel, an Aramaic translation that appears in the Targum Jonathon, provides support for this interpretation. Compare the translation with the original:

EZEKIEL 1:26–27

upon this semblance of a throne, there was the semblance of a human form. From *what appeared as his loins up*, I saw a gleam as of amber— what looked like a fire encased in a frame; and *from what appeared as his loins down*, I saw what looked like fire. There was a radiance all about him. Like the appearance of the bow which shines in the clouds on a day of rain, such was the appearance of the surrounding radiance.

TARGUM OF EZEKIEL 1:26–28

above the likeness of the throne there was the likeness of the appearance of Adam[28] above it from on high. I saw something like the *hashmal* like the appearance of fire from the midst of it round about, *an appearance of glory which the eye is unable to see, and such that it is impossible to look at it and upward; an appearance of glory which the eye is unable to see, and such that it is impossible to look at it and downward . . .* I saw what appeared to be fire; and it was surrounded by splendor. Like the appearance of the rainbow that is in the cloud on a rainy day, so was the appearance of splendor round about. [29]

Halperin regards the Aramaic translation as attempting to soften the anthropomorphism of Ezekiel's vision through a "fog of euphemisms," and there is evidence elsewhere in this Targum of a desire to avoid anthropomorphisms; for example, it generally does not give literal translations for references to the face of God or the eye of God (Halperin 1988, 89; Levey 1987, 14). But were the exclusive or primary motivation to avoid anthropomorphisms in general, the translation would surely eliminate the suggestion that God looked like Adam. Instead, what it eliminates is the reference to God's loins, for which it substitutes "a glory (*yakar*) that the eye is unable to see." The Targum makes an identical substitution when translating Ezekiel 8:2. This avoidance of the reference to God's loins contrasts with the way in which this translation deals with the term "loins" elsewhere. In all but one other instance, it employs forms of the word *ḥrṣ* (Isa. 20:2, 21:3, 45:1; Jer. 13:1, 2, 4, 8, 11; Ezek. 29:7, 23:15, 44:18, 47:4). Only in reference to the loins of the Messiah do we find a similar kind of avoidance (Isa. 11:5). In addition to the avoidance of the word "loins," it is interesting to note the doubling that occurs in the translation. "An appearance of glory which the eye is unable to see, and such that it is impossible to look at it." The inability to gaze is underscored through iteration. It is interesting that the substitution of "the glory" (*yakar*) for the loins occurs throughout later mystical writings, including the Hekhalot texts and the Shiur Qomah, the mystical text which describes the size of God's limbs.[30]

Indeed, worries about sexual improprieties motivated the rabbis to consider treating other scriptural passages as too esoteric for general consumption. The same early rabbinic laws that restrict discussion of the chariot vision also prohibit the public study of the forbidden sexual relationships listed in Leviticus 18 and 20 (M. Hag. 2:1; T. Hag. 2:1). This concern with the public consumption of sexually provocative passages is also reflected in rabbinic debates about which scriptural passages may be read and translated in the synagogue into the vernacular (M. Meg. 4:10; T. Meg. 3:31–38; and a baraita in BT Meg. 25a–b).[31] The scriptural passages are grouped into three categories, those that may be read in Hebrew and translated into Aramaic, read but not translated, neither read nor translated. Together these lists discuss fifteen different scriptural passages (Halperin 1980, 52). They include the creation story (Genesis 1); the story of incest between Lot and his daughters (Gen. 19:30ff); the story of Reuben having intercourse with Bilhah, his father's wife (Gen. 35:22); the story of Tamar's seduction of her father-in-law (Gen. 38); the first telling of the golden calf story (Exod. 32:1ff); the second telling of the calf incident (Exod. 32:21ff); "warning and punishments," which Halperin identifies as the list of prohibited sexual relations of Leviticus 18 and 20; the priestly blessing (Num. 6:24–26); the rape of the concubine at Gibeah (Judges 19); David's adultery with Bathsheba (2 Sam. 11–12); Amnon's rape of Tamar (2 Sam. 13); Absalom having intercourse with David's concubines (2 Sam. 16:20–23); Ezekiel's chariot vision (Ezekiel 1); and his vision of Jerusalem as a promiscuous woman (Ezekiel 16). Although the sages decide that most of these passages may be read and translated, "the fact that they had to be explicitly permitted shows that their suitability for synagogue use had been questioned" (Halperin 1980, 52). The rabbis do not worry about censuring scriptural stories that involve questionable moral behavior of a nonsexual nature. Most interpreters see no link between this worry about the public discussion of sexual impropriety and the worries about Ezekiel's chariot vision. But Ezekiel's vision is the most explicit reference to the deity's loins, and the other passage from Ezekiel that is discussed involves not only the promiscuous behavior of the woman Israel, but a graphic depiction of God having intercourse with her.

It is thus significant that there is almost no rabbinic commentary on Ezekiel 1:27 and 8:2, the two verses that mention the deity's loins.[32] There are no references in all of rabbinic literature to Ezekiel 8:2. Ezekiel 1:27 is cited only twice, and one of these citations is of an extremely late date and appears in a context that deals with merkabah speculation.[33] The lack of commentary on what are extraordinary statements of Ezekiel strongly suggests a process of censure. Whatever discussions sages may have had about the verses left no trace in rabbinic literature. In contrast, Ezekiel 1:26 is cited a dozen times, despite its reference to God's appearance in human form.[34] The anthropomorphic image did not deter rabbinic interpretation, just as it did not bother the Targum translators. But the reference to God's loins was clearly another problem.

The idea that the rabbis thought about divine genitals may seem completely absurd on the face of it. But there are at least a few indications that the sages thought discretely about such matters. There is, for example, a famous rabbinic idea that the Messiah will not come until the souls which are stored in God's *guf* have come to an end (BT Yeb. 62a; A.Z. 5a; Nid. 13b) (Urbach 1967, 237). The term *guf* normally means "body." Jastrow describes the "*guf* of God" as the fictitious place in which souls are stored. But *guf* is also a rabbinic euphemism for penis (PT Ber. 1:3, 3:3; LevRab 25:6). For example, Abraham is regarded as fit to sacrifice only after circumcision of the *guf* (LevRab 25:6). It is certainly reasonable to translate *guf* as God's metaphorical penis.[35] And in another passage, the sages imply that God's phallus may be circumcised. Commenting upon what it means for Adam to be made in the image of God, one rabbi explains that Adam is born circumcised (ARNA 2:58) (Schechter 1887, 12; Goldin 1955, 23). In part the implication is that Adam is created perfect like God. But one cannot avoid seeing here the suggestsion of a divine circumcision. Nor would this be foreign to rabbinic theology, which imagines God as performing all the other rabbinic obligations, including wearing phylacteries, studying Torah, and so forth. This would also be consistent with the view that Hillel regarded bathing himself as important because his body was made in the divine image.

All of this suggests that the explicitness of Ezekiel's visions, in particular the reference to God's loins, was what perturbed the rabbis. It is clear that the rabbis viewed Ezekiel's vision as more explicit than other visions (GenRab 27:1). But if Ezekiel's vision was considered the most stark among the prophets, it was believed to be dwarfed by what the Israelites saw at the crossing of the Red Sea. There, even the maidservant saw more than Isaiah and Ezekiel had seen (Mek. Shirah 3).

I do not see the rabbis' avoidance of God's loins as simply another example of their discomfort with sexually explicit material, for the rabbis forbade the public discussion of Ezekiel's vision while permitting the reading and translation in the synagogue of most sexually explicit material in Scripture. The mention of God's loins was more provocative, I submit, because it evoked the issue of male homoeroticism. And we shall now see just how erotic an experience the sighting of God was considered in rabbinic imagination.

The Chamber of the King

Consider once more the four sages who enter *Pardes*. The story itself suggests that the garden in question is the one described in the Song of Songs, the garden in which God and Israel meet each other as lovers. In describing Aqiba's successful entrance and exit from the garden, the story quotes the woman's words to her beloved: "Draw me after you, let us make haste. . . . [The King has brought me in his chambers]" (Song 1:4). It thus compares Aqiba's entrance into the garden with the woman's entering the private chambers of her lover, the king. And it suggests that while all the sages entered the orchard, only Aqiba entered the king's chambers.[36] Indeed, it is significant that Aqiba, the one sage to survive this experience unscathed, is cited in rabbinic literature of the same period as viewing the Song of Songs as the holiest part of Scripture: "The entire world is not worth the day on which The Song of Songs was given to Israel. For all the scriptures are holy but The Song of Songs is the holy of holies" (M. Yad. 3:5).[37] If the Song of Songs is the holy of holies, it is imagined to be the place where God resides and which only the high priest may enter. Aqiba is thus depicted as a kind of high priest among the rabbis, the only one to successfully enter the scriptural holy of holies.

Moreover, the Song of Songs contains one of the three biblical references to a *pardes*, the word used to describe the orchard that the sages have entered. The term *pardes* is also used to describe the limbs of the female lover, which are said to be like an orchard of pomegranates. To enter into *Pardes* perhaps implies taking the position of or embodying the female lover. Indeed, if we examine this passage of the Song of Songs more carefully, we see that there are other indirect allusions to it in the story of the four sages. It is as if the story has a subtext, a subtext that is only hinted at, because of its esoteric nature.

> You have captured my heart,
> My own, my bride,
> You have captured my heart,
> with one [glance] of your eyes,
> with one coil of your necklace.

How sweet is your love,
My own, my bride!
How much more delightful your love than wine,
Your ointments more fragrant
than any spice!
Sweetness drops
from your lips, O bride;
Honey and milk are under your tongue,
and the scent of your robes is like the scent of Lebanon.
A garden locked is my own, my bride,
a fountain locked, a sealed-up spring.
Your limbs (*šelāḥayik*) are an orchard (*pardes*) of
    pomegranates,
and of all luscious fruits. . . .
Awake, O north wind. Come, O south wind!
Blow upon my garden,
That its perfume may spread.
Let my beloved come to his garden
And enjoy its luscious fruits. (Song 4:9–16)

According to the story, Ben Zoma gazed and was smitten and concerning him Scripture says, "If you have found honey, eat only enough for you, lest you be sated with it and vomit it" (Prov. 25:16). In itself, this is an odd way to describe Ben Zoma's sin, but it makes a great deal of sense when we read the Song of Songs as background. Ben Zoma is like the female lover of the Song: "Sweetness drops from your lips, O bride; honey and milk are under your tongue." This is a decidedly erotic image and may even allude to a woman's vagina (Pope 1977, 458), as may the subsequent reference to "a garden locked is my own, my bride, a fountain locked, a sealed-up spring." The image of honey in the mouth may also be a reference to Ezekiel's vision. During that vision, God hands Ezekiel a scroll and instructs him to eat it. Upon doing so, Ezekiel has the taste of honey in his mouth (Ezek. 3:2). Given these associations, it is not surprising that the image of honey under the tongue is later used to justify the esoteric nature of the chariot vision, which should be like honey under the tongue, savored alone (BT Hag. 13b).[38]

The mouth dripping with honey is not the only oral image in this story. Regarding Elisha's sin, the story applies the following verse of Scripture: "Let not your mouth lead your flesh (*běśārekā*) into sin" (Eccles. 5:5). In the context of Ecclesiastes, this is an instruction not to leave a vow unfulfilled, a meaning that makes no sense in the context of the sages' story. But the association of the mouth and sensual pleasure can without exaggeration be read into the rabbis' choice of Scripture to describe Elisha's transgression. Indeed, metaphors of eating are sometimes used to describe an inappropriate gaze, as is suggested in a rabbinic parable that is told immediately after the story of the four sages and apparently is meant to illustrate Aqiba's role in the story.

> To what is the matter like? To a royal garden with an upper room built over it [to guard it]. What is [the guard's duty]? To look but not to feast his eyes on it. (Tos. Hag. 2:3–5)

Aqiba is here imagined as the one guard who does not gaze too greedily in the royal garden. By contrast, the other sages are like guards who "feast the eyes," an oral metaphor that echoes the images of Ben Azzai whose mouth drips with honey and Elisha whose mouth leads him into sin.

But what sin exactly did Elisha commit? The story says cryptically—or should I say esoterically—that he "cut down shoots." This expression can be interpreted several ways.[39] Some view cutting down shoots as a metaphor for one who does not practice the Torah he has learned. Others note that "shoots" can be a reference to the righteous of God (PT Ber. 2:8), and cutting down shoots is applied to their deaths. But it is also possible that cutting shoots is another specific allusion to the Song of Songs' description of the female lover, whose "limbs are an orchard of pomegranates." The word translated as "limbs" (*šelāḥayik*) poses difficulties. The verb, *šelāḥ*, is used of trees sending forth roots (Jer. 17:8; Ps. 80:12), and the noun refers to branches (Isa. 16:8) (Pope 1977, 490). Thus some interpreters translate the verse this way: "You are a park (*pardes*) that puts forth (*šelāḥayik*) pomegranates." Others understand it as an allusion to the woman's limbs, and perhaps to her intimate parts: "Your limbs are an orchard of pomegranates."

If we read the shoots of the rabbinic story as a reference to the poem, to cut down shoots is to do damage to the collective body of female Israel. This is an apt metaphor for apostasy, for which Elisha is later condemned. By leading students astray, he destroys Israel's youth, and indeed, shoots is sometimes a metaphor for children.[40] In one source at least, the shoots of Israel are explicitly imagined as her sons. The Targum of the Song of Songs, which may be of a very late date, interprets her shoots this way: "Regarding thy young men, rich in the fulfillment of precepts like pomegranates, they are attached in love to their wives, and beget children righteous as themselves."[41] The metaphor of cutting down shoots may also be a veiled allusion to an act performed on the male sexual organ, whether circumcision or castration.

Only one incident in the story of the four sages remains to be interpreted. With regard to Ben Azzai, the story quotes the scriptural verse "Precious in the eyes of the Lord is the death of his righteous" (Ps. 116:15). It should come as no surprise that an encounter "of the fourth kind" sometimes results in death. Biblical myth regards the sighting of God as a life-threatening experience (Exod. 19:21, 33:20). Only the select few are able to see God and live (Exod. 24:11). But why is the death of Ben Azzai considered precious? Some interpreters see here a reference to martyrdom. The sage's commitment to Scripture (the garden) was said to have resulted in his martyrdom at the hands of Rome.[42] But there is another common rabbinic understanding of this verse: "What is *precious in the eyes of the Lord is* [shown at] *the death of the righteous* (GenRab 62:2; ExodRab 52:3). In other words, at the moment of death, God shows the righteous their reward. In one context, moreover, this understanding of the verse is attributed to Ben Azzai himself and the righteous who dies is imagined as a woman:

> It is written *She is clothed with strength and splendor; She looks to the future cheerfully* (Prov. 31:25). The entire reward of the righteous is kept ready for them for the hereafter, and the Holy One,

blessed be He, shows them while yet in this world the reward He is to give them in the future; their souls are then satisfied and they fall asleep. (GenRab 62:2)

The verse cited is part of the famous proverb that discusses the virtues of a good wife. In this case, she is a metaphor for the soul of the righteous. The Hebrew word for soul is *nefesh*, a feminine noun. But before the reader reaches the reference to the soul, the text has already encouraged an identification of the righteous man with the "she" of the proverb.

"Precious (*yakar*) in the eyes of the Lord is the death of his righteous" thus refers to something that the righteous, now feminized, will be shown at the moment of death. It is possible that there is a double entendre in this verse, at least as the sages use it in the story of the four sages. The word *yakar* is one of the Aramaic words that the Targumim (the Aramaic translations) often use to describe God. And as previously noted, it is this word in particular that is used to circumvent the reference to God's loins. In short, what is shown to the righteous at the moment of death is everything Ezekiel saw.

The meaning of the story of the four sages is veiled in subtle associations, truncated scriptural verses, and obscure allusions. In part, this is true of rabbinic literature in general. But in this story in particular, a story that deals with an esoteric subject, the hints of eroticism, and the fear of homoeroticism, can only be approached indirectly. Later references to the study of the chariot vision underscore the eroticism of visionary experience.[43] And this experience, as rabbinic reflections on the God sightings at Sinai indicate, threatened death unless it could be mediated or approached with proper decorum. Indeed, the rabbinic heroes in the orchard story find their doubles in rabbinic musings about biblical characters who entertain a vision of God.

The Insatiable Gaze

In reflections on biblical reports of God sightings, the rabbis make it clear that they view the erotic as present in the relationship between

God and Moses, the biblical figure who has the most intimate relationship with the deity, and the one character who speaks with God "mouth to mouth."[44] The rabbis give conflicting accounts of this relationship. According to one view, God refuses to show Moses the divine face (Exod. 33:20) because Moses earlier did not want to look upon God at the burning bush. "When I desired it, you did not desire it. Now that you desire it, I do not" (Ber. 7a; ExodRab 3:1). God withholds divine intimacy and does not show his face to Moses because of Moses' earlier hesitation. According to another view, however, Moses is rewarded for his modest behavior.

> As a reward for three [actions] he was privileged to obtain three [rewards]. In reward for *And Moses hid his face* (Exod. 3:6), he obtained the brightness of face (Exod. 34:29–30).[45] In reward for *he was afraid* (Exod. 3:6) he obtained the privilege that *they were afraid to come near him* (34:30). In reward for [being afraid] *to look upon God* (Exod. 3:6) he obtained the privilege of *he beheld the likeness of the Lord* (Num. 12:8). (BT Ber. 7a; ExodRab 3:1)

According to this view, Moses' hesitation about intimacy, his modesty, and his fear of looking at God are rewarded with the brightness of his own face, with the people's fear of approaching him, and with beholding God. Another version of the same idea puts it this way: "R. Joshua of Siknin in the name of R. Levi [commented] 'Moses did not feed (*znw*) his eyes on the Shekinah [and because of this] he derived benefit from the Shekinah. He did not feed his eyes on the Shekinah, as it says *And Moses hid his face* (Exod. 3:6). And he derived benefit from the Shekinah as it says *Moses knew not that the skin of his face sent forth light* (Exod. 34:29)'" (LevRab 20:10). In still another version, God says to him: "'Since you showed me respect (*kavod*) and hid your face when I would show Myself to you, I assure you that you will be near Me on the mountain for forty days and forty nights. You will not eat nor drink, but will feast on the splendor (*zyz*) of the Shechinah,' as it is said, *And Moses knew not that the skin of his face sent forth beams* (Exod. 34:29)" (ExodRab 47:5).

Beneath this disagreement about whether God exposed or hid himself in reaction to Moses' modesty is a shared presupposition: the issue of God's veiling or showing the divine body revolves around matters of proper decorum in intimate relations. And this decorum involves in part a regulation of eroticism, albeit of an order different from that operating between people. The issue of eroticism, which is left implicit in these statements about the relationship between God and Moses, is more fully expressed in a closely related set of reflections that contrast the behavior of Moses with Nadab and Abihu, two other Israelites who were also privileged to gaze at God.

Recall the myth in Exodus 24 in which Moses and Aaron, Nadab, Abihu, and seventy leaders of Israel ascended to the mountain top, where "they saw the God of Israel: under His feet there was the likeness of a pavement of sapphire, like the very sky for purity. Yet He did not raise His hand against the leaders of the Israelites; they beheld God and they ate and drank" (Exod. 24:9–11). It is clear in later rabbinic reflections that the sages believe this sighting of God is similar to that described by Ezekiel. Several rabbinic reflections on this passage link the pavement of sapphire with the sapphire that Ezekiel sees in his vision.[46] What the rabbis have to say about this vision is therefore relevant to their understanding of the chariot vision. According to the sages, Nadab and Abihu do not handle their God sighting with the required delicacy. Like the three sages in the orchard, they gaze inappropriately at God and suffer punishment.[47]

The biblical myth does not explain who Nadab and Abihu are, although a later source identifies them as sons of Aaron, the high priest, and describes how they are killed by God for offering a strange fire before the Lord (Lev. 10:1–3). What this strange fire is and why they make the mistake of offering it, the biblical myths do not say. Rabbinic interpretation offers a number of explanations of their sin. Among the more ingenious suggestions is that Nadab and Abihu are put to death for "feasting their eyes" on God.

> *Yet He did not raise His hand against the leaders of the Israelites* (Exod. 24:11). Said R. Phinehas, "From here [we learn] that they deserved to have a hand laid against them, for Rabbi Joshua said,

'Did provisions go up with them on Sinai, as it is written *They beheld God; [and they ate and drank]* (Exod. 24:11)? [Surely not]. Infer that they sated their eyes on the Shekinah, like a person who
looks at another while eating and drinking.'" R. Yohanan said,
"They derived actual nourishment, thus it is written *The light of
the King's face is life*" (Prov. 16:15). Said R. Tanhuma, "Infer that
they uncovered their heads, became bold, and feasted their eyes
on the Shekinah." (LevRab 20:10)[48]

There is no indication in the biblical text that Nadab and Abihu did
anything improper. But the sages understand matters otherwise. Since
the story says that God did not raise his hand against the elders, it suggests that God withheld a punishment that was in fact warranted.
Since Moses is not mentioned here, the sages assume that the elders
alone must have acted inappropriately, and they single Nadab and
Abihu out as the primary culprits.

Nadab and Abihu are biblical parallels to the sages who gazed at
God and perished in the king's orchard. In this case, the metaphor of
feasting the eyes is based explicitly on the end of the myth: "They beheld God and they ate and drank." The sages construe this statement
symbolically. Nadab and Abihu and the others feasted, not on real
food, but on the sight of God. According to one sage, this gaze provided them with actual sustenance.[49] Consider, too, the odd metaphor of a person who gazes at another while eating and drinking. It suggests that Nadab and Abihu are violating the bounds of etiquette by
staring at God, who is metaphorically eating and drinking the sacrifice
that has been offered (Exod. 24:5–6).[50] But their transgression must
be more than improper etiquette, for the punishment of death does not
seem to fit the crime. The image of feasting the eyes on the Shekinah,
however, suggests what that transgression might be. The Hebrew word
for feasting *znw* (from the stem *zwn*) can be construed as a pun on the
word for "lusting after" or "whoring" (from the stem *znh*), which is
used in biblical Hebrew to describe Israel's lusting after other gods.
This link between words which derive from different consonantal
stems would be perfectly consistent with the rabbinic understanding
of language (Eilberg-Schwartz 1988). Indeed, these two different

words are spelled identically in the third masculine plural, the form that is used here. Nadab and Abihu are feasting their eyes and gazing lustily at God, like a person who gazes at another while eating and drinking, and they are acting boldly by not averting their eyes. The expression "became bold" (*hgysw 't Lbn*) is also used sometimes to describe a person who becomes bold in making sexual advances (BT Ket. 12a, 28a) (Jastrow [1903], 224). "Uncovering their heads" also signifies their boldness and lack of respect. The association of unbound hair with unrestrained sexuality is known in both psychoanalytic and ethnographic studies, and is evident in biblical rules pertaining to hair as well. Samson's long hair is a sign of his strength and his virility. When a woman is suspected of adultery, she is put through a trial by ordeal in which her hair is exposed or unbound, apparently in allusion to the inappropriate exposure of other parts of her body (Num. 5:18). In rabbinic literature as well, it is shameful for a woman's hair to be exposed (M. B.Q. 8:6; Ket. 7:6; BT Ket. 66a, 72a; B.Q. 91a). Nadab and Abihu, then, refuse the priestly duty of being like women and keeping their heads covered or bound. They let their hair down just as they do not restrain their insatiable desire.[51]

In this case, they gaze at the Shekinah, and here a feminine noun is used to describe God's presence. In mystical tradition, the Shekinah is the feminine aspect of God. Although it is not clear that it has such feminine implications in rabbinic literature (Scholem 1991), the use of the term may be significant here. As in the case of female Wisdom in Proverbs the homoerotic nature of the gaze may be softened by the use of a feminine noun to describe God's presence.

Sating themselves on God is not the only sin the sages attributed to Nadab and Abihu. They are also said to have drunk wine, lacked the prescribed number of priestly garments, entered the sanctuary without washing their hands and feet, and to have had no children (LevRab 20:9). These were classic sins that priests had to avoid, and the proscriptions have biblical warrants (M. Kel. 1:9; Tos. Ker. 1:5; BT San. 83a–b). Yet there may have been a link in rabbinic thought between some of these violations and their insatiable gazing at God. That they drank wine would fit their inappropriate behavior in God's presence and recalls the story of Noah's drunkenness. In proving that they lacked the requisite number of priestly garments, the sages cite "They shall be worn by Aaron and his sons [when they enter the tent of meeting]" (Exod. 28:43). This citation concludes a lengthy section describing priestly attire. But it may be significant that the preceding verse reads "You shall also make for them linen breeches to cover their nakedness, they shall extend from the hips to the thighs" (Exod. 28:42). If this is the garment which the two young priests failed to wear, a reasonable conclusion from the citation, then the sexual nature of their sin is again underscored. They approached God with their nakedness uncovered. Indeed, one wonders whether their action of "uncovering their heads" may allude to the exposure of their nakedness. For the word "uncovering" is used to refer to uncovering one's nakedness in God's presence when there is a need to urinate (BT Yoma 77a). The same term is used to describe uncovering the corona of the penis in circumcision (M. Shab. 19:2, 6; BT Shab. 137b; Yeb. 71b; NumRab 11). It is possible that this sexual meaning of "uncovering their heads" explains why in some versions of this story Nadab and Abihu "stand on their feet" rather than "uncover their heads" (NumRab 2:25), another possible euphemism for the sexual organs.[52]

It is significant, moreover, that Nadab and Abihu never took wives because they thought no women worthy of their pedigree.

> Rabbi Levi said, "They were pompous. Many women remained unmarried waiting for them. What did they say? 'Our father's brother is a king, our mother's brother is a prince, our father is a High priest, and we are both deputy High priests; what woman is worthy of us?' " Rabbi Menahma in the name of Rabbi Joshua b. Nehemiah quoted: "*Fire devoured their young men* (Ps. 78:63). Why had *fire devoured their young men*? Because *their virgins had no marriage song* (Ps. 78:63)." (LevRab 20:10)[53]

In a stunning interpretation of Ps. 78:63, the sages understand "fire devoured their young men," as referring to the death of Nadab and Abihu (Lev. 10:1–3) "and their maiden remained unwed" as providing an explanation for why they were killed. The refusal of these young men to marry may be related to their lust for God, for immediately following this statement, the text turns to Nadab's and Abihu's inappropriate gaze at God. It is as if they direct their desire in the wrong direction. God is the object of their gaze rather than human women.

Moses, because he is allowed to gaze at God, is justified in abstaining from sexual relations. According to some rabbinic commentaries, Moses never again had sexual relations with his wife after his encounter with God. Recall that this is how the rabbis understand Miriam's and Aaron's protest "on account of the Cushite woman" (Num. 12:1). Miriam and Aaron are upset on behalf of Zipporah, Moses' wife, because Moses has ceased to have sexual relations with her. The rabbis treat Moses' sexual abstinence as one of the three decisions that he made on his own but with divine approval (BT Yeb. 6:6; ARNA 2:29–33).[54]

In one context, Moses' decision to become celibate is recounted in the process of defining how a man discharges his obligation to be fruitful and multiply. According to the Mishnah (Yeb. 6:6), the school of Shammai rules that a man fulfills his obligation when he has two sons. The school of Hillel rules that a man must father a son and a daughter. The Talmud explains the reasoning of both schools as follows. "What is the reasoning of the house of Shammai? We make an inference from Moses, regarding whom it is written *The sons of Moses: Gershom and Eliezer* (1 Chron. 23:15). And [what is the reasoning of] the house of Hillel? We infer from the creation of the world. [Just as God made male and female (Gen. 1:26–28), so a man must have a son and daughter]." The Babylonian Talmud then asks why the school of Hillel did not deduce the answer from the example of Moses.

> They can answer you [that] Moses did it with His [God's] consent. For it was taught: Moses did three things on his own initiative and his opinion coincided with that of the Omnipresent. He separated himself from his wife, broke the tablets of testimony (Exod. 32:19), and added one day [to the prescribed period of sanctification that preceded the revelation on Sinai] (Exod. 19:10, 15).
>
> He separated himself from his wife. What was his reasoning? He said, "If to the Israelites with whom the Shekinah appears

only for a while and for whom a designated time [for that appearance] was fixed the Torah nevertheless said, *Come not near a woman* (Exod. 19:15), how much more so to me, who may be spoken to at any moment and for whom no designated time has been set. And his view coincided with that of the Omnipresent; for it is said *God said to them: Return to your tents; but you remain here with Me [and I will give you the whole instructions]* (Deut. 5:27). (BT Yeb. 62a; see also BT Shab. 87a)

The schools of Hillel and Shammai disagree as to which biblical character is the most exemplary model for fathers. The house of Hillel believes men should emulate God and should father a son and daughter just as God created a man and a woman. But the school of Shammai views Moses as the perfect human model, and after having two sons, Moses kept himself from his wife. The house of Hillel rejects this reasoning, according to the Talmud, because it views Moses as an irrelevant exception. Moses infers that he should be permanently celibate because God's presence may appear to him at any time. Celibacy and contact with God go hand in hand. Moses therefore cannot serve as an example for other men who do not come in contact with God regularly.

Moses bases his judgment, however, on something that Scripture never explictly attributes to God. Recall that God never said "Come not near a woman." Those words are attributed to Moses. It is difficult to imagine that the rabbinic commentators failed to notice that Moses and not God spoke the words "Come not near a woman." They surely must have seen the deviation from God's word regarding purity. Indeed, it is possible that the sages were struggling to divert attention from Moses' interpretation of God's instruction. In any case, the sages explain Moses' abstention from sexual relations as reflecting his desire to be in a constant state of purity, always ready to be in God's presence. Since sexual intercourse is contaminating, Moses decides to desist from marital relations. But as I have tried to show, Moses is the only biblical figure that the rabbis imagine feasting appropriately on the sight of God. His abstention from marital relations takes place in the context of his intimate relations with God.

This link is suggested in another version of this story in which one sage claims that Moses did not make the decision about celibacy on his own. "Rabbi Judah ben Bathyra says, 'Moses kept away from his wife only because he was told by the mouth of the Almighty, as it is said, *With him I do speak mouth to mouth* (Num. 12:8), mouth to mouth I told him 'Keep away from thy wife,' and he stayed away'" (ARNA 2:31–32). It is interesting that this verse is cited to prove that God demanded Moses' abstinence (Goldin 1955, 19; Boyarin 1993). This is God's response to Miriam and Aaron's protest. On this interpretation, Miriam and Aaron cannot already be protesting Moses' celibacy since God has not yet given him such instructions. More important, it associates Moses' celibacy with the most intimate depiction of God and Moses' relationship. When God speaks intimately to Moses in a way that he speaks to no other prophet, he tells him he must have no contact with his wife. Moses thus exemplifies the tension between being an intimate of God and a husband to a wife, a sentiment shared by the apostle Paul: "The unmarried man is anxious about the affairs of the Lord how to please the Lord but the married man is anxious about worldly affairs how to please his wife" (1 Cor. 7:32).

Moses, I suggest, is a symbol of a very general rabbinic anxiety about the conflict of being married and loving God. The dilemma is not only about conflicting demands made on one's time. Nor is it simply about how familial duties compete with sacred duties. That kind of conflict is often expressed as a tension between the obligations of Torah study, personified as a woman, and the obligations to one's wife.[55] Rather, Moses' position involves a contradiction in the very essence of what it means to be a man, for being a husband to a wife is in tension with being a wife of God. At times this tension can be reduced, by feminizing the man through circumcision or other symbols, or by hiding God's body. But the dilemma does not go away without repudiating the image of masculinity which creates it. And woven into that image is the assumption of heterosexual desire, both of human men and the male God they love.

Moses is an ideal figure who can transcend the dilemma contained in the image of masculinity by forgoing sexual relations with his wife.

Other men have to live with the ambiguity. They have to love God and procreate. The resolution of this dilemma will be left to the time to come when the righteous will become like angels who do not procreate and who are satisfied by the sight of God (GenRab 2:2, 8:11).

For the rabbis of late antiquity, being a man of God, as this chapter shows, was in part an imaginative act that involved putting oneself figuratively in the place of a woman. This process of feminization was linked to the dilemma involved for a man in imagining himself in intimate relationship with or in the presence of the heavenly king. The God of Israel, however, was not just the lover of men. He was also the ideal to which men aspired. And as we shall now see, the identification with a sexless Father generated another set of tensions for men as well.

PART IV

*Like
Father,
Like
Sons?*

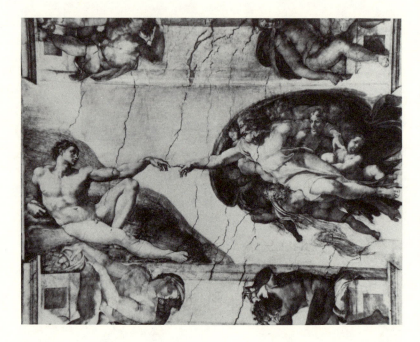

The Creation of Adam by Michelangelo. Sistine Chapel, Vatican.
Photograph from Alinari/Art Resource, New York.

Chapter Eight

A Sexless Father and
His Procreating Sons

> *Let us make Adam in our image, after our like-*
> *ness. They shall rule the fish of the sea, the birds of*
> *the sky, the cattle, the whole earth, and all the*
> *creeping things that creep on earth. And God cre-*
> *ated man in His image, in the image of God He*
> *created him; male and female He created them.*
> *God blessed them and God said to them, "Be fer-*
> *tile and increase, fill the earth and master it; and*
> *rule the fish of the sea, the birds of the sky, and all*
> *the living things that creep on earth."*
>
> GENESIS 1:26–28

A SYMBOL OF A father God, like many religious symbols, is as much an ideal that cannot be achieved as an affirmation of what already is. Thus the symbol of a male God is not simply a legitimation of masculinity or an object of male desire. It is also an image against which men must measure themselves and by whose standard they fall short. For how can men, who are expected to procreate and reproduce the lineage of their fathers, be made in the image of a sexless God?[1]

As a symbol to be emulated, a sexless father God naturally provides an ideal of male asceticism. To be really like God, a man should have no sexuality. Israel's God thus generates very different consequences for masculinity than a religious system in which the phallus and sexuality of the male gods are the subject of speculation, as in Hinduism for instance.

It makes a difference for masculinity whether a religious system imagines male deities with phalluses. We might call those that do "phallocentric" because the phallus is a symbol of male power, sexuality, domination, and even divinity. But in some cases, Jewish monotheism being one important example, masculinity must contend with the disappearance of the deity's phallus. The divine word, the Logos, takes the phallus's place. The disappearance of the phallus does not undo male domination in the social or symbolic system, but it does create a different kind of masculinity with its own distinctive problems. Human men, because they do have penises, can only partially assume the power invested in a sexless God. When it comes to a man's penis and his sexual desire, there is a fundamental difference between him and God.

An ascetic male God, of course, would have posed much less of a problem for human masculinity had reproduction been less central to what ancient Israel understood by manhood. Israelite men were caught: to be most like God they had to renounce their sexuality; but they could not be truly men unless they fulfilled their obligations to continue the generations. In this chapter, I explore some of these tensions of masculinity, which are expressed most clearly in the biblical myths reflecting on what it means to be made in the image of God.

Masculinity and Procreation

In much of the literature of ancient Israel, as we've seen, masculinity, heterosexuality, and reproduction are closely associated. Recall how the earliest myth of creation explains that the original physical unity of Adam and Eve accounts for marriage and sexuality. Because they originally were of the same flesh and bone, "a man leaves his father and mother and clings to his wife, so that they become one flesh" (Gen. 2:24). Sexuality and marriage represent a return to the primordial unity of Adam and Eve. But it is clear that Israelite religion regards the issue of reproduction as critical for men in particular. So important is it for a man to reproduce himself that should he die without offspring, his brother or a near kinsman bears the responsibility of levirate marriage, that is, of marrying his widow and conceiving sons in his name (Gen. 38; Deut. 25:5; Ruth 4:5, 10, 17). During her husband's lifetime, of course, sexual union between a man and his sister-in-law would be considered incest (Lev. 18:16, 20:21). But after his death, the union is what makes possible the continuation of his name.[2]

The identification of masculinity with procreation is clearest in the scriptural writings that derive from the priestly community.[3] The priestly myth of creation (Gen. 1:26–28) treats the complementarity of men and women as essential to human nature, occurring at the very moment of human creation. The importance of human fertility is underscored by its close and frequent association with divine blessing. But again, it is clear that the blessing of fruitfulness is addressed particularly to men. Thus after the flood, God tells Noah and his sons to be fruitful and multiply. Noah's wife and his sons' wives are not included in the blessing (Gen. 9:1, 7). The blessing of fertility is also central to the covenant that God makes with Abraham and his male descendants.

> As for Me, this is My covenant with you: You shall be the father of a multitude of nations. And you shall no longer be called Abram, but your name shall be Abraham, for I make you the father of a multitude of nations. I will make you exceedingly fertile and make nations of you and kings shall come forth from you. (Gen. 17:4–6)

The priestly writings trace the fruition of this blessing in Abraham's descendants. When Isaac gives Jacob his final blessing, he prays that God "bless you, make you fertile and numerous, so that you become an assembly of peoples. May God grant the blessing of Abraham to you and your offspring, that you may possess the land where you are sojourning, which God gave to Abraham" (Gen. 28:3). This wish is subsequently granted upon Jacob's return to Canaan, when God blesses him with fertility (Gen. 35:11). As his own death approaches, Jacob recalls this blessing when he adopts Joseph's sons, Jacob's grandchildren, into his patrilineage (Gen. 48:3–5). The book of Exodus begins by noting that this blessing has been fulfilled (Exod. 1:6).

The priests' preoccupation with male procreation is intimately tied to the issue of descent. The priestly writings are interested in reproduction as the means through which the genealogy of Abraham and Jacob (Israel) is perpetuated and expanded. In particular it is the patriline, the line of male descendants, that concerns the priests. The priestly genealogies generally list only male names; the names of wives and daughters are absent.[4]

The intertwining of masculinity and procreation are nowhere more evident than in the priestly understanding of circumcision. In the priestly writings, circumcision is treated as a symbol of male fertility, of God's promise to make Abraham a father of multitudes. It is no accident that the symbol of the covenant is impressed on the male organ of generation, rather than the ear or nostril. By exposing the male organ, the rite of circumcision makes concrete the symbolic link between masculinity, genealogy, and reproduction.[5]

The close association of masculinity with genealogical proliferation, however, conflicts with the image of a sexless father God. The two myths of human creation, as stories that define what it means to be a human being, must struggle somehow to make sense of the contradictory nature of masculinity, of being both a man who reproduces and one made in the image of God.

Androgyny, Ambiguity, and Disembodiment

The two myths of human creation in Genesis 1 and 2 have been extensively analyzed for what they have to say about the image of women.[6] But these myths also reveal something about the nature of masculinity. And each deals in its own way with the masculine dilemma of being obliged to procreate while emulating a father God who has no sexuality. Indeed, one of the purposes of these myths may be to ponder this tension and to obscure it. We have learned from Claude Lévi-Strauss that myth often functions to hide basic contradictions of the cultural and social system. In fact, it may be because there is no solution to this contradiction of monotheism that there is more than one myth of human creation. Each of the creation myths struggles to reconcile an ascetic male God with a masculine ideal of procreation. Nor is it an accident that the two myths involve ambiguities related to the nature of bodies, both human and divine.

In what is generally regarded as the earlier of the two myths (Gen. 2:4–24 J), God creates a single creature called Adam and subsequently divides it in two to form a new creature named "Eve." According to the most familiar interpretation of this story, the first creature is male. It is from the side of this male creature that woman is taken. But as feminist interpreters have pointed out, the sex of this first earthling creature is not specified (Trible 1983; Bal 1987). Adam is identified as male only after Eve comes into being. Then Adam says, "This one shall be called Woman for from man (ʾîš) was she taken." This is the first time that the word "man" is used unambiguously. Previously, the creature is called "Adam," which, because of its phonetic similarity to the word for earth (*adamah*), may simply be translated as "earthling."

The ambiguity as to whether the word Adam is to be understood as generic "man" or as "earthling" may be one of the mechanisms by which this myth accomplishes its work. Assuming for a moment the traditional interpretation that Adam is male, this myth establishes a near perfect parallel between human and divine masculinity, as feminist interpreters make clear.[7] The male God who creates is mirrored in the human realm by the single man from whom all humanity is descended. Adam is split in half to produce two human beings. Since fission requires no female partner, it is the perfect vehicle of reproduction in a symbolic system where God does not reproduce. There is seemingly no tension between creation and procreation, between the God who creates alone and the male human who needs no sexual partner. According to this understanding, the myth affirms human masculinity at the expense of femininity and sexuality. Sexuality is secondary, not part of God's original intention in creating man. Eventually, of course, God decides it is not good for man to be alone (Gen. 2:18) and that a human partner must come from man's own flesh. The legitimation of marriage and sexuality at the end of this myth destroys the symmetry—short lived, to be sure—between God and man. In this first reading of the myth, then, the parallelism of man and divine father are promoted over sexuality and marriage. The first Adam is an ascetic male. Sexuality and marriage are divine after- thoughts or concessions, and not part of the founding moment of hu- man creation.

The vagueness about Adam's sex, however, undermines the perfect correspondence between a human and divine masculine. Some femi- nists view the androgyny of Adam as affirming the equality of man and woman in the natural order. They regard the view that Adam was an original male from whom a female was subsequently formed as an an- drocentric interpretation which imports the biases of male interpret- ers (Trible 1983). But the question of whether Adam is male or an- drogynous also allows for a vacillation between incompatible assertions: on one reading of the myth, the first person is male and as- cetic like God; on the other reading, men must marry and procreate. The myth's ambiguity enables both of these assertions to be posited at the moment of human creation.

In the other myth of human origin, which serves as epigraph to this chapter, the question is not of Adam's sex, but of whether God has a body. There are a number of issues raised by the statement in Genesis 1 that God made Adam in the divine image. First, and perhaps fore- most, is whether the human body is regarded as made in the divine im- age.

Most interpreters think not and favor a spiritual interpretation: hu- mans resemble God in some qualitative sense only.[8] Nahum Sarna is representative of this view when he writes "the idea of man 'in the im- age of God' must inevitably include within the scope of its meaning all those faculties and gifts of character that distinguish man from the beast and that are needed for the fulfillment of his task on earth, namely, intellect, free will, self-awareness, consciousness of the exis- tence of others, conscience, responsibility and self-control" (1970, 15–16). Other interpreters suggest that humans are like God in that they rule over creation: "They shall rule the fish of the sea, the birds of the sky, the cattle, the whole earth, and all the creeping things that

creep on earth."[9] Still other arguments point to those sources in Israelite religion that imagine God in human form, sources already considered in chapter 3 (Exod. 24:9–11, 33:23ff.; 1 Kings 22:19; Amos
9:1; Isa. 6:1–2; Ezek. 1:26–28; Dan. 7:9–11). In fact, the most detailed description of God is given in the book of Ezekiel. Since Ezekiel
was a priest, it is possible that his image of God was shared by the narrator of the priestly myth of creation.[10]

Given these other sources that imagine God in human form, the
"image of God" passage in Genesis is said to presuppose a resemblance
between the human body and divine form. The use of the word "image" (ṣelem), which most interpreters construe to mean a physical likeness, supports this view. Furthermore, in Genesis 5:1–3, the terms
"image" and "likeness" are used to describe the resemblance between
Adam and his son Seth. The use of the terminology here suggests that
humanity resembles God in the same way that Seth resembles Adam,
including their physical characteristics.[11]

In all of this debate about whether God's image is that of a human
form, the deeper and more difficult question about God's anatomical
features is obscured. Indeed, it is significant that interpreters who favor the embodied image of God never consider this question. So
preoccupied are they with contesting the spiritual interpretation of
God's image that the most troubling issue of all—what features God
has—remains nearly invisible.

Those favoring a spiritual interpretation mainly argue that human
sexuality differentiates humanity from God. Embodiment and sexuality are traits that humans share with animals (Sarna 1970; Bird 1981).
On this reading, the image of God does not parallel the human differentiation into male and female. It is somehow the idea of generic man
that is in the image of God, not sexually differentiated humankind.
The "image of God refers neither to Adam alone nor to Eve, but only
to the two of them together" (Sapp 1977, 10).

But even on the spiritual interpretation sexuality is not necessarily
a sign of the difference between humans and God. It is possible to understand Genesis 1:26–28 as suggesting that men and women, and by
implication procreation itself, are somehow contained in the idea of

God's image. Phyllis Trible's *God and the Rhetoric of Sexuality* is the most articulate exposition of this argument. In Trible's view, the division into male and female is what distinguishes humans from animals. "Procreation is shared by humankind with the animal world . . . sexuality is not" (1978, 15). That is, although Genesis 1 says that both animals and humans reproduce, the attributes of male and female are exclusively human characteristics, at least in Genesis 1.[12] Through a literary analysis, Trible goes on to suggest that "male" and "female" correspond structurally to "the image of God." Sexuality is thus one of the human experiences that point toward an understanding of Israel's transcendent deity. Trible develops her argument by exploring the metaphors used to depict God. Not only is God metaphorically a father, husband, king, and warrior, but a woman who conceives, gives birth, and nurses and mothers children.

Trible's interpretation is self-consciously an attempt to recover female imagery and motifs within the Hebrew Scriptures. As suggested by the title of her book, her project is to redeem human sexuality and reconcile it with the conviction that humans are made in the image of God. It is striking, however, that Trible ignores the interpretation that ascribes a form or body to God. It is clear that such an omission is necessary for her reconciliation of the sexual division of humanity and the image of God. Since God has relationships with no other gods in the literature of the Hebrew Bible, God's act of copulation can only be metaphoric. Recall how Ezekiel invokes the metaphor of sexual intercourse to depict the covenant between God and Israel (Ezek. 16:8). While such metaphors do validate human sexuality in important ways, they still do not allow for God to have an embodied sexual experience. If the relation of God to Israel is analogous to that of husband and wife, then what parallels the human act of intercourse is revelation, the insemination of Israel with God's will. It is impossible to simultaneouly embrace the idea that God has a body and that God is a sexual being. In order for God to have sex, God must not have a body, and to have a body God can have no sex.

It is thus not surprising that the "image of God" passage is so ambiguous. As James Barr observes, "There is no reason to believe that this writer [of the priestly creation myth] had in his mind any definite idea about the content or the location of the image of God." According to Barr, this hesitation stemmed from a "delicacy and questionability . . . of any idea of analogies to God" (1968–69, 13). I would argue instead that the passage attempts to hide the fundamental tensions in the religious symbol system of the priests, and in Israelite monotheism in general.

The priests were a community of men who presided over the sacrifices and purity of the Temple cult. Priestly status was passed from father to son. As we have seen, only male names tend to be recorded in the priestly genealogies, for women had no significant role in genealogical reckoning. Moreover, in the priestly myths, circumcision represents God's promise of male fertility and patrilineal continuity. The priestly inclusion of the feminine in God's image is part of an attempt to reconcile their definition of masculinity with the divine image. The simultaneous creation of man and woman and the inclusion of both in the image of God valorizes reproduction as part of the fabric of creation.

The shifting noun and verb tenses is another means by which the Genesis 1 myth negotiates the conflict between a sexless God and a humanity that is sexually divided. The plural "Let us create" has always been puzzling to interpreters.[13] Is the plural referring to other divine beings? Is it a royal "we" or a "plural of deliberation"? However this question is answered, the construction glosses the problematic fact that there is only one God but two sexes of human beings. Phyllis Bird writes that " 'Let us' cannot be a slip . . . it appears also to have been selected by P as a means of breaking the direct identification between adam and God suggested by the metaphor of image, a way of blurring or obscuring the referent of *ṣelem*" (1981, 148). A similar obfuscation is accomplished by the shift from singular to plural in speaking of humanity (He created *him/it*, male and female he created *them*). The use of two nouns, "image" (*ṣelem*) and "likeness" (*děmût*), the former implying a concrete representation and the latter a more abstract, qualitative similarity, also contributes to the ambiguity.[14]

A second "image of God" passage (Gen. 5:1–3) also employs the term "likeness" to describe the similarity between God and humanity, as mentioned earlier: "This is the record of Adam's line—When God created man, He made him in the likeness of God; male and female He created them." But the passage then goes on to use the terms "likeness" and "image" to describe the similarity of Adam and his son Seth: "When Adam had lived 130 years, he begot a son in his likeness after his image, and he named him Seth." If Genesis 5:1–3 is read by itself, it seems to suggest that the likeness between God and humanity (dĕmût) is of a different order than the likeness between a father and son (ṣelem and dĕmût). But if Genesis 5:1–3 is read as a supplement to Genesis 1:26–28, the opposite is the case: for ṣelem is used both to describe the resemblance between Adam and Seth (Gen. 5:3) and between God and humanity (Gen. 1:26–27). Once again, the point of these myths may be to avoid being too specific about what God's image means.

I have argued that the centrality of procreation in the ancient Israelite definition of masculinity conflicted with the image of a sexless father God. The nature of this tension changed, however, as procreation lost some of its importance and came to play a different role in the definition of masculinity. This reconfiguration of masculinity partially explains the emerging shame over male nakedness in God's presence that characterized rabbinic Judaism. Once celebrated as a symbol of the patrilineage and bearer of the covenantal sign, the penis had to be hidden from God. Though the patrilineal identity was never denigrated entirely, its diminished importance allowed men to act more and more like their celibate father.

The Veiled Penis

It is an irony worth pondering: though circumcision marked the covenant between God and Abraham, rabbinic Judaism defined circumcision as a sign that must be hidden when praying to God. The penis had to be vanquished from sight whenever a Jewish male said the Shema, the prayer in which he expressed his love for God:

Hear, O Israel! The Lord is our God, the Lord alone. You shall love the Lord your God with all your heart and with all your soul and with all your might. Take to heart these instructions with which I charge you this day. Impress them upon your children. Recite them when you stay at home and when you are away, when you lie down and when you get up. Bind them as a sign on your hand and let them serve as a symbol on your forehead; inscribe them on the doorposts of your house and on your gates. (Deut. 6:4–9)

The hiding of circumcision and the penis in prayer could be interpreted as a result of a general discomfort with nakedness, and part of a general inclination to keep the naked and the sacred apart. But the penis was not simply naked flesh for ancient Jews, it was also the covenant with God inscribed on the body, a symbol that alluded to God's promise to multiply the seed of Abraham. Yet at the very moment that a man expressed his profound fidelity and love to his one God, he could not see the organ marked by the token of that love. This veiling of the penis during prayer delineated the male body, dividing it into upper and lower parts which were invested with differing religious meanings, meanings that were entangled in images of gender, desire, and sexuality.

The Mishnah and the Tosefta, the earliest rabbinic legal documents, enumerate a series of laws regulating the recitation of the Shema. The rules which govern the proper etiquette for this prayer reflect on possible situations in which a Jewish male might have occasion to recite the Shema without his clothes on. For example, suppose a man has had intercourse or a nocturnal emission during the night. He is not allowed to pray until he has bathed and purified himself (M. Ber. 3:4–5). But suppose that the morning light is about to dawn as he is emerging from this ritual purification. Since the Shema is supposed to be recited before the morning light appears, he might not have adequate time to properly clothe himself. In this situation, he may not recite the Shema while he is naked. He must cover his genitals either with some handy material (M. Ber. 3:5; Tos. Ber. 2:14) or stand in the water up to his waist (M. Ber. 3:5) so that his penis is not visible. For similar reasons, he may not recite the Shema while taking his garment off over his head, unless he is wearing an undergarment which keeps his nakedness covered (Tos. Ber. 2:15). And a man may not recite the Shema in a bathhouse (Tos. Ber. 2:20). It would be difficult to find a more graphic image of the division of the male body than that of a man praying in water up to his waist. Only with his lower body covered, and his nakedness out of sight, may a man proclaim his fidelity to God.

In part, the motive behind this ruling does belong to a larger concern with proper etiquette during prayer. It is clear that the sages believe that a man should not say his prayers in the presence of a variety of offensive things (Tos. Ber. 2:16). Furthermore, the requirement to hide the penis is linked to a tradition which associates nakedness with shame (see M. A.Z. 3:4), a view with biblical roots (Gen. 2–3; Exod. 20:26).

The historical situation of the Jews further illuminates this shame over male nakedness. In the Jewish encounter with Greco-Roman society, from the second century B.C.E. through the second century C.E., political persecution of Jews sometimes included bans on circumcision. [15] Since neither Greeks nor Romans were circumcised, participation in Greek athletics and the use of Roman baths made Jewish men conspicuous. Greeks and Romans considered a circumcised penis ugly; they regarded the narrow uncircumcised penis as aesthetically more pleasing. Jewish texts of the period suggest that not only were some Jews failing to circumcise their male children but that some adult Jewish men were practicing epispasm, the surgical reversal of circumcision, and infibulation, a procedure that concealed circumcision. The same procedure was used by Greek males who were embarrassed about defectively short foreskins. [16]

Social pressures could easily have generated feelings of shame over the appearance of the circumcised penis, yet the rabbinic rules regarding nakedness are precisely the opposite of what would be expected if external social pressures alone were responsible for their rulings on prayer. After all, while nakedness is proscribed during the privacy of prayer, a man is permitted to remove his clothing when going to the bathhouse (M. A.Z. 3:4). Indeed according to later sources, going to the bathhouse and cleaning the body are regarded as treating the male body with the respect it deserves as the image of God (LevRab 34:3). As noted earlier, one rabbinic source implies that it is Adam's circumcised flesh that makes him like God (ARNA 2:58; GenRab 54–55). If embarrassment about circumcision motivated rabbinic laws, the rules would have been reversed: one would cover up in front of others and uncover in front of God. The encouragement to appear naked when others are naked (Tos. Ber. 2:21) actually promotes a display of ethnic distinctiveness. Rabbinic law thus forbids the display of nakedness only in the company of God. It does not try to hide the difference of male Jews from their male neighbors.

It is necessary, therefore, to search for other cultural reasons inherent in early Judaism that made the division and veiling of the body desirable. One of these reasons was the reevaluation of procreation.

Spiritual Sonship and the Demotion of the Lineage

The priestly community of ancient Israel defined itself through kinship. The priests claimed to be direct descendants of an ancestor in the tribe of Levi, some tracing the patrilineage back to Aaron, some to Moses, still others to Levi.[17] Like all communities in which descent defines the boundaries of the community, the priests found issues of reproduction and lineage central to their understanding of Israel's history. They were the ones who were preoccupied with the begats of Genesis. In the priestly creation story, God immediately commands Adam and Eve to be fruitful and multiply, emphasizing that procreation is central to what it means to be human.

In contrast, the early rabbis, like other groups of late antiquity, rejected descent as the exclusive method of defining status in their community. To be sure, the rabbis still recognized descent from Abraham as determining whether a person belonged to the social entity called Israel. But the sages also recognized conversion as a means whereby a person could become a Jew (S. Cohen 1989). Conversion did not entitle one to be inscribed in the genealogy of Abraham (M. Biq. 1:4). In reciting prayers, converts were not permitted to say, "O God of our fathers." Instead they had to say, "O God of your fathers." But though the language of descent continued to operate in Israel's conception of itself, actual descent was no longer a prerequisite for membership in the community.

Unlike the priests, the sages did not acquire their status by birth. The rabbinic status was based on mastering Torah and the traditions of its interpretation. It involved becoming a disciple of older sages and learning through apprenticeship what it meant to be a student of Torah. A boy did not inherit the status of sage from his father, although rabbis often taught their sons Torah and sons often became sages (Alon 1977, 436–57; Aberbach 1976). It is clear, moreover, that the wisdom one acquired through Torah study held greater prestige than the status acquired by lineage (M. Hor. 3:8).

Thus the sages conceptualized Israel as concentric circles, in which the larger inclusive category of Israel was defined by a model of descent, while the inner circle of the sages' own community was determined by individual achievement. This configuration contrasted with that of the priestly community, for whom both of the circles—the one defining Israel and the one defining the priests' own community—were identified by the patrilineage. Consequently, procreation was not crucial for the reproduction of the sages' community in the same way it had been for the priests.

Nevertheless, the sages described their own community in language drawn from the domain of procreation, sexuality, and kinship. They imagined their own activities as sages as a kind of cultural or religious reproduction in which Torah would be disseminated and students would be multiplied. Safrai, writing with other matters in mind, describes it this way: The aspiration of a sage was "to disseminate Torah and raise many disciples, to inspire every person to realize his right and duty 'to make Torah increase,' and to encourage the asking of questions" (1987, 69). The rabbinic community thus formed a set of Torah ties that competed with and in some cases superseded kinship loyalties. Rabbis fathered "children" through teaching Torah. As the learning of Torah emerged as the paradigmatic religious act in the rabbinic community, it absorbed the symbolic capital which had earlier been invested in procreation. Concerns about reproduction and lineage were symbolically extended from the human body to Torah knowledge itself. For the rabbis, the reproduction of Torah knowledge and clear lines of Torah dissemination were of paramount concern.

This symbolism is already evident to some extent in the Mishnah (ca. 200 C.E.), the earliest rabbinic document, and is even clearer in Avot, the first rabbinic text (early third century) to reflect in a sustained way on the meaning of Torah study. Early rabbinic law developed an analogy between teacher-disciple and father-son relationships (Eilberg-Schwartz 1990; Aberbach 1976). As the Mishnah puts it, one's father brings one into this world, while one's teacher brings one into the world to come (M. B.M. 2:11; M. Ker. 6:9). By ignoring the role of the mother, a symmetry is established between being a father and being a sage. In addition to the analogy between birth and rebirth, which is explicit here, there is an implied comparison between procreation and Torah study. This relationship between a rabbi and his "son" takes precedence over the real father-son relationship.

> [In a case where a man finds] the lost possession of his father and a lost possession of his teacher, [the return of] his teacher's takes precedence. For his father brought him to this world, and his teacher who taught him wisdom brings him to the world to come. If his father is a sage, [the obligation to return] his father's takes precedence.
>
> If his father and teacher were carrying loads, he should help put down his teacher's and afterwards his father's. If his father and teacher were in captivity, he redeems his teacher and afterwards his father. But if his father is a sage, he redeems his father and afterwards his teacher. (M. B.M. 2:11; Ker. 6:9)

A disciple's responsibilities are analogous to those of a son. Just as a son must perpetuate his father's lineage and protect its purity, a disciple must preserve his rabbi's teaching and transmit it without contamination to posterity (Avot 1:11; M. Eduy. 1:3). The genealogy of Torah knowledge is thus imitative of priestly genealogies. "Moses received the Torah from Sinai and transmitted it to Joshua, and Joshua to the elders, and the elders to the Prophets and the Prophets transmitted it to the men of the Great Assembly" (Avot 1:1). This concern with Torah genealogy manifests itself in the rabbinic concern with attributions: rabbi so and so said in the name of rabbi so and so. According to the Tosefta, one who does not raise up disciples in effect loses his status as rabbi. "If a scholar has disciples and disciples of disciples, he is quoted as Rabbi; if his direct disciples are forgotten, he is quoted as Rabban; if both are forgotten, he is quoted by his name" (Tos. Eduy. 3:4).

Not surprisingly, the explicit aspiration of the sages is to increase and disseminate Torah and raise many disciples. "One who does not increase [Torah knowledge] decreases it. One who does not learn is worthy of death" (Avot 1:13). Given their preoccupation with reproducing Torah knowledge, it is not surprising that the sages were haunted by the various ways in which Torah study might be interrupted or Torah knowledge diminished. One who forgets a single matter of what he has learned or one who interrupts his memorization of Torah to admire a blossoming tree is compared to a person who has committed a capital offense (Avot 3:7, 8). The sages' obsessive concern about the loss of Torah knowledge is reminiscent of their concerns about the waste of semen (M. Nid. 2:1). One sage is even praised for never losing "a drop" (Avot 2:8). It is hard to miss the association between this "drop" of Torah and "a drop" of semen referred to by the same document several passages later (Avot 3:1). Torah production, then, was the cultural equivalent of physical reproduction. A sage created a genealogical line through the transmission of Torah. His link to perpetuity was dependent on the success and commitment of his intellectual heirs.

The rabbis thus imagined themselves as belonging to two overlapping communities with dual expectations. As a member of Israel, the sage was expected to procreate and reproduce the lineage of Abraham. Yet as a sage, his duty was to multiply disciples and propagate Torah. The sages mapped this dual set of expectations onto the male body. The lower body was the symbolic site for those obligations pertaining to a man's covenantal obligations to replenish Israel. The circumcised penis, the symbol of procreation and kinship, became a hidden sign as these matters lost the prominence they had held earlier in the Israelite imagination. If the lower body was marked by God's promise that Israel would increase, the upper body provided the means for the sage to increase Torah. In particular, rabbinical knowledge was disseminated as "oral Torah" (Torah *šbʿl ph*), which literally translated means "Torah that is on the mouth." As the organ that transmits the Torah, the mouth thus became a symbol of reproduction competing with the penis as a symbol of masculinity.

This shift in symbols and attitudes made it easier for the rabbis to reconcile human masculinity with the image of a sexless God. Whereas previously God's sexlessness posed a problem that had to be veiled, it now functioned as an ideal for a moderate asceticism. But although the dual obligations of reproducing Israel and reproducing Torah were theoretically compatible, the sages may have experienced more ambivalence about the former demand than their analogies suggest.

Procreation and the Image of God

Consider the Mishnaic law which is generally regarded as the classical justification for a man's obligation to procreate.[18]

> A man may not desist from being fruitful and multiplying unless he has children. The House of Shammai says, "Two males." The House of Hillel says, "A male and a female," as it says *male and female he created them* (Gen. 5:2).
>
> If a man married a woman and he stayed with her for ten years and she did not bear, he is not permitted to desist. If he divorces her, she is permitted to marry another. And [her] second husband is permitted to stay with her for ten years [as well]. If she has a miscarriage, one calculates the period of ten years from the moment of miscarriage.
>
> A man is commanded to be fruitful and multiply. But not a

woman. R. Yohanan ben Beroka says, "Regarding both of them Scripture says *And God blessed them . . . and he said to them be fruitful and multiply*" (Gen. 1:28). (M. Yeb. 6:6)

This law may not be the strong endorsement of procreation that it seems. In fact, the Mishnah can be read as suggesting that if a man fathers only two children, he fulfills his obligation to be fruitful and multiply. This law, then, might be more a justification for ceasing procreation early. Indeed, in another early version of this dispute, the house of Hillel requires a man to have only one child, a son or daughter (Tos. Yeb. 8:4).[19]

The interpretation of the Mishnah as approving a *limitation* of procreation is consistent with the ruling that a man may stay married to a woman for ten years, even though they have not been able to have children. And in permitting a woman who has not had children in ten years to remarry, the sages allow men to marry women who are already suspected of being barren. Indeed, later rabbinic sources record tales of rabbis who did not want to leave wives after ten years and how God intervened and gave them children (Baskin 1989, 101–14). These are hardly positions that reflect a desire for large families. If the Mishnah is in fact specifying the minimum number of children a man must father, but actually wants men to have more, it is strange that it never explicitly encourages larger families. This passive position of the Mishnah regarding procreation contrasts sharply with its position on other religious duties, such as Torah study: "These are the things that have no measure [i.e., maximum]: food left in the corner of the fields for the poor, first fruit dedicated to God, appearances before God on festivals [alternative: sacrifices during festivals], acts of generosity, and the study of Torah" (M. Peah 1:1). Strikingly, the law which spells out the obligation to procreate gives no indication that it favors more than a minimum compliance. It does not say, "and one who has more children is praiseworthy," as it does with regard to other practices (M. Ter. 4:6, 9:3; M. San. 5:2; M. Nid. 2:1). Nor does it specify a penalty for a man who stops trying to have children.

Reading the Mishnah this way puts in a completely different light the claim that to be fruitful and multiply is to imitate God's act of creation, for one can be like God by fathering only two children. To have more than two children would mean that one has in some sense failed to be like God, who created only Adam and Eve. Appealing to God as a model, rather than, say, Abraham (Gen. 25:1) or Jacob, who each fathered many children, may thus endorse a limitation of one's fertility.

In addition to defining what it means to "be fruitful," the Mishnah records a dispute about whether the obligation devolves upon men alone or also upon women. The anonymous view, which is generally assumed to be the majority opinion, treats procreation as an exclusively male obligation. The secondary literature tends to focus on discovering reasons why women are excluded from the religious obligation to procreate.[20] The real question, I suggest, is not why women are exempt, but why there is a minority view that considers them obligated at all?

To answer this, one needs to understand the growing dissociation between the rabbinic idea of masculinity and the requirements of procreation and genealogy. Note that the majority view—that men alone are obligated to procreate—receives no explicit scriptural warrant. It is presented as so self-evident that it needs no justification. The minority view, which suggests that women, too, are subject to a religious obligation to have children, challenges the traditional identification of masculinity with the continuity of the male line. It is this view that requires a scriptural foundation. The suggestion that women like men are obligated to procreate is another symptom of a shifting conception of masculinity. As the lineage loses its definitive place in the representation of masculinity, reproduction begins to be associated with femininity.

In later rabbinic discussions of this same issue, the view that men are obligated to procreate even needs to be defended:

> From where does one derive this view [that men alone are obligated]? Said Rabbi Eliezer in the name of Rabbi Eleazar in [the name of] Rabbi Simeon, "Scripture says *Be fertile and increase, fill the earth and subdue it (kibĕšūhā)* (Gen. 1:28). It is the nature of a

man to subdue and not the nature of a woman. Nonetheless, the word subdue is plural implying two [man and woman]." Said Rabbi Nahman bar Isaac, " 'You subdue it' (*kibĕšūhā*) is written [i.e., in the singular, not the plural]."[21]

   Rabbi Joseph said [one can derive it from here]: "*And God said to him [Jacob] I am El Shaddai be fertile and increase* (Gen. 35:11)." (BT Yeb. 65b)

The scriptural citation used in this Talmudic defense of the majority view seems weak, for it has already been used in the Mishnah to justify the inclusion of women in the obligation to procreate. "Be fertile and increase" is in the plural and addressed to men and women. Attempting to undercut that interpretation, emphasis is drawn here to the second part of the verse, "fill the earth and subdue it," which is said to be directed primarily to men, because the act of subduing is typical of men not women (see also GenRab 8:12). But this interpretation hardly counters the force of the earlier one. For even if the end of the verse is addressed to men alone, the words "God blessed them and said to them, 'Be fruitful and multiply' " are clearly in the plural and addressed to both sexes. More compelling is the other verse the Talmud cites in justification of the "men alone" principle: "And God said to him [Jacob] I am El Shaddai be fertile and increase" (Gen. 35:11). This is a stronger proof text since the blessings of fertility that God promised Abraham applied specifically to men (Gen. 9:1, 7; 28:3; 35:11).

This unfolding debate in the rabbinic texts suggests that the mandate of male procreation could no longer be taken for granted. The view that women were equally obligated was clearly getting a hearing. Indeed, the Babylonian Talmud cites a series of cases where women who have not yet had children ask for their marriages to be dissolved so that they can find another husband with whom they can conceive (see also Baskin 1989, 106–7). Whether women actually brought such cases before the sages is impossible to know. But even if these are "just so" stories, they indicate the receptiveness of rabbinic imagination to the view that women also were bound by the obligation to produce children. The increasing emphasis on mothering corresponded to the loss of significance of physical fatherhood.

This is one of the reasons why the status of the mother was increasingly taken into account in genealogical reckonings. In early rabbinic law, the status of a child followed the father only when a valid marriage was contracted. When an illegitimate marriage occurred, the child's status followed that of the parent judged to be inferior (M. Qid. 3:12). Thus when an Israelite man married a gentile woman, the child was considered gentile, reflecting the decreasing concern with the father's genealogy.[22]

A similar process explains in part the rabbinic view that women have a sexual desire that must be satisfied. This is evident in the law of *onah*, which required a man to have sexual intercourse with his wife on a regular basis. The law is presented as attempting to protect the interests of the wife:

> One who takes a vow that his wife not benefit from sexual intercourse—
> the House of Shammai says, "Two weeks [he may abstain]."
> the House of Hillel says, "One week."
> Disciples may go forth to Torah study without permission [from their wives] for thirty days. Workers for one week.
> "The *onah* [obligation to have conjugal relations] which is mentioned in the Torah (Exod. 21:10)
> travellers—are obligated every day,
> workers—twice in a week,
> ass drivers—once a week,
> camel drivers—once in thirty days, ·
> sailors—once in six months,"
> these are the words of Rabbi Eliezer. (M. Ket. 5:6)

The sages find justification for this ruling in the scriptural injunction that a husband "must not withold from this one her food, her clothing or her *onah*" (Exod. 21:10). It is not at all certain whether the Hebrew term *onah* implies conjugal rights in this biblical context. Nonetheless, by linking the obligation to this verse, the sages treat the act of sexual intercourse as a right that a married woman possesses, like her right to be clothed and fed. Some interpreters regard the law of *onah* as a forward-looking law that recognized and protected the woman's individual desires and needs (Feldman 1974, 60–80; Biale 1984, 121–34).

But consider, too, how the obligation of conjugal duties also shaped the idea of masculinity and male desire.[23] As Foucault (1978) noted about the modern period, laws that seem to repress desire may actually be one of the mechanisms by which a particular kind of desire is itself created. In this case, the law of *onah* presupposes the need to protect women from husbands who either withhold sexual favors, lack strong sexual desire, or are not available for intercourse. The law of *onah*, then, protected women from the kind of men that rabbinic law was interested in creating: Men who were more interested in their professions or Torah study than in their wives. Indeed, the exemption for Torah study is revealing, for it associates the labor of Torah with the kinds of work that involve heavy labor or take a man away from home. Through its articulation of a theory of female desire, this law helped to create an ascetic image of rabbinic masculinity.

The Mishnah discussed above is not the only instance in rabbinic literature where procreation is imagined as imitating God. In several different contexts, rabbinic literature ascribes such a view to Ben Azzai (Tos. Yeb. 8:4; GenRab 34:14; BT Yeb. 63b; GenRab 17:2), one of the sages who entered the orchard of heavenly delights.[24] But this very same sage remains unmarried.

> Rabbi Eleazar ben Azariah expounded, "Anyone who desists from being fruitful and multiplying diminishes[25] the image [of God]. What is the reasoning? Because *in the image of God He made the man* and it is written afterward *be fruitful and multiply*."
>
> Ben Azzai expounded, "Anyone who desists from being fruitful and multiplying [is like one who spills blood][26] and diminishes the image. [What is the reason celibacy is like murder]? *whoever sheds the blood of man, by man shall his blood be shed; for in His image did God make man* (Gen. 9:6). What is the reasoning [celibacy di-

minishes the image?] *In the image of God He made the man* and afterwards it says *and you be fruitful and multiply*" (Gen. 1:26–28).

Rabbi Eleazar said to him, "It is nice when one practices what one preaches. Ben Azzai has nice things to say but his practice leaves something to be desired."[27]

[Ben Azzai] said to him, "because my soul desires Torah. The world can be sustained by the hands of others." (GenRab 34:14; following Theodor and Albeck 1965, 1:326–27)

This source carries to the logical conclusion the claim that to be made in the image of God involves procreating. If so, then abstention from procreation constitutes a diminishment of the divine image. For this reason Ben Azzai is accused by Rabbi Eleazar of not practicing what he preaches. He remains celibate despite his belief that to father children is an act of *imitatio Dei* and that celibacy is like murder. But there is another way of reading this story that makes Ben Azzai's position more comprehensible. That is, Ben Azzai's behavior may suggest a radical alternative: that the desire for Torah may supersede the obligation to procreate. In other words, Ben Azzai is not necessarily a hypocrite. In endorsing the view that procreation is an act of *imitatio Dei*, he nonetheless believes that other kinds of religious commitments transcend that value. Moreover, the fact that he does not marry suggests that he does not really think celibacy is murder. His actions, rather than contradicting his words, provide a context for understanding them. And what his actions show is that the comparison of celibacy to murder is not to be taken that seriously and that desire for Torah supersedes the desire to be like God. What is striking about this source, then, is not the association of procreation with God but the portrayal of a sage whose desire for Torah surpasses his desire to be made in God's image.

Ben Azzai does not feel compelled to marry, despite his view that procreation is an act of imitating God. Imagine, then, the consequences of viewing procreation as a "creaturely" dimension of the human being, a view that appears in other rabbinic sources:

Rabbi Joshua son of Rabbi Nehemiah said in the name of Rabbi Hanina son of Rabbi Isaac, and the Rabbis in the name of Rabbi

> Leazar said: "He [God] created him [Adam] with four character-
> istics of the higher [beings, i.e., angels] and four characteristics
> of the lower [beings, i.e., the beasts]. [Those of the higher
> beings]: he stands upright, speaks, understands, and sees like the
> ministering angels. But do not animals also see? [Unlike animals]
> this [human] one has peripheral vision. The four attributes of
> below: Adam eats and drinks like an animal, reproduces like an
> animal, defecates like an animal, and dies like an animal.
> (GenRab. 8:11, 14:3)[28]

The dissociation of procreation from the divine image in rabbinic sources was thus the logical extension of views reflected in the rules governing prayer. The lower body, already divided from the upper, became associated with the "animal" in man. It was this understanding that led some sages to refer to procreation as a sin (BT A.Z. 5a).

It would be incorrect to leave the impression that these views alone dominated rabbinic consciousness. There are important endorsements of marriage and procreation that compete with these more ambivalent views (e.g., GenRab 17:2). But the endorsements have a long biblical tradition, and it is the views that deviate from that tradition which require explanation. The symbolic splitting of the male body was a symptom of an impulse toward asceticism that could never be fully realized as long as the ideology of reproduction remained central to the idea of the covenant. At the same time, as Torah study came to be emphasized as a means of fulfilling one's covenantal obligations, genealogical descent was no longer the only—or even the primary— idiom of self-understanding in rabbinic Judaism. Ironically, these changes in what it meant to be a man of God—the ascetic emulation of the deity and the devaluing of the patriline—would allow the conceptualization of a God who fathers a human child with no help at all from the seed of man.

Chapter Nine

The Virgin Birth and
the Sons of God

When your days are done and you lie with your fa-
thers, I will raise up your offspring after you, one
of your own issue, and I will establish his kingship.
He shall build a house for My name, and I will es-
tablish his royal throne forever. I will be a father to
him, and he shall be a son to Me.

2 SAMUEL 7:14

Gᴏᴅ's ᴘʀᴏᴍɪsᴇ ᴛᴏ Dᴀᴠɪᴅ—that he will establish a king from
one of David's line—evokes an image of fatherhood that is consistent
throughout the sources that make up the Hebrew Bible. The Israelite
people are said to be the children of the union of God and the feminine
collective Israel (e.g., Hos. 1:4; Jer. 3:2–4; Ezek. 23:4). God is responsible for blessing the wombs of the matriarchs, Sarah, Rebekkah,
Leah, and Rachel, and enabling them to conceive (Gen. 21:1–2,
25:21, 29:31, 30:22). In establishing a king, God is said to father him,
and he regards God as his father (Ps. 2:7, 89:27).

In all these cases, divine fatherhood is compatible with and works
through human fatherhood.[1] Indeed, the role of the human father is
central in the genealogy of Abraham and David. This is the meaning
of God's promise to David: God is not going to choose just anyone as
king. His adopted son will be one of David's "own issue."

How, then, did God's promise to David come to be construed in the

223

Gospels as a prediction of the birth of Jesus—conceived, not by man, but by God. To begin to answer this question, we return to an early myth that establishes a precedent of divine-human union, the myth of the sons of God in Genesis. We examined this story in chapter 6 in the context of repressed male fears of being made redundant by a male God. It can be said that those fears were realized in the story of the virgin birth.[2]

There are obvious and important differences between the myth of the sons of God and the story of the virgin birth, and we shall come back to them in due course. It is nevertheless striking that interpreters of the Gospels have generally ignored the Genesis myth, despite an ongoing debate about Jewish and pagan precedents for the story of Jesus' divine conception.[3]

I recognize that the debate about whether the virgin birth is authentic is of central importance to many, but here I wish to set the question of authenticity aside. In this context, I take the virgin birth story as a product of the religious imagination. Rather than try to prove or disprove the story, I want to speculate instead about why the Christian religious imagination found it persuasive. In my view, the story of a virgin conception was a perfect founding myth for Christianity, for it captured the differences emerging Christian communities were trying to assert as they separated from Judaism.

The Sons of God and the Holy Ghost

The sons of God myth tells how divine beings take human women for wives, and giants are the offspring of their union. The ancient Israelites blamed the divine-human union for the origin of human sin and suffering. In contrast, Christian communities treated the idea of a divine-human union as the beginning of redemption: Jesus, born of the Virgin Mary, conceived by the Holy Ghost, is the Messiah. What made this change possible? I believe it was the decreasing importance of the patriline in determining the boundaries of the community. While for Jews, the father's genealogy defined Israel, for Christian communities descent through the father's line became irrelevant. The idea of union between a divine male and a human female, which displaced the human male, thus posed a threat in Judaism in a way that it did not in Christianity.

Consider the role of the sons of God in the book of Jubilees. Written by a Palestinian Jew sometime in the second century B.C.E., Jubilees retells and embellishes the stories of Genesis. The sons of God myth is developed in some detail. According to Jubilees, God originally sent angels, or Watchers, to earth "to teach the sons of man, and perform judgment and uprightness upon the earth" (Jub. 4:15). But the Watchers father children with human women and "injustice increased upon the earth and all flesh corrupted its way" (Jub. 5:2). Human evil and misfortune are the consequence of the angels' coupling with human women. When bringing the flood, therefore, God singles out the Watchers for punishment. "And against his angels whom he had sent to the earth he was very angry. He commanded that they be uprooted from all their dominion. And he told us [the uncorrupted angels] to bind them in the depths of the earth, and behold, they are bound in the midst of them, and they are isolated" (Jub. 5:6). But the spirits of the Watchers' offspring wander the earth as demons and plague Noah even after the flood.[4] Noah prays to God that they be shut up and no longer cause corruption (Jub. 10:4–5). But Mastema, the chief of the spirits, pleads on their behalf, and God capitulates to his request, leaving one-tenth of the spirits to roam the earth. While these spirits oversee the other nations, Israel is ruled by God alone (Jub. 15:32). Mastema continues to bring misfortunes upon Israel. It is he who convinces God to test Abraham, who provokes the Egyptians to pursue Israel (Jub. 48:12), and who seeks to kill Moses on the way to Egypt (Jub. 48:2).

The threat of the Watchers' intrusion into the human realm and the implied redundancy of human men dovetails with Jubilees' larger worries about threats to Israel's ethnic and religious purity. Jewish fears about the integrity of Israel as a national and cultural unit are expressed in a variety of ways. The author of Jubilees traces the fate of Abraham's lineage in great detail, reminiscent of the priestly writings discussed earlier. Indeed, there is evidence that this writer may have been from a priestly family or was attempting to generalize priestly law to the whole community (Wintermute 1985, 45; Endres 1987, 142). There is no scriptural precedent, for example, for Jubilees' distinctive treatment of Levi, the ancestor of the priestly line, who is given priority over the other sons of Jacob (Jub. 45:16, 32:21–26). The concern for the genealogical purity of Abraham's seed is also evident by which biblical stories Jubilees passes over in silence. For example, Jubilees does not mention the stories in which Sarah, Abraham's wife, is taken into the court of foreign kings, stories that could suggest that Sarah's offspring were not Abraham's.

Similarly, in Jubilees' conception of the religious universe, Israel is ruled by circumcised angels (Jub. 15:27). As far as I know, this is the first explicit allusion in Jewish sources to the idea of a divine being with a penis. These male angels, however, need not be feared, for they do not take human women for wives. Just as Israel's men should not cross boundaries, Israel's angels do not intrude into the human realm. They do not threaten to disrupt the genealogical lines of descent that define Israel.

By contrast, Jubilees imagines gentile nations as ruled by spirits who are the offspring of the union between the Watchers and human women. The author of Jubilees in effect declares: Our God and his angels have never taken human wives, but the gods of the gentiles are the product of such unholy unions. Can it be entirely accidental that Christian communities that repudiated genealogical descent as a marker of identity would one day worship a son of a divine-human union? I think not. It is only outside a community that defines itself in terms of pure genealogical descent that such a symbol makes sense. Within such a community, the union of a divine male and a human female is an abomination.

I am by no means the first to notice this incompatibility between the idea of a virgin conception and the Jewish emphasis on genealogy. Machen, for example, argues that the virgin birth could not have been a Jewish idea, especially in light of the Jewish belief that the Messiah would be a descendant of David: "Surely that expectation would constitute a powerful barrier against any evolution of the idea of the virgin birth on Jewish Christian ground. . . . How then, except under the compulsion of fact, would Jewish Christians like the authors of these narratives, Jewish Christians who laid such stress upon the Davidic descent of Jesus, ever have evolved the notion that Jesus was not the son of Joseph, after all, but was born without human father, being conceived by the Holy Ghost?" ([1930] 1965, 285). In a similar vein, Schaberg also argues that that the idea of a virginal conception is foreign to Jewish theology: "There is no text in that earlier literature in which the action of God or the Spirit of God is said to replace or cancel natural human sexual activity in a way as to render the human role superfluous . . . the notion of virginal conception seems to say something negative about human sexuality, something opposed to the positive aspect of major Israelite and Jewish tradition" (1987, 3).

Both of these writers, I believe, are right in thinking that a virginal conception is incompatible with earlier forms of Judaism. But they draw radically different, and in my judgment mistaken, conclusions from this fact. Machen believes his argument helps prove the historicity of the virgin birth. Since Jews would have had no motivation to make up this story, it strengthens the probability that it happened. And Schaberg assumes that if the idea of a virginal conception was foreign to Jewish soil, the texts must have originally referred to an illegitimate conception that was covered up. What both these writers fail to see, though, is that the very reason that Jews would not have come up with the image of a virgin birth explains why Christians might have. For if Jews felt threatened by a myth which eliminated the human father and his seed, the same myth provided a founding ideology for communities that included Jews and gentiles together.

Spiritual Sons

Early Christianity was originally one of the many varieties of Judaism in the first century C.E. But this form of Judaism began to differ from its siblings in the role that genealogy played in identifying its community.[5] At some point, descent from Abraham ceased to matter for this group of Jews, and one did not have to be a physical descendant of Abraham to be a Christian. The inclusion of gentiles on equal footing with Jews meant that genealogy no longer defined one's status in the community of those who followed Jesus' teachings. By the same token, the fact that one was born a Jew did not guarantee membership in Christ. Precisely when the mission to the gentiles began is difficult to pinpoint exactly, but the book of Acts reflects on the tension in the early church between those who believed that the gospel should be directed primarily to Jews and those who believed it should be extended to the gentiles.

The apostle Paul was a significant, if not primary, force in the movement to include the gentiles. Paul insisted that one could be a descendant of Abraham without belonging to his genealogical line: "For not all who are descended from Israel belong to Israel, and not all are children of Abraham because they are his descendants; but 'Through Isaac shall your descendants be named.' This means that it is not the children of the flesh who are the children of God, but the children of the promise are reckoned as descendants" (Rom. 9:6–8).[6] It is clear that Paul is here contesting the significance of genealogy. One can be heir to all the promises of Abraham by being a descendant in faith. Hence the refrain in Paul that there is "no distinction between Jew and Greek" (Rom. 10:12). For Paul, "all who are led by the Spirit of God are sons of God" (Rom. 8:4). While Paul believes that the gentiles share in the promises to Abraham, he also believes that the Jews should follow their traditional obligations. In other words, Paul imagines the Christian community as two complementary communities. Jews by birth should continue to practice all the instructions of the Torah, including circumcision. The gentiles, who are spiritual descendants of Abraham, are not obliged to follow Jewish law: "Or is God the God of Jews only? Is he not the God of Gentiles also? Yes, of Gentiles also, since God is one; and he will justify the circumcised on the ground of their faith and the uncircumcised through their faith. Do we then overthrow the law by this faith? By no means! On the contrary, we uphold the law" (Rom. 3:29–31). Thus although Paul repudiates genealogy as a defining feature of the Christian community, he does not totally eliminate it. Jews by birth retain an identifiable status with distinctive obligations.

Paul's ambivalence about genealogy is reflected in his understanding of Jesus. As many interpreters have pointed out, Paul nowhere mentions the virgin birth and does not seem familiar with the idea.[7] Rather, he describes Jesus as "descended from David according to the flesh and designated Son of God in power according to the spirit of holiness by his resurrection from the dead" (Rom. 1:3). The Jesus of Paul has a genealogy that goes back to David, and it is a tie of the flesh, what we would call a biological relationship. We have no intimations here of a virgin birth that will later appear in the gospels of Matthew and Luke. If Jesus is the direct descendant of David, he is the spiritual son of God. And what makes him God's son is the resurrection. In other words, the idea of Jesus as God's son in this case is not altogether different than the Hebrew Bible's claim that David's descendant will be the son of God. God has conferred the status of son, but he has not been involved in any unusual way in Jesus' conception. Paul thus reflects a stage in the tradition in which the fatherhood of God has not yet been pushed back to Jesus' birth (Brown 1977, 134; Fitzmyer 1981, 306). Jesus has not yet been imagined as the actual son of the divine because Paul stands at the beginning of the mission to the gentiles. And the full significance of that inclusion has not yet impressed itself on Christian thought.

Paul's attitude toward circumcision, however, shows how the decreasing importance of genealogy began to reshape the conception of masculinity and prepare the way for the myth of the virginal conception. Where genealogy remained dominant, circumcision was the symbol par excellence of the covenant with God. The male sexual organ carried the ultimate symbol of the religious community.[8] But with Paul, male sexuality lost its close assocation to religious faith, for to be a member of his community did not involve pedigree: "Circumcision indeed is of value if you obey the law; but if you break the law, your circumcision becomes uncircumcision. So, if a man who is uncircumcised keeps the precepts of the law, will not his uncircumcision be regarded as circumcision? . . . For he is not a real Jew who is one outwardly, nor is true circumcision something external and physical. He is a Jew who is one inwardly, and real circumcision is a matter of the heart, spiritual and not literal" (Rom. 2:25–29). Circumcision, therefore, itself depends on faith. If one is circumcised in the flesh and has no faith, he is uncircumcised. But if he is uncircumcised in the flesh but has faith, he is circumcised. In light of this understanding, Paul rethinks the meaning of Abraham's circumcision. He wishes to show that gentiles need not be circumcised to be descendants of Abraham, so he argues that Abraham's circumcision was not a symbol of his faith in God, for his faith was reckoned to him before circumcision: "The purpose was to make him the father of all who believe without being circumcised and who thus have righteousness reckoned to them, and likewise the father of the circumcised who are not merely circumcised but also follow the example of the faith which our father Abraham had before he was circumcised" (Rom. 4:9–12).

This demotion of circumcision, like the hiding of the penis in rabbinic Judaism, signifies that male procreation had lost the significance it once had. The male organ of generation was no longer the primary symbol of the covenant with God, because the Christian community did not define itself through the father's line. Paul's demotion of circumcision also anticipates the elimination of the human father and his seed from the story of Jesus' birth. The Messiah has no human father, at least not in a genealogical sense. Thus the virgin birth carries to its logical conclusion a symbolic shift that was initiated in Paul's writings and in his mission to the gentiles.

It is only in the Gospels of Matthew and Luke that Jesus' status as son of God is associated with his conception by a virgin woman. These gospels were both written after the letters of Paul and the Gospel of Mark, though they rework older stories. The fact that both gospels recount the story of Jesus' miraculous birth shows that it had gained some currency by the time of the gospels' writing. Both gospels appear to have addressed communities in which gentiles played a significant if not dominant role (Brown 1977; Fitzmyer 1981). As we shall see, the virginal conception of Jesus provided a compelling myth for the legitimation of communities with a significant gentile presence.

The Gospel of Matthew begins with "the book of the genealogy of Jesus Christ, the son of David, the son of Abraham" (Matt. 1:1). It starts with Abraham and traces his line through David to Jesus. A Jew reading Matthew's account would have found it similar in most formal respects to the genealogies of the Hebrew Bible. For the most part, it is composed of a series of male names. Somewhat unexpectedly, however, Matthew also includes in the genealogy the names of four women, in addition to Mary, the mother of Jesus.[9] The reference to these women—Tamar, Rahab, Ruth, and the wife of Uriah (Bathsheba)—clearly anticipates the role of Mary at the end of the genealogy. But the author of Matthew may have included them for another reason. In the Hebrew Bible, and in Jewish imagination of the first century C.E., these women were apparently understood to be of non-Israelite origin, that is, of gentile stock. Moreover, there is something irregular or even scandalous about the sexual behavior of three of these women. Tamar conceives her son, Perez, with her father-in-law, Judah. Bathsheba conceives Solomon through an adulterous relationship with David. Rahab, who is described as a prostitute in the Hebrew Bible, is here viewed as the mother of Boaz. These are telltale signs that something is different about Jesus' genealogy. The presence of these women's names probably underscored the fact that God had previously guided the genealogy of David in unexpected ways. "These women were held up as examples of how God uses the unexpected to triumph over human obstacles and intervenes on behalf of His planned Messiah" (Brown 1977, 74).[10]

But the punch line has not yet been given away. On reading the genealogy, it is easy to assume that Jesus is a direct descendant of David. Only after the catalog of names do we learn of Mary's virginal conception through the Holy Spirit (Matt. 1:18–25), that Joseph played no role in fathering Jesus. The story of Jesus' conception totally undermines the expected reading of the genealogy that precedes it. For this reason, some scholars conclude that the genealogy contradicts the virginal conception story and reflects an older tradition, like that found in Paul, that presupposed Jesus' physical descent from David's seed. But there are good literary and linguistic reasons to think the genealogy is meant to go with the virgin birth story. Among other things, the genealogy breaks a recurring linguistic pattern when describing Joseph's relation to Jesus. Brown writes that "If Matthew meant [that Joseph was the biological father] why would he have departed from the usual formula which would have affirmed it clearly: 'By her Joseph was the father of Jesus, called the Christ.' The very shift of pattern implies that Matthew did not want to say that Joseph was the biological father of Jesus" (1977, 62).[11]

What, then, was the point of tracing Jesus' genealogy to David and Abraham through Joseph when Joseph did not father him? Some interpreters conclude that the author of Matthew simply tolerated the tension because of a fidelity to recording "tenacious traditions with respect to ancestry among the Jews at the time of Jesus" (Albright 1971, 6). Others view it as a "paradox in the ancient sense of marvel or wonder that should inspire" awe and reverence (H. Milton in Johnson 1969, 186). But there may be no contradiction or paradox here at all. The point may have been to dismiss descent through the male line as central to Jesus' status. In other words, Jesus was the son of David and Abraham in a spiritual sense only. His spiritual father, the man his mother was eventually to marry, was a descendant of David. Matthew was thus showing that descent was not communicated through natural sexual relations. For this reason, some describe the relationship between Joseph and Jesus as one of "legal paternity."[12]

Technically, there is not much difference between the idea of spiritual and legal paternity. Both imply that paternity is not a relationship that is dependent on the father's seed but a status that can be conferred. The idea of Joseph's legal paternity, however, carries with it some inappropriate historical assumptions, namely, that Jews of the first century c.e. would have found this legal status comprehensible. As evidence, interpreters cite a passage of the Mishnah (which is certainly later than 70 c.e.) which deals with matters of inheritance: If a man says "this is my son he is to be believed" (M. B.B. 8:6). This supposedly proves that Jews of Jesus' time recognized legal paternity. But this quote is taken out of context. This Mishnaic passage is not talking about legal fatherhood, but about a witness's credibility in matters of inheritance. According to this ruling, when a man identifies a particular boy as his son, he should be believed that the boy is actually his son. In other words, the issue is not about a father conferring the status of son but applies to situations in which a man may be believed when he claims to have fathered a child.

In my judgment, then, the point of Matthew's genealogy was to contest the Jewish conception of paternity which until that time had been figured through the male line. Jesus is said to be the son of David in exactly the way that gentiles are said to be Jews. Just as gentiles are spiritual heirs of Abraham, Jesus is incorporated into a lineage that is not his by birth. Jesus is thus the spiritual descendant of both God and David. His human father is completely irrelevant to his status both as son of God and as Messiah. It is no accident that Matthew recorded the genealogy first and then appended the story of the virgin birth subsequently. In ordering things in this way, the virgin birth story would have shocked Jewish readers into rethinking what the genealogy meant.

The Gospel of Luke does not mislead the reader in the way that Matthew does, although it makes the same point about genealogy. Here the story of the virgin birth (Luke 1:26ff.) precedes the genealogy of Jesus (3:23ff.). Originally, the gospel may have begun with the genealogy, and the infancy narratives may have been appended only later.[13] But once they were appended, the genealogy takes on a very different meaning. The reader encounters the genealogy already knowing of Jesus' virginal conception. There can be no misunderstanding the intent of the author of Luke: the genealogical background of Jesus is secondary to his spiritual identity.

The Lucan genealogy differs significantly from the one in Matthew. Not only is it longer and more detailed, but it traces Jesus' lineage through different figures. There have been many ingenious attempts to reconcile the two genealogies. But these need not detain us, for their primary motivation is to prove the historicity of the accounts, which is not our concern. What is interesting is how the Gospel of Luke makes the same points about genealogy through the infancy narratives. Here, the birth of John the Baptist precedes and is entwined with the virgin birth of Jesus. The story of John's conception is clearly modeled on similar stories in the Hebrew Bible. In particular, there are allusions to the divine intervention in the pregnancies of Sarah and Hanah (Fitzmyer 1981, 317). The story of John the Baptist begins by explaining that the priest Zechariah and his wife, Elizabeth, a woman of priestly descent, have no children. Like Abraham, Zechariah encounters an angel, who tells him that his wife will bear him a son and instructs him what the child's name should be. Echoing Abraham's words nearly verbatim, Zechariah says to the angel, "How shall I know this? For I am an old man and my wife is advanced in years." And Elizabeth, like Sarah, does conceive, as the angel has promised.

The account of Jesus' divine conception follows John's story.[14] Through this juxtaposition, the Lucan gospel reminds the reader of how God has helped barren women conceive throughout Israel's history and prepares the way for a more miraculous intervention. This is stated explicitly in the words of John: "He who is mightier than I is coming, the throng of whose sandals I am not worthy to untie" (Luke 3:16). In other words, the complete elimination of the human father signals the birth of a more important figure. But the miraculous conception of Jesus suggests something else as well. It defines the changing nature of the Jewish-Christian community. For if the old community traced status through the male line, the new community would worship the son of God who was born to a virgin. It is no accident that an angel announces John's conception to his father but the conception of Jesus to his mother. And John, who represents the last example in a long-established tradition, articulates the new notion of fatherhood: "Bear fruits that befit repentance and do not begin to say to yourselves, 'We have Abraham as our father'; for I tell you, God is able from these stones to raise up children to Abraham" (Luke 3:8). The succession of the infancy narratives in Luke makes the same point as the juxtaposition of genealogy and virgin birth in Matthew. Genealogy is no longer a significant factor in determining identity.

The myth of the virgin birth thus signaled a new attitude toward fatherhood and a transformation in the meaning of masculinity. The reproduction of the father's line was no longer centrally important and this change would have effects on men's attitudes toward their own bodies and to sexuality in general. For if the religious role of masculinity was no longer to continue the lineage of the fathers, then the male organ of generation would begin to lose the positive value it once had. Paul's attitude toward circumcision has already indicated how the sexuality of the male body was being demoted. The circumcised penis was no longer a religious symbol of what it meant to be a member of the community, and as this symbolic link was broken, procreation and sexuality began to move to the woman's domain. This is another reason for the importance of women's names in Matthew's genealogy. Even in the Gospel of Mark, which does not imagine a virgin birth, Jesus is identified as "the son of Mary." Rabbinic Judaism, as we have seen, also began to trace descent through the mother for similar reasons. Procreation and sexuality were feminized, leaving men with a divided understanding of themselves. Their own relationship to their sexual bodies was seen as analogous to their relationships with their wives; their relationship to their intellectual and spiritual selves became symbolic of their relationships to God. In short, procreation and sexuality became foreign elements in the territory of manliness.

This divided image of man is evident in the early Christian sources' interpretation of what it means to be made in the image of God. These Christian reflections make explicit what earlier Israelite reflections could not: man is now divided above and below: the head of man is divine; the sexual part of man is feminine:

> The head of every man is Christ, the head of a woman is her husband, and the head of Christ is God. Any man who prays or prophesies with his head covered dishonors his head, but any woman who prays or prophesies with her head unveiled dishonors her head—it is the same as if her head were shaven. . . . For a man ought not to cover his head, since he is the image and glory of God; but woman is the glory of man. (1 Cor. 11:7)

According to this statement of Paul, there is a hierarchy rising from woman to God in which the head of the inferior is the body of the superior. A man's body is woman, his head is Christ.[15] The body of Christ is man, and Christ's head is God the father.

This way of reconciling man with the divine image was not possible in Israelite religion. In that context, the sexual part of man—bearing the sign of circumcision—could not be divorced from the meaning of being a man in ancient Israelite culture. Only with rabbinic culture did this split begin to be possible. The Christian imagination, however, was far freer to make a male divine body a central metaphor of its religious imagination. Since masculinity was no longer defined in terms of procreation, it did not matter that Christ had no consort. Indeed, Christ's masculinity was not only tolerable but confirmed the configuration of masculinity in the religious community. With Jesus, all genealogies came to an end.

In another respect, though, Christ's body continues to generate a problem for Christian men—the same dilemma of homoerotic desire that a male God posed for Israelite men. This is evident, for example, in one of Paul's letters where he uses the divided image of man—the divine head and female body—to endorse marriage and, presumably, sexuality.

> Wives, be subject to your husband, as to the Lord. For the husband is the head of the wife as Christ is the head of the church, his body, and is himself its Savior. As the church is subject to Christ, so let wives also be subject in everything to their husbands. Husbands, love your wives, as Christ loved the Church and gave himself up for her, that he might sanctify her, having cleansed her by the washing of water with the word, that he might present the church to himself in splendor, without spot or wrinkle or any such things, that she might be holy and without blemish. Even so husbands should love their wives as their own bodies. He who loves his wife loves himself. For no man ever hates his own flesh, but nourishes and cherishes it, as Christ does the church, because we are members of his body. For this reason a man shall leave his father and mother and be joined to his wife, and the two shall become one flesh. This mystery is a profound one, and I am saying that it refers to Christ and the church. (Eph. 5:21–22)

This metaphor recalls passages in Hosea, Jeremiah, and Ezekiel in which Israel is depicted as the wife of God. And like those passages, the homoerotic love of men for Christ is avoided by speaking collectively of the Christian community as a woman. But it is obvious that for Paul a man stands in the same relationship to Christ as a woman to a man. Men are both the body and wives of Christ. This feminization of Christian men imposes heterosexual metaphors of desire on what are male-male relationships.

The exploration of homoeroticism within Christianity is beyond the scope of this inquiry. But taking this issue into account will surely add a further dimension to the already excellent investigations by Caroline Walker Bynum and Leo Steinberg on the nature and meaning of Christ's sexuality.[16] Let me conclude by saying that we must resist the trend in our modern scholarship to underestimate what is erotic. The sensual and the erotic are important in shaping the images we analyze. I think it is no accident, for example, that in Renaissance art we never see the exposed organ of Christ the man, only the penis of the baby Jesus. In my view, the body of Christ continues to pose one of the two dilemmas evoked by monotheism, namely, male homoerotic desire for the divine. But within the matrix of Christianity, in which descent through the male line has ceased to be important, being made in the image of a sexless father God is no longer a problem.

Embracing Our Fathers: Theological Musings of a Son

I N THE COURSE OF writing this book, a colleague asked me why I wanted to see my father naked. Taken aback momentarily, I replied, "Why do you want to imagine your father without a body?" It seems to me that this brief interchange raises some profound issues both about the nature of fatherhood generally and about its expression in religious and theological imagery. A father God who has no body, or one who turns his back so that we cannot see his face, is not a father with whom some of us find it possible to be intimate.[1] Indeed, such a God is like the remote fathers that many of us had as children. At issue, then, is whether the symbol of a father God who has turned his back on us is redeemable, and if so, how?

The image of a male God has clearly been one of the central problems of feminist theology over the past twenty years. In the wake of Mary Daly's *Beyond God the Father*, Jewish feminists—Rachel Adler, Rita Gross, Judith Plaskow, Marcia Falk, and Ellen Umansky, to name only a few—have explored the ways in which a male image of God validates male experience at the expense of women. I find the force of the feminist argument very compelling, and it has contributed to my own growing discomfort with the liturgy of traditional Judaism. Like many other men and women who have found the feminist critique persuasive, I either lapsed into silence or found other language to use to talk about God. But over the course of writing this book, I have come to think differently about images of male gods, about father gods, and about human fathers as well.

I began to see that feminist analyses have not clearly distinguished between images of male deities and images of father deities. The two obviously overlap, but the maleness of God may have different implications than the fatherliness of God. Indeed, it is striking to me that unlike feminist scholarship in general, feminist theology has reflected little on our relationships to both our parents—our mothers and our fathers.[2] I believe these relationships are fundamental to our discussion, for if we agree with nothing else from Freud, he was certainly right about the ways in which divine and parental images are entangled. And the possibility of connecting to divine images, whether male or female, clearly is related to the relationships we have to our mothers and fathers. My father is a wonderful man whom I love. But our connection to each other was nonverbal; as a child, I was closest to my father in sporting events or games. As I grew and we could no longer play games together, there was no vehicle for the expression of feelings of intimacy. It was only in the past few years, while I was going through a divorce, that my father and I were able to reconnect emotionally. The experience of a fatherly figure reaching out to me has made me reflect on the need many of us have for fatherly images that are nurturing and loving. I need to imagine a God with a body, with fatherly arms, who does not turn his back away.

Because of the feminist critique, I had earlier rejected a fatherly image of God, because to evoke such images participates in the oppression of women by deifying masculinity. I remain worried by this problem.[3] There is a real danger that by celebrating fatherly images, we risk reinforcing the symbolic structures that underlie women's oppression. But if we embrace such images with care, we may be able to help realize the goals of the women's movement. "With care" means that fatherly images can be used only if equally powerful female images are also celebrated. And it means that only particular kinds of fatherly images should be used—not the incorporeal majestic God that helped to generate the hierarchical associations of masculinity and spirituality, with the corresponding association of femininity and embodiment (Ruether 1983), but an image of a tender loving Father who faces and embraces the child. A loving and embodied God may support a different kind of masculinity, a masculinity that is capable of intimacy and tenderness. As a new generation of men emerges, men who have grown up with and take seriously feminist concerns—about parenting, about sharing household chores, about sharing the privileges of the religious life—a new generation of masculine images is needed as well. Although I do not presume to speak for all men and women, in the course of talking to people around the country, I have found great receptiveness to the possibility of celebrating a loving father God. Such images are powerful for different reasons: To some, the image of a loving Father offers the possibility of healing their own pain about emotionally distant fathers. To others, such images may be powerful because they were parented by loving fathers. Whether male or female images work at all will depend to a large extent on our individual biographies.

By embracing a fatherly image of God, I by no means intend to suggest that we should abandon serious analyses of patriarchal religion or attempts to reform the liturgy by introducing feminine imagery for God or using more inclusive language. As I have said, the idea of the loving father God is viable only when equally compelling feminine images are employed as well. I imagine a liturgy in which both male and female images are evoked, in which each of us can see God as nurturing and powerful.

In one sense, I am suggesting a reversal of the process of monotheism that I explore in this book. Instead of feminizing men so they can have an intimate relationship with a male God, we might feminize this God, without always making him into a goddess. Indeed, I believe that in many ways the process by which we may now be creating new femininities and masculinities involves redistributing across the genders the traits that previously were thought to inhere in one or the other. As women have learned to be more assertive and powerful, men must learn to be more intimate, more related, more open. Ideally, this process will culminate in the dissociation between aggression and masculinity, on the one hand, and sensitivity and femininity, on the other. Obviously, we still have a long way to go. But I suggest that a different kind of masculinity requires a feminized image of a male God or what one day may simply be recognized as one version of God.

Our relationships to our images of the divine are not only those of child to parent. They are also relationships that are entwined in eroticism, as this study and other feminist writings have suggested (Plaskow 1990; Lorde 1984). As I have argued in this book, I suspect that the image of a distant Father is deeply connected to the male fear of homoeroticism. In other words, as Freud suggested, the suppression of the erotic relationship between father and son is partly responsible for the creation of the authoritative father God. Embracing the Father involves a willingness to see male-male eroticism as an emotionally whole relationship. It does not mean that all men are homosexual, but it does mean that we recognize the part within ourselves that craves intimate bonds with fathers and other men, though those bonds do not take the form of sexual relationships. My analysis, I hope, shows that homoeroticism, though enormously problematic in the Jewish tradition, is also inescapably part of it. My argument may serve as evidence of how deeply homophobia is inscribed in the tradition, but I hope it also provides resources for celebrating homoeroticism.

There is a danger, however, of exalting male-male connections. For it is precisely this "all boys club" to which women rightly object. Indeed, feminist criticism has pointed to the ways that patriarchy is a kind of "homosociality," in which women are exchanged for the creation of male-male bonds (Rubin 1979; Sedgwick 1985; Irigaray 1985a). But it is important not to let this legitimate critique of homosociality be conflated with homophobia. Homophobia should not be enlisted in the efforts to criticize male domination in the social order (Owens 1987).

Homoeroticism, however, applies not just to men's relationship with male religious symbols. The same kind of process is at work between women and female images of deities. Thus far feminist analysis has tended to focus on the process of identification: how women's lives are deepened by being able to imagine themselves in the image of a female God. But if eroticism is part of our relationships with divine images, then women's relationships to goddesses potentially involve female homoeroticism. The turn to goddess imagery does more than celebrate women's power and identity; it also celebrates female-female eroticism.

But the larger point is this: the use of both masculine and feminine images by both men and women opens up the possibility of various forms of intimate relations to the divine. I see this "polymorphously perverse theology" as extremely liberating. It will mean that all identities can find their rightful place in our contemporary theological expression and that we can celebrate all the cravings for intimacy that we have and wish for. For all of those reasons, it is time to reembrace our fathers, to find a place for them in our contemporary pantheon, not as dominating or distant others, but as the loving, nurturing fathers we wish them to be.

Notes

Introduction

1. For Lacanian readers I deal with the issue of the penis/phallus distinction in chapter 1.
2. Most influential for me were Adler 1977; Daly 1973; Delaney 1977, 1990, 1991; Falk 1987, 1989; Gross 1983; Ruether 1983; Ochshorn 1981; Plaskow 1983, 1990; and Umansky 1984. For a discussion of God's fatherhood and its implications in a broader perspective, see Metz and Schillebeeckx 1981.
3. I disagree with Halperin (1990), who argues that "heterosexual" and "homosexual" are strictly modern categories, the employment of which is limited to the last hundred years. It is true that ancient Jews would not have used these terms. It is also true they would not have made sexual identities into essences that defined them as people. But the emphasis on procreation and fathering children was central to the definition of masculinity, as they construed it. And male-male sexual acts were considered an abomination. The best translation of this image of masculinity is the modern term "heterosexuality." Indeed, in many contexts both ancient and modern masculinity is constructed through a repression of male-male eroticism (Rubin 1975; Butler 1990; Sedgwick 1985). On the complementarity of men and women in Judaism see also Alpert 1989, 1992.
4. I develop this point at greater length in Eilberg-Schwartz 1990, 87–114.
5. For example, although Bakan's work (1979) is suggestive in a variety of ways, he does not provide a thorough analysis of the sources he analyzes and hence is unconvincing. His central thesis, following one line of Freud's thought, is that Israelite religion originated before men's role in conception was understood. The discovery of paternity led to a transformation in the nature of Israel's myths, but traces of the earlier stages of thought and its subsequent transformation are still present in the Hebrew Bible.

6. See in particular Lakoff and Johnson 1980 and Fernandez 1974, 1977, 1982, 1986.

7. This view owes obvious debts to Lévi-Strauss's thinking (1963, 1973, 1978) about the ways myth and ritual express contradictions of the symbolic or social system.

8. This is one of the rich ethnographic and theoretical points of the British school of social and symbolic anthropology. See, for example, Evans-Pritchard 1976; Turner 1967; Douglas 1966. See my own use of this insight in Eilberg-Schwartz 1990, 115–94.

9. I have developed this point in more depth in Eilberg-Schwartz 1990 and 1992.

10. For treatments of this initial contact between Greeks and Jews and the way in which Greeks interpreted the Jewish prohibition against images, see Gager 1972 and Stern 1974.

11. On Philo's problem with anthropomorphism see Williamson 1989, 28–85, and Tobin 1983, 36–55. I explore possible meanings of this interpretation before contact with the Greeks in chapter 4.

1. Feminism, Freud, and the Father God

1. How this complicated reversal came about is an interesting story in its own right but is not immediately relevant to the present concerns (Gay 1966, 1968; Manuel 1959, 1983; Eilberg-Schwartz 1990, 31–67).

2. Some in the object relations school see religion as reflecting the pre-oedipal relationship with the mother. Rizzuto (1979) has explored in a clinical setting the way in which the evolving relationship with both parents impinges on the individual's relationship to God.

3. There is now a well-developed tradition of feminist psychoanalytic criticism. See Mitchell 1974; Mitchell and Rose 1985; Chodorow 1978; Irigaray 1985a, 1985b; Butler 1990. For an approach to the Hebrew Bible informed by feminist reflections on psychoanalysis, see Bal 1987, 1988. This interaction between feminist criticism and psychoanalysis, however, has only begun to rethink the issue of religion. See van Herik 1982, Goldenberg 1990, and the recent illuminating reflections on feminism, psychoanalysis, and religion by Jonte-Pace (1987, 1992a, 1992b).

4. See, for example, Delaney 1991.

5. Bynum (1986) anticpates me in talking about the complex ways in which religious symbols function.

6. An interesting exception is Bal (1988, 88, 104–6), who is herself influenced by Freud. See also Adler 1977, 239; Ruether 1983, 93; Plaskow 1990, 186; Starhawk 1979, 9.

7. See, for example, Chernin 1981; Kuhn 1985; and Wolf 1991.
8. See Bal (1988, 88, 104–6), who discusses how Manoah has to leave the act of fathering to a messenger of God and how this represents a failure of fatherhood. Pardes (1992, 44–45) also notes the way in which Adam is rendered irrelevant when Eve says she "co-created" Cain with God. But Pardes does not develop the implications of this insight for the threat it poses to human masculinity.
9. See, for example, Williams 1986 and duBois 1988.
10. Alcoff 1988; Butler 1990; Fuss 1989; Gagnier 1990; Spelman 1988.
11. See Gallop's (1988, 91–100) interesting reading of Irigaray as a post-essentialist.
12. Irigaray offers a different theory. Unlike de Beauvoir, she does not view women as other, but as unrepresentable, as totally excluded (Butler 1990, 9).
13. The history of Israel's monotheism is a complex subject that I take up in chapter 4. Theorists of religion have tended to assume that from the first Israel believed in the existence of only one God. But this belief developed only after a long period of evolution, and for a long part of its early history Israelite religion included more than one deity in its pantheon.
14. Most of my quotations from Freud are taken from the standard edition of his works (Strachey 1953–74), which comprises 24 volumes. Volume numbers of individual works are provided in the references.
15. There are some exceptions to this view. See, for example, Trible 1983 and Mollenkott 1986. I believe Trible overstates the feminine gendering of God and I specifically engage her view in chapter 8, where I discuss an alternative understanding of what it means for men and women to be made in the image of God. Frymer-Kensky (1992) argues that various qualities of the goddesses are incorporated into the images of Yahweh.
16. For a critical assessment of this tendency to identify Judaism and patriarchy, particularly with the way this feeds into and draws upon a discourse of anti-Judaism, see Kellenbach 1990.
17. Daly 1973; Collins 1976; Lerner 1986; Kristeva 1982; Ruether 1983.
18. See, for example, Adler 1977; Ruether 1983; Daly 1973; Bynum 1989.
19. Adler 1977; Delaney 1977, 1986, 1990, 1991; Ochshorn 1981, 139.
20. Unless otherwise noted, all translations follow the Jewish Publication Society translation of the Scriptures (JPS 1985).
21. See Butler 1990, 6–7; Laqueur 1990; Epstein and Straub 1991.
22. See Devor's 1989 study of women who are commonly mistaken for men.
23. Walter Williams (1986, 116–20) explores this theme. The recent movie *The Crying Game* is a well-known example of this potential discrepancy.

24. Walter Williams (1986) argues that the dichotomies of male/female thus make it impossible to really understand practices such as the berdache, which involve a kind of third gender. This privileging of the genitals in assigning gender reflects the importance that heterosexual and reproductive assumptions exert on the notions of what it means to be a man or woman.

25. Trible 1983 and Mollenkott 1986. Trible herself admits that God is predominantly gendered masculine (1983, 22).

26. As Rachel Adler put it, "we should expect that in patriarchal monotheism, where the self-sufficiency of the deity is of the utmost theological importance, the creative aspect of the female role will be claimed by the masculine deity, and hence by his male worshippers, who know themselves to be made in his image" (1977, 239). See also Miller 1986, 611, 614–15.

27. It is misleading, therefore, to say as Arthur Green recently has, that the God of the Jews is "a relatively genderless masculine deity" (1986, 34–35). Given the predominantly masculine gendering of God in ancient Judaism, I find implausible the suggestion that Israelites imagined the deity as either a female or hermaphroditic body, a possibility entertained by late antique interpreters. The veiling of God's sex, of course, makes the final verification of my assumption of God's maleness impossible, but the same is true of any other conclusion one makes about the divine anatomy. This study explores the implications of one very reasonable assumption about how Jews imagined their God.

28. Rachel Adler, for example, noted early on that "it is true that Jewish sources de-emphasize or moderate anthropomorphisms. In none of the Biblical source documents, therefore, is God male, although He is masculine in all" (1977, 239). And Rosemary Ruether (1983, 93) has noted how a spiritualized masculinity creates a dualism in men between an upper and lower masculine self. But she is more interested in the consequences for women than with the effects of this conflict on masculinity, a point I develop in chapter 9. Judith Plaskow has also noted that "while God is sexual in the sense that 'he' is gendered, in biblical and rabbinic thought God is free from sexuality in the narrower sense of engaging in sexual acts" (1990, 186). But it seems to me that this insight requires a significant nuancing of her claim that "when God is pictured as male in a community that understands 'man' to have been created in God's image, it only makes sense that maleness functions as the norm of Jewish humanity" (1990, 127). It is a particular image of maleness that God represents, one that is also at odds with the image of what men are supposed to be.

29. See Gallop 1982, 96 and Ragland-Sullivan 1987, 273. For other views of what the phallus means, see Wilden 1968, 186–88; Gallop 1981; Gallop 1985, 133–56; Mitchell 1985, 39–44; and Butler 1990, 43–44.

2. Analytic Phallusies

1. Jay Geller's work (1992, 1993a, 1993b) has much influenced my whole way of thinking about Freud. We have been working on parallel issues from the very start. But the following chapter could not have been written without a familiarity with the substance of Geller's analyses and, perhaps more importantly, with his way of thinking about Freud.

2. Robert 1976; Krüll 1986; Yerushalmi 1991; Geller 1993a, 1993b.

3. Like Yerushalmi (1991, 7), I disagree with Robert's argument (1976, 150) that Moses' Egyptian origin expresses Freud's ambivalence about his own Jewish identity. Below, I will explore the way in which Freud's theory of monotheism's Egyptian origins allows him to ignore the psychodynamic situation in which monotheism arose.

4. Oring (1984, 95) also suggests that Freud's explanation for the delays in publication do not ring true. For example, in the second preface to the third essay, Freud entitles the recapitulation of those arguments as "the historical premise" (1939, 58). On the fears about anti-Semitic reaction, see Robert 1976, 147–48, and Yerushalmi 1990, 14, 42–43, 46–50, 96–100.

5. I would like to thank Van Harvey for drawing my attention to Rizzuto's work.

6. See Mitchell 1974, 66–67, 89, and van Herik 1982, 93–94. In addition to the case studies discussed below, Freud discusses this passive Oedipus complex in several contexts (1919, 198; 1921, 105–6; 1923, 33).

7. In what follows, I rely in part on Chabat 1982.

8. Wilden (1972) argues that the "voluptuousness" means more broadly "lust for life" and is not limited to the erotic connotations that guide Freud's interpretation.

9. There is some debate about how the term *Entmannung* should be translated and understood. Macalpine and Hunter (1955) argue that Freud treats the term as emasculation, that is, as signifying castration and loss of manhood. But they argue that for Schreber turning into a woman is not the same as castration. Schreber's wish to become a woman is positive because it is associated with gaining a womb and hence being able to conceive. For a discussion, see Bregman 1977, 127, and Geller 1993a.

10. For a history of the analytic treatment of homosexuality, see Lewes 1988. For recent positive analytic views of homosexuality, see Isay 1989 and Corbett 1993.

11. Schatzman 1973. See also Israëls 1981 for a thorough treatment of the relationship between Schreber and his father.

12. Wilden 1972 and Bregman 1977. See also the work of Geller (1993a), who examines Freud's marginal notes in Schreber's memoirs and shows how Freud suppresses other ways of reading the case in his efforts to impose his analytic assumptions.

13. Freud [1914] 1918, 7–122. See also Rizzuto 1979, 31–35.

14. On the complexity of this issue, see Tyler 1991, 32–41. See also Corbett's 1993 study on an important rethinking of the relationship of masculinity and passivity in light of his work with gay patients. Isay (1989) explores the issue of gay men's fantasies of becoming a woman or taking a passive dependent relationship to father figures. It is important to note that Freud sometimes distinguished passive and active homosexuality. Passive homosexuality, the desire to be entered by a man, he associated with femininity more than active homosexuality. By contrast, Freud did not view as feminine the man who wished to enter another male, for in Freud's terms, this homosexual desire was active and hence more masculine. Moreover, Freud distinguished a pregenital form of homosexuality, in which the man wished to be entered in the anus, from the inverted Oedipus complex in which a man wished to be castrated so as to be the object of his father's desires.

15. See, for example, W. Williams 1986, 144. I develop this point in the context of Judaism in part 3. See also Isay 1989 on the way in which such images sometimes structure gay male fantasies. Corbett 1993 provides an important critique of the assumption that homosexuality is necessarily linked to femininity or passivity.

16. Van Herik (1982) develops this point extensively.

17. As Rieff (1979, 267–68), Roazen (1974, 251), and van Herik (1982) point out, Freud's view of religion is completely different in *Moses and Monotheism* than in *Future of an Illusion*. In the latter work, Freud treats religion as feminine, passive, and compliant. Judith van Herik notes that "when Freud detects religion offering the believer a consoling, loving paternal God, he exposes it as the servant of wish fulfillment. The illusion of the existence and tender loving care of this sort of god is mentally like a feminine attitude towards fathers" (1982, 191–92).

18. Jay Geller (1992, 1993a, 1993b) has been exploring this in a fascinating series of essays and in his forthcoming book. See Gilman 1985, 1991.

19. Freud 1900, 197 and Robert 1976, 20.

20. It is clear, moreover, that the association of Jews and femininity was familiar to Freud from Otto Weininger's book *Sex and Character* (1903),

which was widely read and whose central ideas Freud himself was indirectly responsible for. Among other things, Weininger argued that "Judaism is saturated with femininity" and that the "most manly Jew is more feminine than the least manly Aryan." Like women, Jews were said to be "wanting in personality" and to show a tendency "to adhere together." For background on Weininger, who was himself a Jew, see Janik and Toulmin 1973, 71–75.

21. See McGuire 1974, 353. Chabat (1982, 36) drew my attention to this letter.

22. Emphasis in original. Jones 1955, 2:92, and Masson 1985, 2.

23. Masson 1985, 4 n. 3, citing unpublished letter to Ferenczi later that same month.

24. For an account of these fainting spells, see Jones 1953, 1:317; Jones 1955, 2:146; Jung 1961, 156–67; Roazen 1974, 247–48, 257; and Rosenberg 1978, 194ff. See also Jung's letters to Freud after the incident (McGuire 1974, 524ff.). Jung clearly interprets the fainting as an oedipal struggle in which Freud treats him as the threatening son.

25. Cited in Roazen 1974, 249.

26. Roazen 1974, 249, 257, and Jones 1953, 1:317. See Rosenberg (1978, 234), who anticipates some of this analysis, although he emphasizes the oedipal struggle with Jung. Shengold is one of the few interpreters to emphasize that "Freud's fainting involved both sides of the Oedipus complex: punishment for death-wishes toward rivals for the exclusive possession of the mother, and homosexuality associated with passive surrender to them—in short, the basic bisexuality of man" (1972, 140).

27. Jones 1955, 2:146, and Roazen 1974, 247–48, 257. Shengold (1972) and Rosenberg (1978) both note the importance of Freud fainting while having this discussion but interpret this incident primarily in the context of Freud's oedipal struggles with Abraham.

28. Jung 1961, 157; Roazen 1974, 247–48.

29. Shengold (1972) also writes about the meaning of this oversight. He interprets it as evidence of hostile feelings to Abraham.

30. See note 3 above.

31. Freud 1939, 28. Shengold interprets Freud's reaction to the sun slightly differently. Schreber claimed he could look into the sun. "The delusional privilege of being able to gaze at and defy the father-sun with open eyes is to be contrasted to Freud's attitude to his own father as expressed after the latter's death in a dream: I found myself in a shop where there was a notice up saying 'You are requested to close the eyes'" (Shengold 1972, 129).

32. These views appear in order in the following: Jones 1955, 2:365–66; Krüll 1986, 187; Bakan 1958, 156; Robert 1976, 143–44; Yerushalmi 1991, 76; and Oring 1984, 93–94.

33. Krüll (1986, 184) compares Freud's desire to publish this anonymously with his desire to hide the autobiographical character of his screen memories. Robert (1976, 141) and Oring (1984, 95) also draw a parallel to Freud's reluctance to publish parts of *Moses and Monotheism.*

34. For a comprehensive discussion of the conflict between art historians and psychoanalysts growing out of the Freud-Schapiro dialogue, see Eissler 1961; Farell 1963; and Gombrich 1963, 30–44.

35. See Liebert 1983, 4, on the primary data available.

36. On Michelangelo's relationship to the pope, see Liebert 1983, 140–64. For a discussion of the artist's passionate male relationships, see Liebert again and Walters 1978, 128–52. For Freud's citations of Vasari and his knowledge of Michelangelo's heterosexual relationships, see the Leonardo essay (1910, 64, 71, 109, 111, 121, 124, 127, 128, 133).

37. Reprinted in Bayer 1987, 27.

38. Masson 1985, 291–95, 436, 331. Jay Geller drew my attention to the issue of left-handedness in the Freud-Fliess correspondence.

39. Masson remarks that this joke is about Freud himself.

40. For discussions of this dream, see Robert 1976, 83, 90–92, and Krüll 1986, 41–43, 179. Both Robert and Krüll discuss the significance of the variations between the way Freud reports the dream in his letter to Fliess and his retelling of it in his *Interpretation of Dreams.* Robert notes that in German the phrases "close your eyes" and "close the eyes" of someone else are indistinguishable. She interprets this dream as reflecting Freud's need to close his eyes to his own oedipal conflicts, which he had not yet fully brought into view. Krüll sees here an injunction not to investigate Jacob Freud's past.

41. For Freud's views on paternity, see Freud 1909, 33, and Freud 1939, 118, among other works.

3. The Averted Gaze

1. My notion of myth is inspired by Lévi-Strauss's claim that myths struggle with contradictions and find ways to overcome them (1963, 1973, 1978). I do not embrace, however, Lévi-Strauss's assumptions about universal principles of the mind.

2. The Hebrew term translated here as "elders" is a hapax. For a discussion, see Vriezen 1972, 110, and Nicholson 1974, 83.

3. Henton David quoted in Vriezen 1972, 101.
4. Interpreters have debated whether this myth belongs to J or E. Beyerlin (1965, 17) assigns it to E. For a discussion of the dating, see Nicholson 1974, 79; Childs 1974, 500; and Vriezen 1972, 105. Beyerlin (1965, 28) argues that the reference to the elders of Israel and the term "God of Israel" point to a premonarchic origin for this story, to the time when elders held a role under Israel's sacred tribal union. The dating, however, needs to be taken with caution. Interpreters have assumed it is old because it refers to the sighting of the deity, which they regard as a primitive idea.
5. Most interpreters regard the sacrifice in verses 3–8 as a covenantal sacrifice and see the story of leaders seeing God as another version of this covenant (Nicholson 1974, 79). See, however, Hendel 1989 for an alternative treatment of this sacrifice.

   On the notion of a covenantal meal, see Beyerlin 1965, 33; Noth 1962, 195; Childs 1974, 507; and a review of the issue in Nicholson 1974, 1975, 1986, 121–33. Nicholson himself argues that it is not a covenantal meal but a celebration in God's presence.

   For a discussion of Nadab and Abihu, see Vriezen 1972, 106–7. It is interesting to note that a Samaritan manuscript, as well as a manuscript of Exodus from Qumran with Samaritan affinities, adds to this myth the names of Aaron's other two sons, Eleazar and Ithamar. I develop the rabbinic reading of this myth in chapter 7.
6. The meaning of the Hebrew is uncertain.
7. See also Eichrodt 1967, 2:21: "That such language is not meant to be taken as an adequate description of the divine nature can be seen from the way in which, by blurring the details rather than presenting them with precision, the account stresses the parabolic character of the appearance."
8. A developmental perspective developed in the modern period when interpreters began to take seriously the idea that religions evolved. But this developmental perspective has often served apologetic purposes. See Eilberg-Schwartz 1990, 49–66.
9. Eichrodt (1967, 2:23) goes on to list various signs of increasing spiritualization, including the appearance of angelic mediators, the development of a Name theology, increasing references to God's "glory" or "presence" (kavod), the metaphorical uses of God's face, and so on. For similar considerations of these theological terms, see Mettinger 1982; Vriezen 1970, 207–9; and Weinfeld 1972, 191–209. Weinfeld, in con-

trast to many interpreters, regards the Kabod (Glory) theology as presupposing an anthropomorphic image of the deity. I will discuss these theological developments in chapter 5.

10. For a discussion of these different interpretations, see Mettinger 1982, 42, and Weinfeld 1972, 191–209. Mettinger reviews other interpreters who endorse the developmental view.

11. Interpreters disagree as to whether God was imagined as an embodied or an invisible deity. Weinfeld (1972, 191ff.) argues that "the Divinity is personalized and depicted in the most tangible corporeal similitudes." Mettinger (1982, 23), by contrast, argues that God is invisibly enthroned as king.

12. See, for example, Beyerlin 1965, 104–9. Beyerlin argues that this image is particularly connected to ark theology.

13. See also Terrien (1978, 144–47), who suggests that the back of God is a temporal reference.

14. Modern interpreters follow this lead. Terrien, for example, writes that "the idiom *panim el panim*, 'face to face,' should not be taken literally, especially when it is used with a verb of speaking and hearing. It means 'directly' and 'without intermediary' " (1978, 146).

15. Vriezen 1972, 101; Nicholson 1974, 89; Wevers 1990, 384–87.

16. Maimonides (Guide 1:4) 1963, 1:28.

17. See Nicholson 1974, 81–83, for a discussion of these emendations and their problems. Cassuto (1967, 314) offers a different way of dismissing this sighting of God. He suggests that the leaders saw not God but a divine phenomenon like a devouring fire. This is why the word Elohim (God) and not Yahweh is used in the myth. Childs, in a manner reminiscent of Maimonides, writes that "the shift from the verb r'h to ḥzh, the latter word being the technical term for prophetic clairvoyance, again appears to be an attempt to characterize this viewing as a special category of perception" (1974, 507).

18. I agree with Noth (1962, 195), who suggests that the gaze of the Israelite leaders and that of the narrator should not be conflated. The leaders saw the God of Israel; the narrator reports only what is under the deity's feet.

19. On sapphire being linked to heaven, see Noth 1962, 195, and Nicholson 1974, 91. Beyerlin (1965, 31) discusses the connection of the Kabod, the light suggested by the sapphire pavement, and the deity's feet, which are all associated with ark theology.

20. See note 5.

21. Some interpreters see this as originally a story about a demon that attacks Jacob and tries to keep him from crossing the stream. For a discussion of

the issue, see Westermann 1984, 2:517–19. In chapter 6, I provide an alternative interpretation.

22. There are reasons to believe that Jacob did in fact wrestle with God. The renaming of Jacob is reminiscent of God's changing Abram's and Sarai's names to Abraham and Sarah. Nowhere else in the Hebrew Bible does a divine being other than God change a human name. In addition, Jacob's surprise that he has seen the face of this being and survived is obviously part of the same set of ideas encountered earlier concerning God. Indeed, this story may very well be from the same source as the myth in which Moses is forbidden to see the deity's face. And there are other incidents in which other characters, such as Abraham, Sarah, and Lot, see divine beings yet express no worry about seeing their faces.

The Jacob myth has a very strong resemblance to the story in which a messenger of God comes to the barren wife of Manoah and promises her that she will bear a child (Judges 13). The messenger explains that the child, who is named Samson, must be dedicated to God and become a Nazarite. In this case, the text makes explicit that we are dealing, not with God directly, but with "a messenger of God." Like the Jacob myth there is initial confusion about the nature of the man who appears; the man refuses to tell anyone his name, and Manoah and his wife, like Jacob, see "Elohim." Yet the story of Manoah's wife is from a later source and may already represent an attempt to tone down the Jacob story. In the end, there can be no final certainty as to whether Jacob is imagined to have seen an angel's or God's face.

23. See the Letter of Aristeas (140–62) in Shutt 1985, 140–41.

24. For a more detailed discussion of the ways in which Israelite religion has been privileged in modern interpretation, see Eilberg-Schwartz 1990.

25. See also Janowitz (1992), who makes a similar point but draws very different conclusions.

26. Eichrodt, for example, notes that "there is an absolute bar on the idea of his becoming visible in animal form" (1967, 2:22).

27. See Barr 1959, developing views similar to Otto and Eliade.

28. As mentioned, God is frequently imagined as a king enthroned in the Temple. Mettinger (1982) develops this point.

29. But the notion of deference does seem to leave certain facts unaccounted for. It does not explain why God allows Moses to gaze on the divine back. And if the issue is deference, why is Moses not expected to bow? Moreover, images from the ancient Near East depict other human figures face to face with their gods. So the question remains why this face-to-face encounter is not possible in Israel.

30. Noth (1962, 258), for example, suggests that "front side" is the primary meaning in Exod. 33:23. The suggestion of God hiding the face in 33:20 is added by a later writer to imply that no one may see Yahweh's face.

31. See Biale 1992, 14, on the use of "feet" for "penis," and Wolfson 1992 on the euphemistic meaning of God's feet in rabbinic and mystical literature. Brown, Driver, and Briggs (1975, 697) interpret Judg. 3:24 and 1 Sam. 24:4 as referring to the evacuation of the bowels.

32. It is interesting to note that in Ezekiel's vision, the seraphs who wait in attendance on God have six wings, two with which to fly, two to cover the face, and two to cover their feet (Isa. 6:2). Some interpreters suggest that in this case feet is a euphemism for genitals. References cited in Wolfson 1992.

33. I would like to thank Amy Levine and Jay Geller for drawing my attention to this book.

4. Indecent Exposures

1. H. Hirsch Cohen (1974, 15) is the only other interpreter that I have discovered to see this connection. Cohen, however, argues that seeing is tantamount to taking possession. Ham, in seeing his father's nakedness, takes possession of his vitality.

2. On the Noah myth, see Noth 1981, 262; Friedman 1987, 87, 247. Noth (271) regards Exodus 33 as a conglomeration which may have been associated with J. Driver (1900, 38–29) assigns it to J as well. Beyerlin (1965, 24) assigns 33:18–33 and a large part of 12–17 to J. Friedman (1987, 251) assigned Exod. 33:12–33 to E, but in a personal communication to me, he writes that he is no longer certain why he did so.

3. Zimmerli 1979, 458; Eichrodt 1970, 307; Wevers 1969, 173.

4. Alt's now dated essay (1966) attempted to show that the God of the fathers was an early form of the patriarch's religion. Alt argued that Abraham, Isaac, and Jacob had each established a cult with its own god and that those gods had later been incorporated into Yahwism. While his historical conclusions are no longer compelling, Alt did draw attention to the way the conception of God was linked to specific patriarchs and father figures. For a more up-to-date picture of how Israelite notions of God developed, see M. S. Smith 1990.

5. Olyan (1987), in a compelling reinterpretation of this passage, argues that Jeremiah is polemicizing against Israelites who used a stone as a symbol of Yahweh. See also Delaney 1986, 1991, for a discussion of how fatherhood and "coming into being" are frequently linked.

6. I would like to thank Carl Bielefeldt and Bernard Faure for drawing my attention to this source.

7. That an act occurred is suggested when Noah curses his son when he "learned what his youngest son had done to him." See Rashi (ad loc.); Leach 1969, 19. Bakan (1979, 77ff.) unconvincingly argues that Noah was originally a story about a female who only later was imagined as male in an attempt to take account of the discovery of paternity.

8. Others argue that it means Ham committed incest with his mother (Allen 1963, 78).

9. Cohen (1974, 14, 15–16) comes to a similar conclusion that the sin was the gaze. But as noted earlier, he argues that the looking is symbolic of acquisition. Ham has acquired his father's potency.

10. Bailey (1989, 162), following Westermann (1984, 1:494), suggests that the concerns of this passage may be related to the commandment of honoring one's father and mother. Westermann writes, "As such, it would be in keeping with a continual theme of the J-Source: the culpability of individuals in the most basic of human relations (between man and woman in Gen. 2–3), between siblings in Gen. 4, and between parent and child in our text."

11. See the interesting essay by Kilborne (1992, 236), who argues that shame involves a reaction formation against the desire to look. He criticizes self psychologists and many psychoanalytic writers for not founding a theory of shame dynamics on the behaviors of looking and being looked at, even though Freud linked shame to exhibitionism and scopophilia.

12. Sarna 1970, 170–71; S. H. Smith 1990; Eilberg-Schwartz 1990, 169.

13. Robert Rubinstein drew my attention to the connection between the snake's shedding of its skin and the theme of transformation.

14. One ancient reading of this story suggests a very similar understanding of the snake's role. In one manuscript of the *Life of Adam and Eve* (ApMos 18:1), a text that retells and significantly embellishes the story of the first human pair, the snake says, "I am grieved that you are like animals. For I do not want you to be ignorant." See Johnson 1985, 279.

15. I follow the translation of Sandars (1972, 65). Oden (1987, 101–2) draws the parallel with Enkidu.

16. Sandars (1972, 30–31) notes this transformation from wild man to human. For other versions, see Heidel 1970.

17. I owe to Lévi-Strauss the insight that fermented beverages are a symbol of culture. It has been applied to Israelite religion by Soler (1979). Bailey

(1989, 161–62) notes that wine sometimes has positive valence in biblical literature, where it is regarded as a symbol of the blessed age to come (Hos. 9:10; Amos 9:13–15), even though excess is condemned. Viniculture, moreover, is presented as an advance in the history of civilization. There is no indication that Noah is to be condemned in this story.

18. For example, Lévi-Strauss argues that the prohibition against incest underlies the exchange of women in marriage and hence the complicated systems of kinship that develop in traditional societies. This point has been developed in the important work of Rubin (1975) and Butler (1990).

19. For another study of sexual diversity, see for example Williams's outstanding study of the berdache (1986).

20. Boswell argues that the term *toevah*, which is normally rendered "abomination" in the laws forbidding male-male sexual acts, is a mistranslation. He suggests that it means "ritually unclean." But while the word is sometimes used to designate impurity, it is also used to refer to objectionable acts such as male cross-dressing (Deut. 22:5), the use of graven images of foreign gods (7:25), witchcraft (18:12), and offerings of children.

21. As Niditch notes (1982), it violates the natural order as Israel conceived it, just as cross-dressing (Deut. 22:5), interbreeding animals, mixing different types of grain in a single field, or weaving a garment of two different types of material (Lev. 19:19).

22. See Eilberg-Schwartz 1990, 183. Horner (1978, 77) minimizes the importance of these laws, seeing them as the product of the exilic period. He argues that these laws originated to combat idolatry. But Horner's view rests on now outdated assumptions about cult prostitution and sexual promiscuity in other ancient Near Eastern religions.

23. Levine writes that "male homosexuality is associated with the ancient Canaanites, if we are to judge from biblical literature. Two biblical narratives highlight this theme, one about the men of Sodom in Genesis 19, and the other concerning the fate of the concubine at Gibeah in Judges 19. Although Gibeah was an Israelite town, the story clearly implies that Gibeah's Israelite residents had descended to the abominable ways of the surrounding Canaanites" (1989, 123).

24. A great deal of interpretive energy has been expended on trying to explain why Canaan was cursed when it was Ham who acted indecently. For a review, see Allen 1963, Cohen 1974, and Bailey 1989. For the present discussion this textual issue is not critical.

25. Leach (1969) in my judgment is right to interpret these sexual violations

as linked to Israelite concerns with differentiating the Israelite line from other genealogical lines.

26. Boswell (1980, 91–101), among others, has argued that the sin of Sodom is not homosexuality but inhospitality, an exceedingly important value in Mediterranean cultures. He notes that all other biblical references to Sodom assume that the people's wickedness involved general immorality, not homosexuality per se (Ezek. 16:49, 23:14). He argues that the term "to know" does not always mean sexual intimacy and therefore should not be understood this way in this story. But as Horner (1978, 50) notes, Lot's response demands the sexual interpretation of the men's words. Boswell notices this potential objection but dismisses it. See also Greenberg's (1988, 195–96) critique of Boswell. See Niditch (1982), who argues that Sodom condemns both inhospitality and homosexual rape.

27. Boswell (1980), as noted above, emphasizes the theme of hospitality. Horner (1978, 47–58) argues that the primary emphasis of the story is not the homosexuality, but the aspect of intended rape and dehumanization rape involves. Ide (1985, 17ff., 42ff.) suggests that the story of Sodom may be referring to heterosexuals who are expressing their power through sexual aggression, much as inmates in a prison say "we're going to make a girl out of you" to a new prisoner.

28. See Horner (1978) for the most compelling reading of David and Jonathan's relationship as involving homosexuality. But as Ron Hendel pointed out to me, Horner's interpretation completely ignores the political dimensions of the story in which David, who is Jonathan's beloved, is being portrayed as the legitimate successor of Jonathan's father. The loving relationship is also about David's right to claim Jonathan's position as Saul's successor.

29. Leach (1969, 19) anticipates me in saying that the affair of the Sodomites and the angels contains echoes of the sons of God myth. Boswell (1980) and Ide (1985) also notice but do not develop the possibility that the story could be interpreted as a rape of divine men. Ide, writing with a very different agenda, observes, "Even if everyone were homosexual in the city, lesbians having sex with the 'angels' (or agents) would have to be considered having 'heterosexual' sex, which, according to the rigid purists of the radical right is to be lauded, accepted, and acknowledged—therefore, the alleged lesbians would not be inviting the wrath of YHWH upon their heads and the city of Sodom" (1985, 18). For an articulation of the literary theory that allows one to take account of different viewpoints, see Bal 1985, 100ff., on focalization.

30. For other essays on "gendered spectatorship," see Doane 1982, 1985; Armstrong 1986; and Gammon and Marshment 1988. Mulvey's essay has now been criticized for exclusively focusing on the male gaze and not theorizing the female heterosexual spectator or the gay spectator (Doane 1982; Stacey 1988). In addition, subsequent critics have drawn attention to the way in which the male is sometimes subject to the gaze (e.g., Dyer 1982; Neale 1983; Walters 1978). See Schwartz 1991 for a suggestive analysis of the issue of spectatorship in relation to God. I begin by assuming that these texts are addressed to a male heterosexual spectator, but I hope this analysis will generate in turn studies that include other forms of spectatorship as well.

31. The one possible exception, already mentioned, is the story of Jonathan and David, which Horner (1978) interprets erotically.

32. Elaine Adler (1989, 42) points out that while God as king is a more frequent metaphor, it is not developed as extensively. Adler provides a detailed treatment of the metaphor of covenant as marriage.

33. Mettinger 1979, 16. Adler (1989) explores some of the ways in which this metaphor is apparent in legal contexts prior to Hosea.

34. The place of sexuality in Canaanite religious practice has been inferred from the Israelite material, and biblical scholars have often naïvely assumed that Israel's image of the Canaanites reflects actual practice (Oden 1987, 131–53). This view ignores the distinctive purposes that the marriage metaphor serves in Israel's religious thought. Finally, a recent reevaluation of Hosea suggests that his polemic against Baal may be an inter-Israelite polemic, against Israelites involved in Baal worship (Halpern 1987). Elaine Adler (1989, 130–250) reviews the various understandings of the marriage metaphor.

35. In their essays on Hosea, Bird (1989, 89) and Leith (1989, 97–98) both notice the feminization of Israelite men but do not see the homoerotic dilemma that this entails. Plaskow (1990, 162) also notes that "she" (Israel) is made up of shes and hes.

36. Andersen and Freedman (1980, 218–19) note in this passage the shifting back and forth between the relationship of Hosea and Gomer, on the one hand, and between God and Israel, on the other. Andersen and Freedman take this first piece to be addressed by Hosea to his children. But I see the ambiguity of who's being addressed as part of the point of this passage. It can just as easily be read as addressed to children of Israel, as Mays (1969, 35) suggests.

37. Andersen and Freedman (1980, 264) construe the "you" as addressed to the mother alone and assumes the children are not being addressed. But

in my view they do not give sufficient consideration to the possibility that the listener identifies with the "you," first as child of Israel and then as the wife who is returning to her husband.

38. Mays (1969, 47) also argues that the rapid change in personal pronouns cannot be taken as a sure guide to the composite nature of the material.

39. See Hendel 1987 for a discussion of scholarship on this story and Halpern 1987, 82, on the presence of other gods in Israel's pantheon.

40. Hendel convincingly rejects the connection of this story to the rebellion in heaven pattern. In Hendel's view, the story is a justification for the flood and finds mythic parallels in other contexts. Hendel suggests that the motivation for the flood was to destroy these demi-gods. Later, it is humanity's evil which becomes the motive.

41. For a similar form of veiling in another context, see Geist's (1988, 173, 230) analysis of how Cézanne carefully veils the genitals of Zola, his close male intimate and possibly lover, in his paintings of the bathers. Geist argues that this is a strategy for deflecting the homoerotic gaze. I would like to thank Arnold Eisen for drawing my attention to this source.

42. Generally these terms are used interchangeably. But see Halpern (1987) who differentiates them. On Israel's monotheism, see Halpern 1987, 83; and M. S. Smith 1990, xix–xxvii, 15. Lang (1983) wants to date the development of a Yahweh-alone party to the ninth century. And Tigay (1986), based on archaeological evidence, claims Israel was monotheistic even earlier. For a survey of various views, see Lang 1983, 14ff.

43. See, for example, Beck 1982; Dever 1984; Olyan 1988; M. S. Smith 1990, 16ff., 80–105.

44. Dover 1989, 6; Graves 1955, 117. Barkan (1991) and Saslow (1986) explore the Ganymede myth in the Renaissance.

45. Friedman (1987, 87) dates J and E to this period.

46. A possible exception is Jer. 2:27. See Olyan 1987.

47. I would like to thank Ron Hendel for bringing this source to my attention.

48. Cross (1973, 22–23) reviews the debate about whether El loses his erection prior to or after intercourse in this passage.

49. M. S. Smith (1990, 9) mistakenly assumes that Yahweh has a beard in Daniel's vision and hence conflates El and Yahweh more than is warranted.

50. Cross 1973, 74, 198; Mettinger 1979, 17; Friedman 1987, 47. M. S. Smith (1990, 51) discusses the bull imagery in relation to Yahweh and Baal.

51. Mettinger (1979, 19–20, 23) argues that the bull was at this point con-

sidered a legitimate symbol for Yahweh, but he also notes that Hosea (8:6) found it necessary to declare that the calf of Samaria was not a god. Mettinger thus sees the story of the golden bull (Exodus 32) as originally having no polemical edge, which was only added later. Halpern, by contrast, argues that the bull was only a footstool for Yahweh's throne.

5. Genital Speculation

1. I depart here from the Jewish Publication Society translation, which has "you shall be devoted" instead of "you shall know the Lord" (JPS 1985).

2. Leith (1989, 103) also notes the ambiguity of the term "knowing." I thus disagree with Andersen and Freedman, who write, "The idiom does not describe sexual intercourse, although the verb is so used elsewhere in the Bible, since in that usage the subject is male." They do admit, however, that "the word 'to know' is rich with intimate personal overtones. It is Yahweh himself who will be known" (1980, 283–84). Wolff (1974, 53) completely ignores the sexual overtones.

3. Wevers 1969, 121; Greenberg 1983, 277; Eichrodt 1970, 205.

4. Biale 1992, 14; Carmichael 1979, 74–93; Carmichael 1980.

5. See also Bal 1985, 100ff., on the issue of focalization.

6. Greenberg (1983, 278) rejects the claim of Eichrodt (1970, 205) and others that this text reflects the form of Israelite or ancient Near Eastern marriage. Greenberg suggests the oath here is an allusion to God's promise to the patriarchs.

7. See Hendel 1988; Mettinger 1979; von Rad 1962, 1:215–18.

8. Hendel 1988, 367. Only three male figures, which may be images of gods, have been found in archaeological strata from the twelfth to tenth centuries B.C.E. Moreover, the sites in which they were found had only become Israelite in that period. The best candidate for a picture of Yahweh is a coin dated to the fifth or early fourth century which is marked with the word "Yehud," the name of the Persian province of Judah. On the coin is a bearded god seated on a winged wheel and wearing a Greek garment (M. S. Smith 1990, 9).

9. For an early dating of this prohibition, see, for example, Halpern 1987. Mettinger (1979), by contrast, sees the aniconic prohibition as a generalization of Hosea's critique of the bull as a symbol of Yahweh. For overviews of how this prohibition has been interpreted, see Hendel 1988 and Childs 1974, 404–8. For specific interpretations discussed below, see von Rad 1962, 1:217; Cassuto 1967, 237; Mettinger 1979, 26; Noth 1962, 163.

10. Hendel (1988) offers a particularly good critique of these views.

11. M. S. Smith 1990, 9; Hendel 1988, 376; Hendel, unpublished.

12. In this case I follow Weinfeld's (1972, 278) translation rather than that of JPS 1985, which draws attention to the dimension of shame. The denigration of images as just human handiwork is apparently a later view of why images are proscribed (von Rad 1962, 1:215; von Rad 1966, 168). Von Rad views the law as ancient. Weinfeld, though admitting the ancient nature of the law, suggests it was reworked for deuteronomic purposes. In the Holiness Code, there is a similar association of ideas (Lev. 19:1–4).

13. The word "dishonor" (*maqĕleh*) as a verbal noun is in fact used on two occasions to mean the sense of shame brought on by the exposure of the genitals, in this case of Israel personified as a woman (Jer. 13:26; Nah. 3:5).

14. Etymologically speaking, the term *yĕqalēl* is not to be confused with *maqĕleh* (Weinfeld 1972, 277). Nonetheless, the two words might have been related in Israelite imagination, which tended to conflate and play on words of different etymologies.

15. It may even be possible that this list in the Holiness Code provided the basis for the curses in Deuteronomy 27 discussed earlier (Phillips 1973, 26).

16. A similar association is evident in other legal codes as well (Deut. 5:6–8; Exod. 34:11–17; and to some extent Deuteronomy 4).

17. Douglas (1966, 49) appropriately challenges the image of "Israel as a sponge" and asks why Israel would have absorbed some things but not others. See also Hendel 1988, 372–73. Obbink has suggested that the original rule was a prohibition, not on images of Yahweh, but on images of foreign gods, whose use was rejected in the Yahweh cult. Childs (1974, 406) discusses reasons why this view is not tenable.

18. Brown, Driver, and Briggs 1975, 888. Mettinger (1979, 18) notes the use of similar imagery in the golden calf incident. When Moses grinds up the bull and gives it to Israel to drink, it is like a test for a woman suspected of adultery (Numbers 5). Greenberg (1983, 297) also notes that the term "jealous" evokes the image of a jealous husband.

19. See Olyan 1993 for an important rethinking of this view of intermediaries.

20. Weinfeld, for example, writes that "these later conceptions . . . are diametrically opposed to the earlier view . . . antedating Deuteronomy. Thus in Exod. 24:9–11 we read about the leaders, etc., seeing God; in

Exod. 33:23 Moses is said to have *beheld God's back*, and Num. 12:8 speaks even more strikingly of Moses as gazing upon 'the form of the Lord' " (1972, 198).

21. I offer here a more literal translation than JPS 1985 to reflect the reference to God's face.

22. On some of the ideas that lead Freud to this insight, see Geller 1992. For a discussion of this upper and lower body displacement in myth and religion, see Eilberg-Schwartz and Doniger 1994.

23. Klein 1979 challenges the characterization of the Targumim as anti-anthropomorphic. Hayward (1981) reviews the literature and claims that the Memra is a theology of divine presence. See Olyan 1993 for a reconsideration of the so-called intermediaries.

24. On this idea, see Gallop 1982.

25. Carmichael (1974, 122) also sees a connection between God causing the divine name to dwell in Jerusalem and the importance of a man's name being preserved through the practice of levirate marriage.

26. Moran (1963, 78) points out that there is no trace of the marriage metaphor and notes that the preferred metaphor is father/son. But if the loving relationship between God and Israel is parallel to that of father/son, the two themes cannot be as compartmentalized as Moran claims.

27. Another possible translation is "circumcise the foreskin of your hearts."

28. Deut. 32:16, 21, belong to early poetry and may not be relevant here.

29. On the various uses of the term "love" discussed here see Moran 1963; Brown, Driver, and Briggs 1975, 12, 179; Weinfeld 1972, 328.

30. This was brought to my attention by Camp (1991).

31. I would like to thank Alice Bach for drawing my attention to this issue.

6. *Unmanning Israel*

1. The epigraph to this chapter is taken from the poem "Annul in Me My Manhood" by Brother Antoninus (1962, 86–87). Brother Antoninus, originally William O. Everson, played a leading role in the San Francisco literary renaissance. In 1949 he became a Catholic and then a Dominican Brother and has served at St. Albert's College in Oakland. I would like to thank Judith Plaskow for bringing this poem to my attention.

2. Bregman (1977) anticipates me in making this point. I would like to thank Ruth Tonner for drawing my attention to this essay.

3. This is in some sense the reverse of the process described by Castelli, who explores the masculinization of women in late antique Christianity. Christian thinkers of that period argued that the female should strive to be more like the male because "the male embodies the generic human

and therefore the potential for human existence to transcend differences and return to the same." Castelli writes that "in the Christian tradition, there is virtually no evidence for the movement across conventional gender boundaries by the 'male' toward the 'female,' except when negatively construed, as in polemics against homosexuality" (1991, 33).

4. Bakan (1979, 23–29, 103–33) anticipates a number of my arguments in this chapter. He, too, notes the way in which the divine role implies the redundancy of human men. And he senses that divine impregnation is in conflict with patrilineality. But Bakan makes a number of assumptions which I regard as problematic. He assumes that stories of divine impregnation reflect a stage in religious reflection in which paternity—the role of the male in conception—had not yet been discovered. In his view, divine impregnation of earthly women both justifies divine descent and is consistent with matrilineal descent. Bakan reads many of the stories of divine involvement in conception, such as the story of Isaac's birth, as originally about divine impregnation. In general, I find Bakan's ideas more compelling than his reading of the texts. I think his historical reconstruction of the discovery of the father's role in conception is mistaken, and I do not agree that stories of divine intervention in conception involve the complete absence of the human father. In these ancient stories, the father must always contribute the seed; God's role is limited to determining whether the woman's womb is open to that seed or not. Moreover, as Delaney (1986, 1991) has shown in a series of important studies, the notion of paternity was not discovered; it was created. It was a symbolic construction that interpreted the biological fact that sperm is required for conception. See also Jay 1992 for a discussion of how patrilineality is always in danger of being undermined by matrilineal connections. The fact that patrilineality was not always assumed in Israelite religion, therefore, need not imply a period in which matrilineality dominated or paternity was unknown.

5. As Michael Williams notes, "There is some diversity among the sources, but most speak of an expected union of Gnostics with their angels. However, the angels usually are said to play the male role of bridegroom, while the Gnostics are the female brides. Therefore, the remarkable thing about our passage in the *Gospel of Philip* is that rather than asserting that all Gnostics (men and women) are females, who must be united as brides with their angelic bridegrooms, this text places far more weight on the actual physical sex of a Gnostic: For a Gnostic man there is a female angelic power with whom he must be united" (1986, 207).

6. The column (1 QapGn, col. 2) of the manuscript in which this story be-

gins is missing. Judging from 1 Enoch, it is Noah's beauty that provokes Lamech's fear. See Fitzmyer 1971, 50–53, 78–79.

7. On the Testament of Reuben, see Kee 1983, 784; on the anticipation of the story of the virgin birth, see Fitzmyer 1971, 79.

8. Bakan (1977) and Bal (1988, 104–6) have noted the way in which the human male is rendered superfluous when God is imagined as a dispenser of fertility. But, as I argue, the human father is never totally dispensable in the Hebrew Bible because of the importance of genealogy, which is traced through the male seed, a point to which I return. See Otwell 1977, 56ff. for similar conclusions. Trible provides (1983, 34) a suggestive analysis of the association of God with wombs. However, she reads this association as stressing the way in which the female is divine, and ignores the way in which a male God controls female fertility. As Adler (1977) and Miller (1972) argue, when God is personified as a woman giving birth, this male God is appropriating female procreative abilities.

9. Teubal (1984, 65) argues that the term *aqarah* means "childless," not "barren." In other words, the women have chosen not to have children. But I do not see warrant in the text for this view.

10. Teubal (1984, 126), following Cyrus Gordon, notes that the term "took note of" (*paqad*) is also used to describe Samson visiting his wife with the intention of conjugal relations in Judges 15:1. On this basis, Teubal argues that Sarah was impregnated by God.

11. Pardes (1992, 44–45) does not pick up on the implications of this potential male redundancy.

12. See W. Williams 1986, 144, for more explicit examples of the feminization of the subordinate partner in intimate male relationships defined by heterosexual representations. Bakan (1979, 143, 28) anticipates me in seeing the feminization of Moses. But he understands the mechanism and motivation very differently. In his view, the discovery of paternity led to an association of the father with procreation, making the father into a "mother."

13. Milgrom (1990, 85) notes that the term translated as "nurse" may simply be "guardian," since it sometimes is used to refer to a male taking care of children (2 Kings 10:1, 5; Isa. 49:23). Trible (1983, 69), however, suggests that despite the masculine noun the image is of a nurse carrying a suckling child. Milgrom also notes that it is unclear whether Moses is angry with the people or with God or both.

14. The story of Hagar may come from the same E source (Friedman 1987, 247).

15. Noth (1962, 267) and Clements (1972, 225) suggest the priestly ele-

ments are later additions and the original is much older. Friedman (1987, 252) attributes the passage to P and thus understands it as serving priestly functions. For discussion of this term and its meaning see Albright 1944; Morgenstern 1925; Propp 1987.

16. Gressmann, Jirku, and Auerbach regard the passage as an etiology for the custom of wearing horned ritual masks in ancient Israel (cited in Propp 1987, 382). Similarly, Noth argues, "the present passage, which says nothing at all about the appearance of this mask, shows that the priest's mask (for Moses here appears in a priestly function) was not totally lacking in Israel even though we can discover no more about the time and place at which it was used" (1962, 267). As is obvious, the historical basis for the existence of such masks is pure speculation.

    In Hab. 3:4, the description of God seems to use the stem qrn in association with light. Cassuto (1967, 448), Noth (1962, 267), and Clements (1972, 225) favor this translation because it makes no sense to say the skin of the face is horned.

17. One interpreter sees here an attempt to tarnish the image of Moses by priests who trace their line to Aaron (Friedman 1987, 202). But there is no indication that the disfiguration of Moses' face is intended to undermine his status. On the contrary, the narrative presents it as a sign of his intimacy with God.

18. In fact, it derives from a stem that is used only on one other occasion, in an early poem in which it is placed in parallel to the word for clothing (Gen. 49:11) (Brown, Driver, and Briggs 1975, 691).

19. This was one of the most basic insights of structural linguistics (Saussure 1966) and social and structural anthropology (Radcliffe-Brown [1952] 1962; Lévi-Strauss 1963, 1973, 1978) and is widely accepted as a principle of literary and cultural interpretation.

20. After developing this argument, I discovered I had been anticipated by J. Sasson (1968). See also Eilberg-Schwartz 1990, 115–40, on the use of bovine images as foundational metaphors for Israelite ritual.

21. Friedman (1987, 251) assigns this passage to J.

22. Milgrom (1990, 394–95) notes that sexual intercourse is forbidden in the war camp, which is also a place of God's presence. Clements gets closer to the issue: "The period of hallowing before God appeared required abstinence from normal sexual relationships. This was to preclude any weakening of the vitality which holiness required, and did not imply that such relationships were regarded as opposed to God" (1972, 117).

23. For example, Sarna (1989, 24) views Eve as exaggerating God's prohi-

bition, but does not come to the same conclusion with regard to Moses (1991, 106).

24. Friedman (1987, 252) assigns this source to E.

25. There is also a place called Cushan in the Bible, which is a region in Midian. The Cushite woman may thus refer to Zipporah's ethnic origins (Friedman 1987, 78). But this explanation is problematic too. Moses' marriage to Zipporah occurred much earlier. Why would Aaron and Miriam suddenly protest the marriage now? It hardly solves the problem to assume that Moses left her behind (Milgrom 1990, 93) when he went to Egypt, since we are told she accompanied him back to Egypt.

26. See, for example, Gen. 21:11, which refers to the matter which distressed Abraham greatly "on account of his son." I come back to rabbinic interpretations of this passage in chapter 8. See also Biale's (1992, 33–34) and Boyarin's (1994) discussion of the rabbinic interpretation of this passage.

27. Gunkel, cited in Westermann 1984, 519, 521, and Noth 1962, 49. Westermann reviews the form critical issues and the suggestion that verses 28–29 are additions.

28. See, for example, Andersen and Freedman 1980, 607, and Mays 1969, 163.

29. See also Gevirtz 1975, 52–53. Sarna (1989, 162; 1970, 170–71), who notes the euphemism elsewhere, does not draw the conclusion that Jacob was struck on the genitals.

30. Smith's argument dovetails with my own analysis of circumcision (Eilberg-Schwartz 1990, 141–76), in which I explore how circumcision is a symbol of God's promise to Abraham of fertility.

31. Malul (1985) reviews the various interpreters who support this reading and, developing Albright's original proposal, discusses the technical etymological issues involved in interpreting this word. He points out that the whole passage has an Aramaic tinge to it. It should be noted that *pahad* is used to mean "thigh" in Job 40:17.

32. Nanette Stahl and I, working independently of each other, found that we were arriving at very similar conclusions. Stahl also notes that the term "thigh muscle" (*gid hannaseh*) derives from a stem (*nsh*) that sometimes means forgetting or oblivion. She observes the importance of this allusion to forgetfulness "given the strong lexical link Hebrew establishes between masculinity and memory in the root *z. k. r.* " She concludes that the term *gid hannaseh* serves both as a mechanism for "memorializing Jacob's struggle and creating distance from it. It also hints at the biblical

ambivalence towards the relationship between God and Israel that is being inaugurated with that very encounter" (1993, 124).

33. Ginsberg 1961, 342; Ackroyd 1963, 248; Andersen and Freedman 1980, 607. Mays (1969, 163) points out the parallelism of womb and manhood. Wolff (1974, 212), by contrast, translates *'ônô* as "in his wealth."

34. Mays, for example writes that "the interpretation of v. 4 is hindered because of the difficulty of deciding who is represented by the pronominal subjects and objects. Who prevails—angel or Jacob? Who finds whom at Bethel and who speaks to whom?" (1969, 163). Andersen and Freedman (1980, 609) suggest it is the angel who is crying.

35. Bakan (1979, 140–44) also notes the connection between circumcision and feminization but understands this as a way of signifying the appropriation by men of women's procreative abilities. Circumcision is one consequence of the discovery of paternity. See also Bettelheim 1962. Bettelheim explores the feminization of circumcision among Australian Aborigines, and views the association of circumcision and menstruation as a symbolic attempt by men to appropriate women's reproductive powers.

36. Friedman (1987, 248) assigns the story to J.

37. Sarna makes a similar point: "The part of the body used by Shechem in his violent passion will itself become the source of his own punishment!" (1989, 236).

38. Friedman (1987, 250) assigns the story to J.

39. Following Robinson 1986, 455; Childs 1974, 103. Childs also notes that Zipporah's central role implies Moses' incapacitation. Propp (forthcoming) arrives at the same conclusion when viewing this story as part of the J source.

40. As Robinson points out (1986, 451), a number of interpreters have drawn attention to the connection of these stories, including Buber, Fohrer, Hyatt, Kosmala, and Reinarch. Propp's (forthcoming) claim that Moses is being attacked for his earlier manslaughter does not account for the similarity of this story to the attack on Jacob. Nor does the interpretation that Moses had failed to circumcise himself or his son.

41. See, for example, Robinson 1986, 447; Childs 1974, 103; and Propp, forthcoming.

42. Kosmala 1962. See Pardes's (1992, 91) intriguing comparison to Egyptian myths of Osiris.

43. Pardes, then, is mistaken when she writes that "it is not a covenant between Yahweh and Moses. If it were, Moses would have had to be defined

as Yahweh's bride, given that it is God who traditionally plays the role of bridegroom in the Bible" (1992, 87).

44. Noth 1962, 50, and Wellhausen, cited in Childs 1974, 97–98. Childs also notes the lack of historical evidence to support these views.

45. This image of Yahweh as a bridegroom of blood has interesting similarities to the image of God adopting the foundling Israel and telling her "in your blood live" (Ezek. 16:6).

7. Women Rabbis and the Orchard of Heavenly Delights

1. See also Boyarin 1990, 1993, for an exploration of the eroticism between Israel and God and its associations with circumcision. Boyarin's primary focus is on how circumcision as a concrete and fleshly sign is linked to the rabbis' nonallegorical interpretations.

2. Pope (1977, 17) argues that the Song may always have had such an allegorical meaning and provides a survey of its various interpretations.

3. Unless otherwise noted, the English translations of SongRab are based on Freedman and Simon, 1983, vol. 9, with some of my own alterations.

4. I am departing from JPS 1985 in this translation in order to make the sages' interpretation comprehensible.

5. Elliot Wolfson (n.d.) has suggested that in mystical sources "eye" is used as a symbol for the phallus because of linguistic associations in Hebrew of "eye" and "fountain."

6. Freedman and Simon 1983, 9:21. The sages suggest several other interpretations of kisses as well. See SongRab 1:2, 4–5.

7. On the significance of parables in rabbinic literature in general, see Stern's excellent study (1991).

8. For the critical edition, see Theodor and Albeck 1965. Translations of GenRab follow Freedman and Simon 1983, vol. 1, with alterations.

9. The bracketed part is added from standard editions and does not appear in Theodor and Albeck. Freedman and Simon 1983, 1:502.

10. For a critical edition of Sifre Deuteronomy, see Finkelstein 1969. For an English translation, see Hammer 1986, 69.

11. See Wolfson's important discussion of this subject. Wolfson first (1987, 197) noted the significance of the feminization of men in a text from NumRab 12:10. He develops this theme at greater length in his important study of eroticism and visions of God in Jewish mysticism (1994). My own thinking about circumcision and feminization evolved at the same time as Boyarin's (1993).

12. In some manuscripts, the names of Ben Azzai and Ben Zoma are re-

versed. See Halperin 1980, 87; Lieberman 1955–73, 1:381; 5:1286–381.

13. In some manuscripts, it says Aqiba "ascended" and "descended" (Halperin 1980, 87; Lieberman 1955–73, 1:381–82; 5:1286–94). These variants are important in the debate over whether this story involves a visionary experience. The terms "ascent" and "descent" fit more readily a context of a vision of heaven.

14. The story actually appears in four different sources with variations (Tos. Hag. 2:3; PT Hag. 2:1, 77b; BT Hag. 14b; ShirRab 1:4). Recent treatments can be found in Scholem 1960, 14–20; Halperin 1980, 86–93; Halperin 1988, 31–37; Rowland 1982, 308–23; Urbach 1967, 1–28. Rowland presents the stories synoptically; Halperin (1980) compares them as well. The Tosefta text cited is found in Lieberman 1955–73, 1:381. The Palestinian Talmud has a significant difference in the final parable. In this context, the guard's duty is to look but not to touch.

15. For a discussion of these visions in more detail, see Gruenwald 1980, 32–71.

16. Translation by Isaac 1983, 20–21. On the dating of Enoch, see Isaac 1983, 7. Similar ascensions appear in the writings of Paul (2 Corin. 12:2), the Book of Revelation (4:2), and the Apocalypse of Abraham (11–28).

17. See Elliot Wolfson's 1994 study, which explores many of the same themes in later Jewish mysticism.

18. Scholem's (1946, 40–79; 1960, 14–20) reading marked an important shift in the interpretation of this story. Prior to his work, the story of the four sages was understood as a parable about the dangers of being involved in certain kinds of metaphysical speculation, such as Gnosticism. Scholem, however, understood this story as referring to a mystical experience similar to those in apocalyptic literature. He viewed the reference to *pardes* as corresponding to the use of Paradise in Paul. And he showed that the Talmudic version of this story could only be understood in light of Hekhalot texts, which were previously thought to date to a later period. See Halperin 1980, 2, for a review of the history of this story's interpretation.

19. And Gruenwald (1980, 48ff.), following Scholem, sees *pardes* as a reference to the heavenly paradise.

20. See Urbach 1967; Halperin 1980, 86–94; Halperin 1988, 31–36; Schäfer 1984; Rowland 1982, 306–23. Various objections have been made against Scholem's interpretation. But it is important to realize that

one interpretation does not rule out the other. *Pardes* may well be a metaphor for the dangers of Torah study, and it might refer in particular to the dangers of studying certain passages of Torah, for example, Ezekiel's chariot vision. A parable about the dangers of Torah study would suggest that the study of certain passages could generate visionary experiences. In general, I believe that many of the objections to Scholem's reading are legitimate. But I also think Scholem is correct to see this story as reflecting a visionary experience. I will develop my own reading of the story below.

21. See Halperin 1988, 200. The anonymous view of the Mishnah, which is often regarded as the majority opinion, forbids the reading of Ezekiel's vision, while R. Judah permits it.

22. Halperin (1988, 108) points out that in the Apocalypse of Abraham, Abraham hears only a voice. Rowland (1982, 280) argues that the avoidance of anthropomorphism accounts for the rabbinic worries about Ezekiel's vision.

23. Halperin 1988, 250. See also the comprehensive discussion of this issue in Marmorstein 1968. See Klein 1979 on the Targumim, and Neusner 1988 and Boyarin 1990 on rabbinic Judaism. For a full discussion of how the sages resist the Hellenistic and Greek philosophical thought of other late antique writers, see Boyarin's brilliant exploration (1993) of this issue.

24. Elliot Wolfson pointed out to me that this rabbinic comment could conceivably be rooted in Hekhalot or Shiur Qomah speculation. ˙

25. For a discussion of these sources from another perspective, see Altman 1944. In rabbinic reflections on what it means to be made in the image of God, the sages never suggest that having a body or form makes Adam different from God. For example, God created Adam of four attributes of the higher and lower beings: like the higher beings he stands upright, speaks, understands, and has peripheral vision. Like animals he eats, drinks, reproduces, defecates, and dies (GenRab 8:11, 14:3). According to another statement, three things were taken away from Adam once he sinned: his luster, his immortality, his height (GenRab 12:6). This suggests that Adam's original size and luster made him resemble God. The loss of these diminished his resemblance to God, but did not destroy the basic similarity in their forms.

26. See Boyarin 1990 for an important treatment of the Red Sea theme. The two versions are cited in Lieberman 1960, 121, and Halperin 1988, 225–26.

27. Halperin (1988, 251) notes that a reportedly early tannaitic source cited

in the Babylonian Talmud (Hag. 13a) does not prohibit the public study of those verses in Ezekiel that describe God: "How far does the 'Work of the Chariot' extend? Rabbi said, 'As far as the second *And I saw*' (Ezek. 1:27). R. Isaac said, 'As far as the word *ḥashmal*' (Ezek. 1:27)." Thus Halperin argues that anthropomorphism cannot be the reason for the restrictions on studying the chariot vision. But it is not in fact clear that in its original form this baraita forbade the study of Ezekiel 1:27. The question "How far does the 'Work of the Chariot' extend?" may itself be a later editorial addition. The original statements may refer to how far one may study, as the Talmud later suggests.

I have my own reservations about Halperin's argument about the calf. The Babylonian Talmud (Hag. 13b) says that Ezekiel pleaded with God to remove the calf face from the chariot because of its association with the golden calf. If the association of the calf in Ezekiel's vision was so problematic and had to be suppressed, it is doubtful that the Talmud would make this connection so explicit.

28. Other manuscripts read "the appearance of a man" (Levey 1987, 22–23).

29. Levey 1987, 22–23 (italics added). For the Aramaic text, see Sperber 1962, 3:267–68.

30. M. Cohen 1985, 127. For example, Sefer Haqqomah describes God this way: "From the place of the seat of His glory and up [is a distance of] 1,180,000,000 parasangs. From the place of the seat of His glory and down [is a distance of] 1,180,000,000 parasangs." Sefer Hashi'ur describes God this way: "The distance from His knees to His thigh(s), may He be blessed, is 244,250,000 sheqalim. The name of His loins is Asam Gig Vahu, may He be blessed—this cover (the space between) His thigh(s) and his neck. From the seat of His glory and up (is a total of) 1,180,000,000 (M. Cohen 1985, 31).

31. Halperin (1980, 39–51) argues that the Talmud preserves the oldest version of this story, which is reshaped and edited in the Tosefta version.

32. See Hyman 1979, 2:227. The 1937 edition of Hyman also cites Pirkei deRabbi Eliezer 4:17, which is not cited in the 1979 edition.

33. B. Hag. 31a, Pirkei de Rabbi Eliezer 4:17 in some manuscripts.

34. Hyman 1979, 2:227: PT Suk. 4:3 16a; BT Sot. 17a; BT Men. 43b; BT Hul. 89a; Mek. de Rashbi, p. 118; SifreNum Beshallah 115; GenRab 27; NumRab 4:12, 19:4; EcclRab 2:20, 8; TanhHukkat 6; TanhBub Bereshit 12b; Beshallah 30a; Pesiqta de Rab Kahana 36b; Pesiqta Rabbati 14:10.

35. Elliot Wolfson pointed out to me that this interpretation of *guf* is also implied in *Sefer Bahir*, a medieval mystical work.

36. Pope (1977, 303) discusses the view that the Song refers to three protagonists: a male lover, female lover, and king. We know that mystical speculation was closely linked to the study of the Song of Songs. Indeed, by the mid third century, Origen reports that Jews prohibited both the study of the Song of Songs and Ezekiel, as well as the beginning of Genesis and the end of Ezekiel, which discusses the building of the Temple (Halperin 1988, 26). Lieberman's 1960 essay, though suggestive, needs to be revised to take account of the problems of dating. Lieberman takes for granted that statements attributed to tannaitic sages in late rabbinic documents were said by those early sages. It is important to consider how the Song of Songs is treated in the earliest documents, and whether its treatment in that context is consistent with the treatment by early sages cited in later documents. See Dan 1992 and Halperin 1980 for judicious treatments of how this early rabbinic mysticism might be related to later developments in Hekaloth literature.

37. Lieberman (1960) notes that the contrast might be between this Song and all the other songs or poems in Scripture.

38. There is another reason the verse from Proverbs is appropriate to describe Ben Zoma. It appears in the context of a proverb that describes being in the king's presence: "Remove the wicked from the king's presence and his throne will be established in justice. Do not exalt yourself in the king's presence; do not stand in the place of nobles. For it is better to be told, 'Step up here,' than to be degraded in the presence of the greater. Do not let what your eyes have seen be vented rashly in a quarrel" (Prov. 25:5–8).

This proverb is interpreted elsewhere as referring to how Moses should conduct himself in the presence of God. Because Moses initially hid his face in God's presence, God decided to send Moses to Pharaoh. Similarly, it is better to be humble at first and be promoted later than to be haughty and asked to step down (LevRab 1:5; ExodRab 35:5). The citation from Proverbs is doubly appropriate. It refers to the proper etiquette in a king's presence and it evokes the image of honey on the lips, an allusion to the Song of Songs and Ezekiel.

39. Halperin 1980, 91; Urbach 1967, 14; Scholem 1960, 14; and Lieberman 1955–73, 5:1289, citing DeutRab 7:4.

40. Jastrow ([1903], 899–900) cites the following examples where "shoots" has this metaphoric meaning: PT Yeb. 1:2 refers to the planting of five sons; BT Tan. 5b: "may all shoots taken from you be like yourself." The verb "to plant" sometimes means "to beget."

41. See Gollancz [1908] 1973, 216, for a translation, and Melamed 1921, 88, for the Aramaic original.

42. Rowland 1982, 320. As Rowland notes, this is speculation because we have no evidence that Ben Azzai died in that way.

43. See for example PT Hag. 77a, which describes a sage's discourse on the chariot vision that causes angels to appear and dance like wedding guests before the bridegroom.

44. On the issue of eroticism and visions of God in rabbinic literature, see Boyarin 1990. Wolfson (1994) explores this issue in detail in later mystical sources.

45. According to Jastrow ([1903], 137–80), *qlstr* is a Greek term for crystal.

46. SifreNum Shalach 115, p. 125; YT Suc. 4:5; BT Sot. 17a; BT Hul. 89a; BT Men. 43b.

47. See Kirschner 1983 as well for a more general exploration of the treatment of Nadab and Abihu in rabbinic thought.

48. For parallel versions of this story, see ExodRab 3:1, 45:3; NumRab 2:25; Pesiqta de Rav Kahana 26:9; Tanh Aharei 6; TanhBub Aharei 7. The expression "uncovered their heads" is missing in other versions of this story. After my work on these sources, I subsequently found them discussed in Chernus 1982a, 74–87, but without attention to the issue of eroticism.

49. This idea of feasting on the vision of God thus explains how human figures like Moses can remain with God for extended periods of time without eating (Exod. 34:28; Deut. 9:9). There is precedent in apocalyptic literature for this idea of feasting on the sight of God. In the Apocalypse of Abraham (12:1), Abraham feasts on the sight of an angel for forty days and nights (Halperin 1988, 106, 111).

50. I believe the text suggests that they are staring at someone who is eating and drinking, but it is possible it means that while eating and drinking they are staring at another person. The latter metaphor, however, does not suggest the same violation of boundaries as the former.

51. A priest incurs the death penalty for entering sacred precincts with unbound or unshorn hair (M. Kel 1:9; T. Ker. 1:5; BT San. 83b). Ironically, this prohibition is based on the biblical law forbidding Aaron and his sons from baring their heads in mourning for the death of Nadab and Abihu (Lev. 10:6). On long hair and sexuality see Leach 1958; Freud [1922] 1950; and the various essays in Eilberg-Schwartz and Doniger 1994.

52. On "uncovering" see Jastrow's citations ([1903], 1235) and Wolfson's

discussion (1994) of a similar nexus of ideas in Kabbalah. Feet is a rabbinic euphemism for the penis. For example, urine is called "water of the feet" (*May raglaim*). See especially Wolfson's superb essay (1992) on the use of feet as a euphemism.

53. Margoliot 1972, 2:110–11. For English, see Freedman and Simon 1983, 4:260.

54. Goldin 1955, 18–19; Biale 1983, 33–34. Boyarin (1993) also deals with these texts in the context of exploring the tension between loving Torah and loving one's wife.

55. See Biale's (1992, 33–57) and Boyarin's (1993) more developed reading of this issue in Talmudic discourse.

8. A Sexless Father and His Procreating Sons

1. I considered the development of Israelite monotheism and the possibility of Yahweh having a consort, Asherah, in chapter 4. The literature of the Hebrew Bible does not reflect the notion of Yahweh as a sexually active God.

2. This is a form of "legal fatherhood," about which I will have more to say later. But it should not be confused with spiritual fatherhood in which a father and son have no genealogical relation. Here, the brother performs the levirate duty so that the deceased will have a son in the patrilineage.

3. I disagree with the view of Daube (1977), who argues that procreation was not a duty but a blessing in ancient Israel. Daube's formulation in my view is too legalistic. The fact that procreation is described as a blessing which God bestows first on humanity and then on Abraham's descendants in particular means that it was viewed as central to the identity of the Israelites. See Eilberg-Schwartz 1990, 141–76.

4. On the blessings of fertility and the importance of male descendants, see Bird 1981, 157; J. Cohen 1989, 13–24; Eilberg-Schwartz 1990, 163–76; Sapp 1977, 10, 12; and Jay 1985, 283–309; 1988, 52–70.

5. My analysis of circumcision in this context is is based on my more extensive treatment in Eilberg-Schwartz 1990, 141–77. It remains unclear, however, whether these meanings of circumcision are superimposed upon or replace the themes of emasculation and feminization that appear in the myths of the Jahwist writer, the Deuteronomist, and in early mythic fragments (see chapter 7). In other words, because of the priests' distinctive concern with reproduction and male lineage, circumcision's meaning may have changed.

6. Adler 1977; Trible 1983, 72–115; Bal 1987, 104–30; Pardes 1992. See

also Boyarin 1993 for an important discussion of how these myths might contrast with Greek views of woman's origin. In my view, some of the differences Boyarin posits between the traditions are located within Jewish tradition.

7. Adler 1977. Delaney (1977, 1986, 1990, 1992) explores the ways in which divine creation is made parallel to the male creative role in procreation.

8. Cassuto 1978, 34–35; Barr 1968–69; and Bird 1981. Westermann (1984, 147) provides a review of interpreters who hold this position. James Barr (1959, 31–38) originally suggested that the "image of God" passage presupposes a resemblance between the human and divine forms. But he subsequently retracted that view based on his historical and linguistic analysis (1968–69, 11–26).

9. Bird 1981, 140; J. Cohen 1989, 16; Miller 1972, 289–304; von Rad 1976, 59. For a review of the relevant arguments and the ancient Near Eastern evidence, see especially Westermann 1984, 150ff.

10. On God's human form see Barr 1959; Kaufman 1972, 236–37; von Rad 1976, 58; Westermann 1984, 149ff.; Miller 1972, 292; Mopsik 1989; Boyarin 1990; Weinfeld 1972, 191–210.

11. Sapp 1977, 8; Mopsik 1989, 52. This is not the only reading of the relation between Gen. 1:28 and 5:1–3. I discuss an alternative below. Furthermore, not all commentators agree with this interpretation of *ṣelem*. For a different reading, see Barr 1968–69.

12. It is interesting to compare Bird and Trible on this issue. Bird notes that in other contexts the priestly writer treats the categories of "male" and "female" as applicable to animals. Trible, for her part, argues that in Genesis 1 the division into "male" and "female" is unique to humankind since the animals are divided "according to their kinds," a type of categorization that does not apply to humans.

Bird has also challenged Trible's interpretation for failing to pay sufficient attention to the place of Genesis 1 in the larger context of the priestly writings. To a certain extent, this criticism is valid. To read Genesis 1 as an example of incipient egalitarianism ignores the fact that the priestly writings generally privilege the male over the female. As noted previously, the priestly genealogies do not even mention the presence of wives. But Trible's reading cannot be dismissed out of hand. As I have suggested, the simultaneous creation of male and female in the myth was motivated by the priests' desire to legitimate procreation. But in order to do so the priests had to tolerate an implication that both male and female are made in the image of God. To reformulate Trible's question, then, it is interesting to ask how and why the priests managed to accommodate the association of "the female" with the image of God.

13. Von Rad 1976, 58; Sawyer 1974, 423–24; Speiser 1964, 7; Trible 1978, 13.

14. Miller 1972, 291. However, Barr (1968–69) argues that ṣelem was the term most apt for avoiding the suggestion of resemblance of the human body and divine form.

15. See 1 Mac. 1:14, 48; 2 Mac. 6:10. Josephus (Jos. Anti. 13:257) also reports that Hyrcanus forced the Idumeans to be circumcised. For a general discussion, see Rubin 1989, 105–17.

16. On these issues, see Harris 1964, 1972, and Lassarrague 1990, 53–82. Rubin (1989) argues that the rabbinic procedure called "periah" was introduced by the rabbis as a way to make circumcision irreversible. On circumcision as a sign of ethnic distinctiveness, see Collins 1985 and J. Z. Smith 1982, 1–18.

17. See Eilberg-Schwartz 1990 for references to the fuller discussion of this issue and for a more detailed version of the arguments below.

18. My own reading of this law developed from a suggestion made by Larry Hoffman. For other interpretations of these laws and the sages' view of procreation in general, see Feldman 1974, 46–59; J. Cohen 1989, 124–33; D. Biale 1992, 43; Daube 1977, 34–39. For the implication of these laws for women, see R. Biale 1984, 198–202. Other interpreters tend to read less suspiciously and take these laws more at face value. However, D. Biale (1984, 33–58) and Boyarin (1993) also explore the tension between Torah study and sexual desire. Both Boyarin and Biale tend to see the rabbis as much more positive about marriage and procreation than I do.

19. It is true that a man might be obligated to have several children if he follows the view of either of the houses on its own. Suppose, for example, a man follows the view of Hillel's house: that he must father a son and a daughter. But his wife gives birth to two or three daughters in succession or two or three males in succession. He must keep on until he has a child of the opposite sex. And on the view of the house of Shammai, if he has daughters, he must keep procreating until he has two sons. But consider the possibility that by recording both views the Mishnah in effect authorizes both as viable options. If so, then the only situation where a man must go on producing children is when he has all daughters. If he has two sons, or a son and daughter in succession, he could cease procreating on the view of at least one of the houses.

It is uncertain how large families were in antiquity. Roman law seems to have regarded a mother of three as having done her duty, but it is more difficult to determine what actual practice was (Veyne 1987, 13). Veyne suggests that the number of children may have increased toward the end of the second century c.e. when Stoic and Christian morality began to take hold. A study is needed to determine how large rabbinic families were and whether they were in line with the typical size of families in Palestine at the time. The wars in 70 and 132–35 did lead to a devastation of the population. Biale (1992, 35) suggests these circumstances may have been linked to a desire to increase the population, but the disruption and dislocation might also have provoked a wish for fewer children. I do not recall very many stories in rabbinic literature of sages with large families.

My interpretation understands the Mishnah to be reflecting a move toward asceticism, which was a much broader trend in the late antique period. See, for example, Brown 1988 and Wimbush 1990. D. Biale (1992, 37–40) explores the ways asceticism underlies rabbinic views. For a general discussion, see Fraade 1986.

20. See Feldman 1974, 54; R. Biale 1984, 202; Baskin 1989, 105–6.

21. This interpretation construes the word "subdue" as a second person singular imperative with pronominal suffix.

22. The issue of status is more complicated than my presentation of it here. For a fuller analysis, see S. Cohen 1985a, 1985b. Cohen argues that this method of figuring descent paralleled Roman law.

23. My thinking about this law was influenced by the comments of one of my students, Laurie Davis, in my course "Women and Judaism."

24. See also J. Cohen (1989, 110–14) for a discussion of this source. In GenRab 17:2 a similar view is reported but not cited in Ben Azzai's name.

25. In the printed edition of the Tosefta, it says "annuls the image" rather than "diminishes" which is in some manuscripts and other sources.

26. Some of the manuscripts of the Tosefta and Genesis Rabbah do not include Ben Azzai's words comparing celibacy to murder. See Lieberman 1955–73, 6:75; Theodor and Albeck 1965, 1:326. In general, Ben Azzai's asceticism is viewed in secondary literature as an exception to the dominant tendencies of rabbinic tradition, a position from which I dissent. See J. Cohen 1989, 113–14; D. Biale 1992, 34, 36; Boyarin 1993; Daube 1977, 37–38. Although in one context Biale treats Ben Azzai as an exception to the rule, in another context he suggests that the depiction of Ben Azzai might be reflecting a more general inclination toward asceticism, a view similar to my own.

27. I translated here into colloquial English. A more literal translation

would be "Teachings are becoming when they are uttered by those who practice them, but you, son of Azzai, preach well, but do not fulfill your teaching" (Freedman and Simon 1983, 1:280).

28. See also J. Cohen 1989, 85–88. GenRab 12:7; PT Ket. 5:7, 37b; and GenRab 76:7 refer to animal behavior for making judgments about regulating human sexuality.

9. *The Virgin Birth and Sons of God*

1. Barkan (1979) also notes the tension between divine and human fatherhood, but he argues that the notion of divine fatherhood developed historically prior to the idea of human fatherhood.

2. Brown (1977) notes that "virgin birth" is technically an incorrect description of the stories of Jesus' conception, which focus on the conception and not the birth itself.

3. The whole issue of precedents is a touchy one because significant theological consequences are at stake. At issue for many Christians has been the virgin birth's possible historicity. Finding or discounting Jewish or pagan precedents serves either to justify or belittle its possible reality. If pagan precedents are discovered (Machen [1930] 1965, 317–79; Boslooper 1962, 135–89), then the historical truth of Jesus' miraculous birth is potentially called into question.

   The possibility of Jewish precedents is somewhat more complex. In this case, the question is whether the idea of the virgin birth is a fulfillment of the Old Testament prophecy. In other words, assuming that the Old Testament is God's word, does Jesus' birth prove his messiahship? More specifically, does Isaiah 7:14 anticipate the virgin birth of the Messiah, as the Gospel of Matthew suggests? Naturally, Jews and Christians have debated the issue. Those with a historical sensitivity tend to believe that Isaiah is referring, not to a virgin, but to a young woman of marriageable age (Brown 1977, 145ff.; Fitzmyer 1981, 336). Apart from the passage in Isaiah and possibly one text from Qumran (Fitzmyer 1981, 339), interpreters tend to agree that the idea of a virgin birth is foreign to Jewish sensibility. The closest we come to this idea are stories about barren women whose wombs God opens. Many interpreters use the lack of precedent as evidence of the virgin birth's facticity, arguing that if the idea was not borrowed from pagan or Jewish sources, there would be no reason to imagine it (Brown 1977, 142 n.).

4. In Jubilees it is not clear where these spirits come from. But in 1 Enoch 15:8ff. these spirits derive from the giants who were destroyed. On the nature of the Watchers in general see Wintermute 1985, 47–48.

5. Lang (1985) makes a somewhat analogous argument in the process of exploring the different images of afterlife, with particular attention to whether procreation and sexuality are imagined as part of an afterlife. I also discuss this point at greater length in Eilberg-Schwartz 1990, 195–216.

6. Unless otherwise noted, I am following the translation of the Revised Standard Version.

7. Brown 1977, 29–47. For an alternative and to my mind less convincing view that argues that Paul and Mark were familiar with the virgin birth, see Edwards 1943, 27–116.

8. See Boyarin 1993 and 1994 for a discussion of how the reading of circumcision and the body was related in late antique Judaism and Christianity to attitudes toward the corporate notions of Israel.

9. On the unexpectedness of their inclusion, see Albright 1971, 5, and Johnson 1969, 146ff. See, however, the objections of Brown (1977, 71–72). When women are mentioned in the genealogies of the Hebrew Bible, it tends to be in contexts where there is a need to distinguish among different groups who were traditionally traced to the same figure in the past (Johnson 1969, 153).

10. Schaberg (1987, 32–33) argues that these women were outside the patriarchal social structure: they risk their status through their sexual relations and are subsequently taken under the protection of some male. In each of these cases, moreover, there is an absence of divine intervention and guidance. This anticipates the illegitimate pregnancy of Mary.

11. See also Schaberg 1987, 35.

12. See Brown 1977, 138; Albright 1971, 9; and Johnson 1969, 185, following Strack and Billerbeck 1965, 1:35.

13. Brown 1977, 239ff., and Fitzmyer 1981, 310. But there is evidence in this case as well that the genealogy and infancy narratives were meant to be read together.

14. There is some debate as to whether the Lucan account contains an idea of a virginal conception or whether it could be understood as a conception in the usual human way. Brown gives the reasons for believing the idea of the virginal conception is present. And he discusses the debate over when the idea was introduced into Luke (1977, 298ff.). Fitzmyer originally argued that Luke did not contain an account of the virgin birth but then retracted in light of Brown's argument (1981, 337).

15. For an important analysis of this passage, which explores how the female head is treated as a sexual member, see D'angelo 1994.

16. Bynum (1989), for example, does not consider the possibility that the

homoerotic dilemma generated for men by Christ may explain why men's religious experience may be less somatic than women's. This is why women are more apt to write in intense bodily metaphors, some suggestive of intercourse. Both Steinberg (1983) and Bynum (1991) in her review of Steinberg fail to consider how the issue of homoeroticism may be involved in the depiction of the naked Christ.

Conclusion

1. This is not necessarily the case for all people. Historically speaking, it seems that many Jews have felt intimate with this impersonal distant Father.
2. Rich (1976) is an example of a feminist writer who dwells on her relationships to her parents and the implications for her feminism.
3. For feminist reflections on similar issues, see Hagan 1992.

References

Aberbach, M. 1976. "The Relations between Master and Disciple in the Talmudic Age." In *Exploring the Talmud*, vol. 1, ed. by Haim Z. Dimitrovsky. New York: Ktav.

Abraham, Hilda, and Ernst L. Freud, eds. 1965. *A Psycho-Analytic Dialogue: The Letters of Sigmund Freud and Karl Abraham 1907–1926*. New York: Basic.

Abraham, Karl. [1912] 1955. "Amenhotep IV: Psycho-analytical Contributions Towards the Understanding of his Personality and of the Monotheistic Cult of Aton." In *Clinical Papers and Essays on Psycho-Analysis*, 262–90. London: Hogarth.

Ackroyd, Peter R. 1963. "Hosea and Jacob." *Vetus Testamentum* 13:245–59.

Adler, Elaine June. 1989. "The Background for the Metaphor of Covenant as Marriage in the Hebrew Bible." Ph.D. diss. University of California, Berkeley, California.

Adler, Rachel. 1977. " 'A Mother-Role in Israel': Aspects of the Mother-Role in Jewish Myth." In *Beyond Androcentrism*, ed. Rita M. Gross, 237–59. Missoula: Scholars.

Albright, W. F. 1944. "The 'Natural Face' of Moses in the Light of Ugaritic." *Bulletin for the American School of Oriental Research* 94:32–35.

Albright, W. F., and C. S. Mann. 1971. *Matthew*. The Anchor Bible Series. Garden City, N. Y.: Doubleday.

Alcoff, Linda. 1988. "Cultural Feminism versus Post-Structuralism: The Identity Crisis in Feminist Theory." *Signs* 13 (3): 405–36.

Allen, Don Cameron. 1963. *The Legend of Noah: Renaissance Rationalism in Art, Science, and Letters*. Urbana: University of Illinois Press.

Alon, Gedalyahu. 1977. "The Sons of the Sages." In *Jews, Judaism, and the Classical World*, trans. Israel Abrahams, 436–57. Jerusalem: Magnes.

Alpert, Rebecca. 1989. "In God's Image: Coming to Terms with Leviticus."

In *Twice Blessed: On Being Lesbian, Gay, and Jewish*, ed. Christie Balka and Andy Rose, 61–70. Boston: Beacon.

———. 1992. "Challenging Male/Female Complementarity: Jewish Lesbians and the Jewish Tradition." In *People of the Body: Jews and Judaism from an Embodied Perspective*, ed. Howard Eilberg-Schwartz, 361–77. Albany: SUNY Press.

Alt, Albrecht. 1966. "The God of the Fathers." In *Essays on Old Testament History and Religion*. Garden City, N.Y.: Doubleday.

Altman, Alexander. 1944. "The Gnostic Background of the Rabbinic Adam Legends." *Jewish Quarterly Review* 35:371–91.

Andersen, Francis I., and David Noel Freedman. 1980. *Hosea*. The Anchor Bible Series. Garden City, N.Y.: Doubleday.

Armstrong, Carol M. 1986. "Degas and the Female Body." In *The Female Body in Western Culture*, ed. Susan Rubin Suleiman, 223–42. Harvard: Cambridge University Press.

Bailey, Lloyd. 1989. *Noah: The Person and the Story in History and Tradition*. Columbia: University of South Carolina Press.

Bakan, David. 1958. *Sigmund Freud and the Jewish Mystical Tradition*. New York: Schocken.

———. 1979. *And They Took Themselves Wives*. New York: Harper and Row.

Bal, Mieke. 1985. *Narratology*. Translated by Christine van Boheemen. Toronto: University of Toronto Press.

———. 1987. *Lethal Love: Feminist Literary Readings of Biblical Love Stories*. Bloomington: Indiana University Press.

———. 1988. *Death and Dissymmetry: The Politics of Coherence in the Book of Judges*. Chicago: University of Chicago Press.

Barkan, Leonard. 1991. *Transuming Passion: Ganymede and the Erotics of Humanism*. Stanford: Stanford University Press.

Barr, James. 1959. "Theophany and Anthropomorphism in the Old Testament." *Vetus Testamentum, Supplements* 7:31–38.

———. 1968–69. "The Image of God in the Book of Genesis—A Study of Terminology." *Bulletin of the John Rylands Library* 51:11–26.

Baskin, Judith. 1989. "Rabbinic Reflections on the Barren Wife." *Harvard Theological Review*. 82 (1): 101–14.

Bayer, Ronald. 1987. *Homosexuality and American Psychiatry*. Princeton: Princeton University Press.

Beck, Pirhiya. 1982. "The Drawings from Ḥorvat Teiman (Kuntillet ʿAjrud)." *Tel Aviv* 9:3–86.

Berger, John. 1972. *Ways of Seeing*. New York: Viking.

Berman, Saul. 1976. "The Status of Women in Halakhic Judaism." In *The Jewish Woman*, ed. Elizabeth Koltun. New York: Schocken.

Bettelheim, Bruno. 1962. *Symbolic Wounds*. New York: Collier.

Beyerlin, Walter. 1965. *Origins and History of the Oldest Sinaitic Traditions*. Translated by S. Rudman. Oxford: Blackwell.

Biale, David. 1982. "The God with Breasts: El Shaddai in the Bible." *History of Religions*. 21 (3): 240–56.

———. 1992. *Eros and the Jews: From Biblical Israel to Contemporary America*. New York: Basic.

Biale, Rachel. 1984. *Women and Jewish Law*. New York: Schocken.

Bird, Phyllis. 1981. " 'Male and Female He Created Them': Gen. 1:27b in the Context of the Priestly Account of Creation." *Harvard Theological Review* 74 (2): 129–59.

———. 1989. " 'To Play the Harlot': An Inquiry into an Old Testament Metaphor." In *Gender and Difference in Ancient Israel*, ed. Peggy Day. Minneapolis: Fortress.

Boslooper, Thomas. 1962. *The Virgin Birth*. Philadelphia: Westminster.

Boswell, John. 1980. *Christianity, Social Tolerance, and Homosexuality*. Chicago: University of Chicago Press.

Boyarin, Daniel. 1990. "The Eye in the Torah: Ocular Desire in Midrashic Hermeneutic." *Critical Inquiry* 16 (3): 532–50.

———. 1992. "The Great Fat Massacre: Sex, Death, and the Grotesque Body in the Talmud." In *People of the Body: Jews and Judaism from an Embodied Perspective*, ed. Howard Eilberg-Schwartz, 69–100. Albany: SUNY Press.

———. 1993. *Carnal Israel: Reading Sex in Talmudic Culture*. Berkeley: University of California Press.

———. 1994. *A Radical Jew: Paul and the Politics of Identity*. Berkeley: University of California Press.

Bregman, Lucy. 1977. "Religion and Madness: Schreber's *Memoirs* as Personal Myth." *Journal of Religion and Health* 16 (2): 119–35.

Brother Antonius [William O. Everson]. 1962. "Annul in Me My Manhood." In *The Crooked Lines of God*. Detroit: University of Detroit Press.

Brown, Francis, S. R. Driver, and C. A. Briggs, eds. [1907] 1975. *A Hebrew and English Lexicon of the Old Testament*. Oxford: Clarendon.

Brown, Peter. 1988. *The Body and Society: Men, Women, and the Renunciation of Sexuality in Early Christianity*. New York: Columbia University Press.

Brown, Raymond E. 1977. *The Birth of the Messiah: A Commentary on the Infancy Narratives in Matthew and Luke*. Garden City, N.Y.: Doubleday.

Bryk, Felix. [1930] 1970. *Sex and Circumcision*. Reprint of *Circumcision in Man and Woman*. North Hollywood, Calif.: Brandon House.

Butler, Judith. 1990. *Gender Trouble: Feminism and the Subversion of Identity*. New York: Routledge.

Bynum, Caroline Walker. 1982. *Jesus as Mother*. Berkeley: University of California Press.

———. 1986. "Introduction: The Complexity of Symbols." In *Gender and Religion*, ed. Caroline Walker Bynum, Stevan Harrell, and Paula Richman, 1–22. Boston: Beacon.

———. 1989. "The Female Body and Religious Practice in the Later Middle Ages." In *Fragments for a History of the Human Body*, part 1, ed. Michel Feher, Ramona Naddaff, and Nadia Tazi. New York: Zone.

———. 1991. *Fragmentation and Redemption*. New York: Zone.

Camp, Claudia V. 1985. *Wisdom and the Feminine in the Book of Proverbs*. Sheffield: Almond.

———. 1991. "What's So Strange about the Strange Woman." In *The Bible and the Politics of Exegesis*, ed. D. Jobling, P. Day, and G. Sheppard, 17–32. Cleveland: Pilgrim.

Campenhausen, Hans Von. 1964. *The Virgin Birth in the Theology of the Ancient Church*. London: SCM.

Carmichael, Calum. 1974. *The Laws of Deuteronomy*. Ithaca: Cornell University Press.

———. 1979. *Women, Law, and the Genesis Traditions*. Edinburgh: Edinburgh University Press.

———. 1980. "'Treading' in the Book of Ruth." *Zeitschrift für Alttestamentliche Wissenschaft* 92:248–66.

Cassuto, U. 1967. *A Commentary on the Book of Exodus*. Translated by Israel Abrahams. Jerusalem: Magnes.

———. 1978. *A Commentary on the Book of Genesis* [Hebrew]. Part 1. Jerusalem: Magnes.

Castelli, Elizabeth. 1991. "'I Will Make Mary Male': Pieties of the Body and Gender Transformation of Christian Women in Late Antiquity." In *BodyGuards: The Cultural Politics of Gender Ambiguity*, ed. Julia Epstein and Kristina Straub. New York: Routledge.

Chabat, C. Barry. 1982. *Freud on Schreber*. Amherst: University of Massachusetts Press.

Chernin, Kim. 1981. *The Obsession: Reflections on the Tyranny of Slenderness*. New York: Harper and Row.

Chernus, Ira. 1982a. *Mysticism in Rabbinic Judaism*. Berlin: de Gruyter.

————. 1982b. "Visions of God in Merkabah Mysticism." *Journal for the Study of Judaism*. 8 (1–2): 123–46.

Childs, Brevard S. 1974. *Exodus*. Philadelphia: Westminster.

Chodorow, Nancy J. 1978. *The Reproduction of Mothering*. Berkeley: University of California Press.

Christiansen, Anthony. Forthcoming. "Masculinity and Its Vicissitudes: Reflections on Some Gaps in the Psychoanalytic Theory of Masculine Identity Formation." *Psychoanalytic Review*.

Clements, Ronald A. 1972. *Exodus*. Cambridge: Cambridge University Press.

Cohen, H. Hirsch. 1974. *The Drunkenness of Noah*. Tuscaloosa: University of Alabama Press.

Cohen, Jeremy. 1989. *Be Fertile and Increase, Fill the Earth and Master It*. Ithaca: Cornell University Press.

Cohen, Martin. 1985. *The Shiʿur Qomah: Texts and Rescensions*. Tübingen: Mohr.

Cohen, Shaye. 1985a. "The Matrilineal Principle in Historical Perspective." *Judaism*. 34 (1): 5–13.

————. 1985b. "The Origins of the Matrilineal Principle in Rabbinic Law." *AJS Review* 10 (1): 19–54.

————. 1989. "Crossing the Boundary and Becoming a Jew." *Harvard Theological Review* 2 (1): 13–34.

Collins, John J. 1985. "A Symbol of Otherness: Circumcision and Salvation in the First Century." In *To See Ourselves as Others See Us*, ed. Jacob Neusner and Ernest S. Frerichs, 163–86. Chico: Scholars.

Collins, Sheila. 1976. *A Different Heaven and Earth*. Valley Forge, Penn.: Judson.

Cooke, G. A. 1951. *The Book of Ezekiel*. The International Critical Commentary. Edinburgh: Clark.

Cooper, Jerrold S. 1989. "Enki's Member: Eros and Irrigation in Sumerian Literature." In *Dumu-E₂*, ed. Hermann Behrens et al. Philadelphia: Occasional Publications of the Samuel Noah Kramer Fund.

Corbett, Ken. 1993. "The Mystery of Homosexuality." *Psychoanalytic Psychology* 10 (3): 345–58.

Cross, Frank Moore. 1973. *Canaanite Myth and Hebrew Epic*. Cambridge: Harvard University Press.

Daly, Mary. 1973. *Beyond God the Father*. Boston: Beacon.

Dan, Joseph. 1992. *The Revelation of the Secret of the World: The Beginning of Jewish Mysticism in Late Antiquity*. Occasional Paper 2. Providence: Brown Judaic Studies.

D'angelo, Mary Rose. 1994. "Veils, Virgins, and the Tongues of Men and Angels: Women's Heads in Early Christianity." In *Off with Her Head: The Female Head in Religion, Myth, and Culture*, ed. Howard Eilberg-Schwartz and Wendy Doniger. Berkeley: University of California Press.

Daube, David. 1977. *The Duty of Procreation*. Edinburgh: Edinburgh University Press.

Dayal, Har. 1975. *The Bodhisattva Doctrine in Sanskrit Literature*. Delhi: Motilal Banarsidass.

De Certeau, Michel. 1986. *Heterologies: Discourse on the Other*. Translated by Brian Massumi. Minneapolis: University of Minnesota Press.

Delaney, Carol. 1977. "The Legacy of Abraham." In *Beyond Androcentrism*, ed. Rita Gross. Missoula: Scholars.

———. 1986. "The Meaning of Paternity and the Virgin Birth Debate." *Man* 21 (3): 494–513.

———. 1990. "Seeds of Honor, Fields of Shame." In *Honor and Shame and the Unity of the Mediterranean*, ed. David Gilmore. American Anthropological Association Special Publications 22. Washington, D.C.

———. 1991. *The Seed and the Soil: Gender and Cosmology in a Turkish Village Society*. Berkeley: University of California Press.

Dever, W. 1984. "Asherah, Consort of Yahweh? New Evidence from Kuntillet ʿArjûrd." *Bulletin for the American Schools of Oriental Research*. 255:26–28.

Devor, Holly. 1989. *Gender Blending: Confronting the Limits of Duality*. Bloomington: Indiana University Press.

Dimrock, Edward. 1966. "Doctrine and Practice among the Vaiṣṇavas of Bengal." In *Krishna: Myths, Rites, and Attitudes*, ed. Milton Singer. Honolulu: East-West Center Press.

Doane, Mary Ann. 1982. "Film and the Masquerade—Theorising the Female Spectator." *Screen* 23 (3–4): 74–88.

———. 1985. "The Clinical Eye: Medical Discourses in the 'Woman's Film' of the 1940s." In *The Female Body in Western Culture*, ed. Susan Robin Suleiman, 152–74. Harvard: Cambridge University Press.

Douglas, Mary. 1966. *Purity and Danger*. London: Routledge and Kegan Paul.

Dover, K. J. 1989. *Greek Homosexuality*. Cambridge: Harvard University Press.

Driver, S. R. 1900. *An Introduction to the Literature of the Old Testament*. New York: Scribner's.

DuBois, Page. 1988. *Sowing the Body: Psychoanalysis and Ancient Representations of Women*. Chicago: University of Chicago Press.

Dyer, Richard. 1982. "Don't Look Now—The Male Pin-up." *Screen* 23 (3–4): 61–73.

Edwards, Douglas. 1943. *The Virgin Birth in History and Faith*. London: Faber and Faber.

Eichrodt, Walther. 1967. *Theology of the Old Testament*. 2 vols. Translated by J. A. Baker. Philadelphia: Westminster.

———. 1970. *Ezekiel*. London: SCM.

Eilberg-Schwartz, Howard. 1988. "Who's Kidding Whom? A Serious Reading of Rabbinic Word Plays." *Journal of the American Academy of Religion* 55 (4): 65–78.

———. 1990. *The Savage in Judaism: An Anthropology of Israelite Religion and Ancient Judaism*. Bloomington: Indiana University Press.

———. 1991. "People of the Body: The Problem of the Body for the People of the Book." *Journal for the History of Sexuality* 2 (1): 1–24.

———, ed. 1991. *People of the Body: Jews and Judaism from an Embodied Perspective*. Albany: SUNY Press.

Eilberg-Schwartz, Howard, and Wendy Doninger, eds. 1994. *Off with Her Head: The Female Head in Myth, Religion, and Culture*. Berkeley: University of California Press.

Eissler K. R. 1961. *Leonardo da Vinci: Psychoanalytic Notes on the Enigma*. New York: International Universities Press.

Eliade, Mircea. 1961. *The Sacred and the Profane*. New York: Harper and Row.

Endres, John C. 1987. *Biblical Interpretation in the Book of Jubilees*. Washington, D.C.: Catholic Biblical Association of America.

Epstein, Julia, and Kristina Straub, eds. 1991. *BodyGuards: The Cultural Politics of Gender Ambiguity*. New York: Routledge.

Evans-Pritchard, E. E. [1937] 1976. *Witchcraft, Oracle, and Magic among the Azande*. Abridged by Eva Gillies. Oxford: Clarendon.

Falk, Marcia. 1987. "Notes on Composing New Blessings: Toward a Feminist-Jewish Reconstruction of Prayer." *Journal of Feminist Studies in Religion* 3 (1): 39–53.

———. 1989. "Toward a Feminist Jewish Reconstruction of Monotheism." *Tikkun* 4 (4): 53–57.

Farrell, B., ed. 1963. "Introduction." In *S. Freud's Leonardo da Vinci and a Memory of His Childhood*. Harmondsworth and Baltimore: Penguin.

Feldman, David M. 1974. *Marital Relations, Birth Control, and Abortion in Jewish Law*. New York: Schocken.

Fernandez, James. 1974. "The Mission of Metaphor in Expressive Culture." *Current Anthropology* 15 (2): 119–33.

———. 1977. "The Performance of Ritual Metaphors." In *The Social Use of Metaphor*, ed. David Sapir and Christopher Crocker. Philadelphia: University of Pennsylvania Press.

———. 1982. *Bwiti: An Ethnography of Religious Imagination in Africa*. Princeton: Princeton University Press.

———. 1986. *Persuasions and Performances*. Bloomington: Indiana University Press.

Finkelstein, Louis. 1969. *Sifre on Deuteronomy*. New York: Jewish Theological Seminary of America.

Fitzmyer, Joseph. 1971. *The Genesis Apocryphon of Qumran Cave I*. Rome: Biblical Institute.

———. 1981. *The Gospel according to Luke, I–IX*. Garden City, N.Y.: Doubleday.

Foucault, Michel. 1978. *History of Sexuality*. Translated by Robert Hurley. New York: Vintage.

Fox, Michael. 1974. "The Sign of the Covenant: Circumcision in the Light of the Priestly 'ot Etiologies." *Revue Biblique* 81:557–96.

Fraade, Steven. 1986. "Ascetical Aspects of Ancient Judaism." In *Jewish Spirituality*, vol. 1, ed. Arthur Green. New York: Crossroad.

Freedman, H., and Maurice Simon, eds. 1983. *Midrash Rabbah. 9 vols.* London: Soncino.

Freud, Sigmund. 1900. *Interpretation of Dreams*. SE 4:1–338; 5:339–625 (SE = *The Standard Edition of the Complete Psychological Works of Sigmund Freud*. Translated and edited by James Strachey. 24 vols. London: Hogarth Press and the Institute of Psycho-Analysis, 1953–1974).

———. [1901] 1905. "Fragment of an Analysis of a Case of Hysteria." SE 7:3–124.

———. 1905. *Three Essays on the Theory of Sexuality*. SE 7:135–243.

———. 1909. "Analysis of a Phobia in a Five-Year-Old Boy." SE 10:5–147.

———. 1910. "Leonardo da Vinci and a Memory of His Childhood." SE 11:59–137.

———. 1911. "Psycho-analytic Notes on an Autobiographical Account of a Case of Paranoia (Dementia Paranoides). SE 12:9–79.

———. 1912–13. *Totem and Taboo*. SE 13:1–161.

———. 1914a. "The Moses of Michaelangelo." SE 13:211–36.

———. 1914b. "Some Reflections on Schoolboy Psychology." SE 14:241–45.

———. [1914] 1918. "From the History of an Infantile Neurosis." SE 17:7–122.

———. 1919. "'A Child Is Being Beaten': A Contribution to the Study of the Origin of Sexual Perversions." SE 17:179–204.

———. 1921. *Group Psychology and the Analysis of the Ego.* SE 18:69–143.

———. [1922] 1923. "A Seventeenth-Century Demonological Neurosis." SE 19:69–108.

———. [1922] 1950. "Medusa's Head." In *Collected Papers*, ed. James Strachey, 5:105–6. London: Hogarth Press.

———. 1923. "The Ego and the Id." SE 19:3–66.

———. 1927. *The Future of an Illusion.* SE 21:3–58.

———. 1931. "Female Sexuality." SE 22:225–43.

———. 1935. "Letter to an American Mother." Reprinted in *Homosexuality and American Psychiatry*, by Ronald Bayer. Princeton: Princeton University Press.

———. 1939. *Moses and Monotheism.* SE 23:7–137.

Friedman, Richard Elliot. 1987. *Who Wrote the Bible?* New York: Harper and Row.

Frymer-Kensky, Tikva. 1992. *In the Wake of the Goddesses.* New York: Free Press.

Fuss, Diana. 1989. *Essentially Speaking: Feminism, Nature, and Difference.* New York: Routledge.

Gager, John G. 1972. *Moses in Greco-Roman Paganism.* Nashville: Abingdon.

Gagnier, Regenia. 1990. "Feminist Postmodernism: The End of Feminism or the End of Theory." In *Theoretical Perspectives on Sexual Difference*, ed. Deborah Rhode, 21–30. New Haven: Yale University Press.

Gallop, Jane. 1981. "Phallus/Penis: Same Difference." In *Men by Women*, vol. 2 of *Women and Literature*, ed. Janet Todd, 242–51. New York: Holmes and Meier.

———. 1982. *The Daughter's Seduction: Feminism and Psychoanalysis.* Ithaca: Cornell University Press.

———. 1985. *Reading Lacan.* Ithaca: Cornell University Press.

———. 1988. *Thinking through the Body.* New York: Columbia University Press.

Gamman, Lorraine, and Margaret Marshment, eds. 1988. *The Female Gaze: Women as Viewers of Popular Culture.* London: Women's Press.

Gay, Peter. 1966. *The Enlightenment: An Interpretation.* New York: Knopf.

———. 1968. *Deism: An Anthology.* Princeton: Van Nostrand.

Geertz, Clifford. 1973. *The Interpretation of Cultures.* New York: Basic.

Geist, Sidney. 1988. *Interpreting Cézanne.* Cambridge: Harvard University Press.

Gellman, Marc. 1989. *Does God Have a Big Toe?* New York: Harper and Row.

Geller, Jay. 1992. "(G)nos(e)ology: The Cultural Construction of the Other." In *People of the Body: Jews and Judaism from an Embodied Perspective*, ed. Howard Eilberg-Schwartz. Albany: SUNY Press.

———. 1993a. "Freud v. Freud: Freud's Reading of Daniel Paul Schreber's *Denkwürdigkeiten eines Nervenkranken*." In *Reading Freud's Reading*, ed. Sander Gilman, Jutta Birmele, Valerie Greenberg, and Jay Geller. New York: New York University Press.

———. 1993b. "A Paleontological View of Freud's Study of Religion: Unearthing the *Leitfossil* Circumcision." *Modern Judaism* 13 (1): 49–70.

Gevirtz, S. 1975. "Of Patriarchs and Puns: Joseph at the Fountain, Jacob at the Ford." *Hebrew Union College Annual* 46:33–54.

Gilman, Sander. 1985. *Difference and Pathology: Stereotypes of Sexuality, Race, and Madness*. Ithaca: Cornell University Press.

———. 1991. *The Jew's Body*. New York: Routledge.

Ginsberg, H. L. 1961. "Hosea's Ephraim, More Fool Than Knave: A New Interpretation of Hosea 12:1–14." *Journal of Biblical Literature* 80:339–47.

Girard, René. 1977. *Violence and the Sacred*. Baltimore: Johns Hopkins University Press.

Glazier-McDonald, Beth. 1987. *Malachi*. Atlanta: Scholars.

Goldenberg, Naomi. 1990. *Returning Words to Flesh: Feminism, Psychoanalysis, and the Resurrection of the Body*. Boston: Beacon.

Goldin, Judah. 1955. *The Fathers according to Rabbi Nathan*. New York: Schocken.

Gollancz, Herman. [1908] 1973. "The Targum to 'The Song of Songs.' " In *The Targum to the Five Megilloth*, ed. Bernard Grossfeld, 171–252. New York: Hermon.

Gombrich, Ernst. 1963. "Psycho-Analysis and the History of Art." In *Meditations on a Hobby Horse and Other Essays on the Theory of Art*, 30–44. New York: Phaidon.

Good, Edwin M. 1966. "Hosea and the Jacob Tradition." *Vetus Testamentum* 16:137–51.

Graves, Robert. 1955. *The Greek Myths*. London: Penguin.

Green, Arthur. 1983. "Bride, Spouse, Daughter: Images of the Feminine in Classical Jewish Sources." In *On Being a Jewish Feminist*, ed. Susannah Heschel, 254–57. New York: Schocken.

———. 1986. "Keeping Feminist Creativity Jewish." *Sh'ma*. 16 (305): 33–35.

Greenberg, David F. 1988. *The Construction of Homosexuality*. Chicago: University of Chicago Press.

Greenberg, Moshe. 1983. *Ezekiel 1–20*. The Anchor Bible Series. Garden City, N.Y.: Doubleday.

Gross, Rita. 1983. "Steps toward Feminine Imagery of Deity in Jewish Theology." In *On Being a Jewish Feminist*, ed. Susannah Heschel, 234–47. New York: Schocken.

Grosz, Elizabeth. 1989. *Sexual Subversions*. Sydney: Allen and Unwin.

Gruenwald, Ithamar. 1980. *Apocalyptic and Merkavah Mysticism*. Leiden: Brill.

Guttman, Joseph. 1971. *No Graven Images*. New York: Ktav.

Hagan, Kay Leigh, ed. 1992. *Women Respond to the Men's Movement*. San Francisco: Harper.

Hall, David. 1988. "Epispasm and the Dating of Ancient Jewish Writings." *Journal for the Study of Pseudepigrapha* 2:71–86.

Halperin, David J. 1980. *The Merkabah in Rabbinic Literature*. New Haven: American Oriental Society.

———. 1988. *The Faces of the Chariot: Early Jewish Responses to Ezekiel's Vision*. Tübingen: Mohr.

Halperin, David M. 1990. *One Hundred Years of Homosexuality*. New York: Routledge.

Halpern, Baruch. 1987. "'Brisker Pipes than Poetry': The Development of Israelite Monotheism." In *Judaic Perspectives on Ancient Israel*, ed. Jacob Neusner, Baruch A. Levine, and Ernest S. Frerichs. Philadelphia: Fortress.

Hammer, Reuven. 1986. *Sifre: A Tannaitic Commentary on the Book of Deuteronomy*. New Haven: Yale University Press.

Harris, H. A. 1964. *Greek Athletes and Athletics*. London: Hutchinson.

———. 1972. *Sport in Greece and Rome*. Ithaca: Cornell University Press.

Hayward, Robert. 1981. *Divine Name and Presence: The Memra*. Totowa, N.J.: Allanheld, Osmun.

Heidel, Alexander. 1970. *The Gilgamesh Epic and Old Testament Parallels*. Chicago: University of Chicago Press.

Hendel, Ronald. 1987. "Of Demigods and the Deluge: Toward an Interpretation of Genesis 6:1–4." *Journal of Biblical Literature* 106 (1): 13–26.

———. 1988. "The Social Origins of the Aniconic Tradition in Early Israel." *Catholic Biblical Quarterly* 50 (3): 365–82.

———. 1989. "Sacrifice as a Cultural System: The Ritual Symbolism of Exodus 24:3–8." *Zeitschrift für Alttestamentliche Wissenschaft* 101 (3): 366–90.

———. N.d. "Images of God in Ancient Israel." Manuscript.

Herdt, Gilbert. 1982. "Fetish and Fantasy in Sambia." In *Rituals of Manhood*, ed. Gilbert H. Herdt. Berkeley: University of California Press.

————. 1987. *Guardians of the Flutes: Idioms of Masculinity.* New York: Columbia University Press.

Horner, Tom. 1978. *Jonathan Loved David.* Philadelphia: Westminster.

Horovitz, H. S., ed. 1966. *Siphre d'Be Rab (Sifrei Numbers).* Jerusalem: Wahrmann.

Hvidberg, F. F. 1962. *Weeping and Laughter in the Old Testament.* Leiden: Brill.

Hyman, Aaron. 1979. *Torah Hakethubah VeHammessurah.* 3 vols. Tel Aviv: Dvir.

Ide, Arthur Frederick. 1985. *The City of Sodom and Homosexuality in Western Religious Thought to 630 C.E.* Dallas: Monument.

Irigaray, Luce. 1985a. *Speculum of the Other Woman.* Translated by Gillian C. Gill. Ithaca: Cornell University Press.

————. 1985b. *This Sex Which Is Not One.* Translated by Catherine Porter. Ithaca: Cornell University Press.

Isaac, E. 1983. "1 (Ethiopic Apocalypse of) Enoch: A Translation and Introduction." In *The Old Testament Pseudepigrapha,* ed. James H. Charlesworth, 1:5–92. Garden City, N.Y.: Doubleday.

Isaksson, Abel. 1965. *Marriage and Ministry in the New Temple.* Lund: Gleerup.

Isay, Richard A. 1989. *Being Homosexual: Gay Men and Their Development.* New York: Avon.

Israëls, Hans. 1981. *Schreber: Father and Son.* Amsterdam: Elandsstraat.

Janik, Allan, and Stephen Toulmin. 1973. *Wiggenstein's Vienna.* New York: Simon and Schuster.

Janowitz, Naomi. 1992. "God's Body: Theological and Ritual Roles of Shi'ur Komah." In *People of the Body: Jews and Judaism from an Embodied Perspective,* ed. Howard Eilberg-Schwartz, 183–202. Albany: SUNY Press.

Jastrow, Marcus. [1903]. *A Dictionary of the Targumim, the Talmud Babli, and Yerushalmi, and the Midrashic Literature.* Brooklyn: Traditional Press.

Jay, Nancy. 1985. "Sacrifice as Remedy for Having Been Born of Woman." In *Immaculate and Powerful,* ed. C. W. Atkinson et al., 283–309. Boston: Beacon.

————. 1988. "Sacrifice, Descent, and the Patriarchs." *Vetus Testamentum* 38 (1): 52–70.

————. 1992. *Throughout Your Generations Forever: Sacrifice, Religion, and Paternity.* Chicago: University of Chicago Press.

Johnson, Marshall D. 1969. *The Purpose of Biblical Genealogies.* Cambridge: Cambridge University Press.

————. 1985. "The Life of Adam and Eve." In *The Old Testament Pseudepi-*

grapha, ed. James H. Charlesworth, 2:249–96. Garden City, N.Y.: Doubleday.

Jones, Ann Rosalind. 1981. "Writing the Body: Toward an Understanding of *L'Ecriture Feminine.*" *Feminist Studies* 7 (2): 247–63.

Jones, Ernest. 1953. *The Life and Work of Sigmund Freud*. Vol. 1. New York: Basic.

———. 1955. *The Life and Work of Sigmund Freud*. Vol. 2. New York: Basic.

Jonte-Pace, Diane. 1987. "Object Relations Theory, Mothering, and Religion: Toward a Feminist Psychology of Religion." *Horizons* 14 (2): 310–27.

———. 1992a. "Which Feminism, Whose Freud?" *Pastoral Psychology* 40 (6): 1–6.

———. 1992b. "Situating Kristeva Differently: Psychoanalytic Readings of Woman and Religion." In *Body/Text in Julia Kristeva*, ed. David Crownfield, 1–22. Albany: SUNY Press.

———. 1993. "Psychoanalysis after Feminism." *Religious Studies Review* 19 (2): 1–6.

JPS. 1985. *Tanakh: A New Translation of the Holy Scriptures*. Philadelphia: Jewish Publication Society.

Jung, Carl J. 1961. *Memories, Dreams, Reflections*. New York: Pantheon.

Kee, Howard. 1983. "Testaments of the Twelve Patriarchs." In *The Old Testament Pseudepigrapha*, ed. James H. Charlesworth, 1:775–828. Garden City, N.Y.: Doubleday.

Kellenbach, Katharina von. 1990. "Anti-Judaism in Christian-Rooted Feminist Writings: An Analysis of Major U.S. American and West German Feminist Theologians." Ph.D. diss., Temple University, Philadelphia, Pennsylvania.

Kerényi, Carl. 1951. *The Gods of the Greeks*. London: Thames and Hudson.

Kilborne, Benjamin. 1992. "Fields of Shame: Anthropologists Abroad." *Ethos* 20 (2): 230–53.

Kirschner, Robert. 1983. "The Rabbinic and Philonic Exegeses of the Nadab and Abihu Incident (Lev. 10:1–6)." *Jewish Quarterly Review* 73 (4): 375–93.

Klein, Michael. 1979. "The Preposition *qdm* ('before'): A Pseudo-Anti-Anthropomorphism in the Targums." *Journal of Theological Studies*, n.s. 30 (2): 502–7.

Kosmala, Hans. 1962. "The 'Bloody Husband.'" *Vetus Testamentum* 12:14–28.

Kosovsky, Chaim. 1956. *Thesaurus Mishnae*. 4 vols. Jerusalem: Massadah.

Kristeva, Julia. 1982. *The Powers of Horror*. Translated by Leon S. Roudiez. New York: Columbia University Press.

Krüll, Marianne. 1986. *Freud and His Father*. New York: Norton.

Kuhn, Annette. 1985. *The Power of the Image: Essays on Representation and Sexuality*. Boston: Routledge and Kegan Paul.

Lacan, Jacques. 1985. "The Meaning of the Phallus." In *Feminine Sexuality: Jacques Lacan and the École freudienne*, ed. Juliet Mitchell and Jacqueline Rose. New York: Norton.

———. 1977. *Écrits*. Translated by Alan Sheridan. New York: Norton.

Lakoff, George, and Mark Johnson. 1980. *Metaphors We Live By*. Chicago: University of Chicago Press.

Lang, Bernhard. 1983. *Monotheism and the Prophetic Minority*. Sheffield: Almond.

———. 1985. "No Sex in Heaven: The Logic of Procreation, Death, and Eternal Life in the Judaeo-Christian Tradition." In *Mélanges Bibliques et Orientaux en l'honneur de M. Mathias Delcor*, ed. A. Caquot, S. Légasse, and M. Tardieu. Kevelaer: Verlag Butzon and Bercker.

Laqueur, Thomas. 1990. *Making Sex: Body and Gender from the Greeks to Freud*. Cambridge: Harvard University Press.

Lassarrague, François. 1990. "The Sexual Life of Satyrs." In *Before Sexuality: The Construction of Erotic Experience in the Ancient Greek World*, ed. David M. Halperin, John J. Winkler, and Froma I. Zeitlin. Princeton: Princeton University Press.

Leach, Edmund. 1958. "Magical Hair." *Man* 88:147–68.

———. 1969. *Genesis as Myth*. London: Jonathan Cape.

Leith, Mary Joan Winn. 1989. "Verse and Reverse: The Transformation of the Woman, Israel, in Hosea 1–3." In *Gender and Difference in Ancient Israel* ed. Peggy Day. Minneapolis: Fortress.

Lerner, Gerda. 1986. *The Creation of Patriarchy*. New York: Oxford University Press.

Levey, Samson. 1987. *The Targum of Ezekiel*. Wilmington: Glazier.

Levine, Baruch A. 1989. *Leviticus*. The JPS Torah Commentary. Philadelphia: Jewish Publication Society.

Lévi-Strauss, Claude. 1963. *Structural Anthropology*. Translated by Claire Jacobson and Brooke Grundfest Schoepf. New York: Basic.

———. 1973. *From Honey to Ashes*. Translated by John and Doreen Weightman. New York: Harper and Row.

———. 1978. *The Origin of Table Manners*. Translated by John and Doreen Weightman. New York: Harper and Row.

Lewes, Kenneth. 1988. *The Psychoanalytic Theory of Male Homosexuality.* New York: Meridian.

Lieberman, Saul. 1955–73. *Tosefta Ki-fshuta: A Comprehensive Commentary on the Tosefta.* 8 vols. New York: Jewish Theological Seminary of America.

———. 1960. "Tannaitic Teachings regarding the Song of Songs." In *Jewish Gnosticism, Merkabah Mysticism, and Talmudic Tradition*, ed. Gershom Scholem, 118–26. New York: Jewish Theological Seminary of America.

Liebert, Robert S. 1983. *Michelangelo: A Psychoanalytic Study of His Life and Images.* New Haven: Yale University Press.

Lorde, Audre. 1984. "Uses of the Erotic: The Erotic as Power." In *Sister Outsider.* Trumansburd, N.Y.: Crossing.

McGuire, William, ed. 1974. *The Freud/Jung Letters.* Translated by Ralph Mannherin and R. F. C. Hull. Princeton: Princeton University Press.

Machen, J. Gresham. [1930] 1965. *The Virgin Birth of Christ.* Grand Rapids, Mich.: Baker.

Maimonides, Moses. 1963. *The Guide of the Perplexed.* 2 vols. Translated by Shlomo Pines. Chicago: University of Chicago Press.

McKenzie, John L. "Jacob at Peniel." *Catholic Biblical Quarterly* 25:71–76.

Macalpine, Ida, and Richard Hunter. 1955. "Discussion." In *Memoirs of My Nervous Illness*, by Daniel Paul Schreber, 401–6. London: Dawson.

Malul, Meir. 1985. "More on Paḥad Yiṣḥāq (Genesis XXXI 42, 53) and the Oath by the Thigh." *Vetus Testamentum* 35 (2): 192–200.

———. 1987. "Studies in Biblical and Legal Symbolism—A Discussion of the terms kānāph, ḥēq, and ḥoṣen/ḥeṣen, Their Meaning and Legal Usage in the Bible and Ancient Near East." *Shnaton* 9:191–210.

Manuel, Frank. 1959. *The Eighteenth Century Confronts the Gods.* Cambridge: Harvard University Press.

———. 1983. *The Changing of the Gods.* Hanover: University Press of New England.

Marglin, Frédérique Apffel. 1982. "Types of Sexual Union and Their Implicit Meanings." In *The Divine Consort*, ed. John Stratton Hawley and Donna Marie Wulff, 298–315. Boston: Beacon.

Margolioth, Mordecai, ed. 1972. *Midrash Wayyikra Rabbah: A Critical Edition Based on Manuscripts and Genizah Fragments with Variants and Notes.* 4 vols. Jerusalem: Wahrmann.

Marmorstein, Arthur. 1968. *The Old Rabbinic Doctrine of God.* Vol. 2. New York: Ktav.

Masson, Jeffrey Moussaief, ed. 1986. *The Complete Letters of Sigmund Freud to*

Wilhelm Fliess, 1887–1904. Cambridge: Harvard University Press, Belknap Press.

Mayne, Judith. 1985. "Feminist Film Theory and Criticism: A Review Essay." *Signs* 11 (1): 81–99.

Mays, James L. 1969. *Hosea*. Philadelphia: Westminster.

Melamed, R. H. 1921. *The Targum to Canticles according to Six Yemen Mss.* Philadelphia.

Mellinkoff, R. 1970. *The Horned Moses in Medieval Art and Thought*. Berkeley: University of California Press.

Meshorer, Yaʿakov. 1967. *Jewish Coins of the Second Temple Period*. Chicago: Argonaut.

Mettinger, Tryggve. 1978. "God-Language and Gender." In *In Search of God*, trans. Frederick H. Cryer, 204–7. Philadelphia: Fortress.

———. 1979. "The Veto on Images and the Aniconic God in Ancient Israel." In *Religious Symbols and Their Functions*, ed. Haralds Biezais, 15–29. Stockholm: Almqvist and Wiksell.

———. 1982. *The Dethronement of Sabaoth: Studies in the Shem and Kabod Theologies*. Lund: Gleerup.

Metz, Johannes-Baptist, and Edward Schillebeeckx, eds. 1981. *God as Father?* New York: Seabury.

Meyers, Carol L. 1988. *Discovering Eve*. New York: Oxford University Press.

Milgrom, Jacob. 1990. *Numbers*. Philadelphia: Jewish Publication Society.

Milhaven, John Giles. 1993. *Hadewijch and Her Sisters*. Albany: SUNY Press.

Miller, J. Maxwell. 1972. "In the 'Image' and 'Likeness' of God." *Journal of Biblical Literature* 91:289–304.

Miller, John W. 1986. "Depatriarchalizing God in Biblical Interpretation: A Critique." *Catholic Biblical Quarterly* 48:609–16.

Mitchell, Juliet. 1974. *Psychoanalysis and Feminism*. New York: Vintage.

Mitchell, Juliet, and Jacqueline Rose, eds. 1985. *Feminine Sexuality: Jacques Lacan and the École freudienne*. New York: Norton.

Mollenkott, Virginia. 1986. *The Divine Feminine*. New York: Crossroad.

Mopsik, Charles. 1989. "The Body of Engenderment in the Hebrew Bible, the Rabbinic Tradition, and the Kabbalah." In *Fragments for a History of the Human Body*, part I, ed. Michael Feher, Ramona Naddoff, and Nadia Tazi. New York: Zone.

Moran, W. L. 1963. "The Ancient Near Eastern Background of the Love of God in Deuteronomy." *Catholic Biblical Quarterly* 25:77–87.

Morgenstern, J. 1925. "Moses with the Shining Face." *Hebrew Union College Annual* 2:1–27.

Mulvey, Laura. 1989. "Visual Pleasure and Narrative Cinema." In *Visual and Other Pleasures*. Bloomington: Indiana University Press.

Neale, Steve. 1983. "Masculinity as Spectacle." *Screen* 24 (6): 2–17.

Neusner, Jacob. 1988. *The Incarnation of God: The Character of Divinity in Formative Judaism*. Philadelphia: Fortress.

Newsom, Carol. 1989. "Woman and the Discourse of Patriarchal Wisdom: A Study of Proverbs 1–9." In *Gender and Difference in Ancient Israel*, ed. Peggy Day. Minneapolis: Fortress.

Nicholson, E. W. 1974. "The Interpretation of Exodus XXIV 9–11." *Vetus Testamentum* 24 (1): 77–97.

———. 1975. "The Antiquity of the Tradition in Exodus XXIV 9–11." *Vetus Testamentum* 25 (1): 69–79.

———. 1986. *God and His People*. Oxford: Clarendon.

Niditch, Susan. 1982. "The 'Sodomite' Theme in Judges 19–20: Family, Community, and Social Disintegration." *Catholic Biblical Quarterly* 44 (3): 365–78.

Noth, Martin. 1962. *Exodus*. Philadelphia: Westminster.

———. 1981. *A History of Pentateuchal Traditions*. Translated by Bernhard Anderson. Chico: Scholars.

Ochs, Carol. 1977. *Behind the Sex of God*. Boston: Beacon.

Ochshorn, Judith. 1981. *The Female Experience and the Nature of the Divine*. Bloomington: Indiana University Press.

Oden, Robert. 1987. *The Bible without Theology*. San Francisco: Harper and Row.

O'Flaherty, Wendy Doniger. 1973. *Asceticism and Eroticism in the Mythology of Śiva*. London: Oxford University Press.

Olyan, Saul. 1987. "The Cultic Confession of Jer. 2, 27a." *Zeitschrift für Alttestamentliche Wissenschaft* 99:254–59.

———. 1988. *Asherah and the Cult of Yahweh in Israel*. Atlanta: Scholars.

———. 1993. *A Thousand Thousands Served Him: Exegesis and the Naming of Angels in Ancient Judaism*. TSAJ 36. Mohr/Siebeck.

Oring, Elliot. 1984. *The Jokes of Sigmund Freud*. Philadelphia: University of Pennsylvania Press.

Otto, Rudolf. 1957. *The Idea of the Holy*. Oxford: Oxford University Press.

Otwell, John H. 1977. *And Sarah Laughed: The Status of Woman in the Old Testament*. Philadelphia: Westminster.

Owens, Craig. 1987. "Outlaws: Gay Men in Feminism." In *Men in Feminism*, ed. Alice Jardine and Paul Smith, 98–110. New York: Methuen.

Pagels, Elaine. 1988. *Adam, Eve, and the Serpent*. New York: Random House.

Pardes, Ilana. 1992. *Countertraditions in the Bible: A Feminist Approach*. Cambridge: Harvard University Press.

Patai, Raphael. 1967. *Hebrew Goddess*. New York: Ktav.

Phillips, Anthony. 1973. *Deuteronomy*. Cambridge: Cambridge University Press.

Philo. 1981. *De Opificio Mundi (On the Account of the World's Creation Given by Moses)*. Translated by F. H. Colson. Loeb Classical Library. Cambridge: Harvard University Press.

Plaskow, Judith. 1983. "The Right Question Is Theological." In *On Being a Jewish Feminist*, ed. Susannah Heschel, 223–33. New York: Schocken.

———. 1990. *Standing Again at Sinai*. New York: Harper and Row.

Pope, Marvin H. 1955. *El in the Ugaritic Texts*. Leiden: Brill.

———. 1977. *Song of Songs*. Garden City, N.Y.: Doubleday.

Prewitt, Terri. 1990. *The Elusive Covenant*. Bloomington: Indiana University Press.

Propp, William H. 1987. "The Skin of Moses' Face—Transfigured or Disfigured?" *Catholic Biblical Quarterly* 49 (3): 375–86.

———. Forthcoming. "The Bloody Bridegroom." *Vetus Testamentum*.

Radcliffe-Brown, A. R. [1952] 1965. *Structure and Function in Primitive Society*. New York: Free Press.

Ragland-Sullivan, Ellie. 1987. *Jacques Lacan and the Philosophy of Psychoanalysis*. Urbana: University of Illinois Press.

Reynolds, Frank, and David Tracy, eds. 1990. *Myth and Philosophy*. Albany: SUNY Press.

Rich, Adrienne. 1976. *Of Woman Born*. New York: Norton.

———. 1980. "Compulsory Heterosexuality and Lesbian Existence." *Signs* 5 (4): 631–60.

Ricoeur, Paul. 1970. *Freud and Philosophy*. Translated by Denis Savage. New Haven: Yale University Press.

Rieff, Philip. 1979. *Freud: The Mind of the Moralist*. Chicago: University of Chicago Press.

Ringgren, Helmer. 1966. *Israelite Religion*. Translated by David E. Green. Philadelphia: Fortress.

Rizzuto, Ana-Maria. 1979. *The Birth of the Living God*. Chicago: University of Chicago Press.

Roazen, Paul. 1974. *Freud and His Followers*. New York: Meridian.

Robert, Marthe. 1976. *From Oedipus to Moses*. Translated by Ralph Manheim. Garden City, N.Y.: Anchor.

Robinson, Bernard P. 1986. "Zipporah to the Rescue: A Contextual Study of Exodus IV 24–6." *Vetus Testamentum* 36 (4): 447–61.

Rosenberg, Samuel. 1978. *Why Freud Fainted*. Indianapolis: Bobbs-Merrill.

Rowland, Christopher. 1979. "The Visions of God in Apocalyptic Literature." *Journal for the Study of Judaism* 10 (2): 137–54.

———. 1982. *The Open Heaven: A Study of Apocalyptic in Judaism and Early Christianity*. New York: Crossroad.

Rubin, Gayle. 1975. "The Traffic in Women: Notes on the 'Political Economy' of Sex." In *Toward an Anthropology of Women*, ed. Rayna R. Reiter. New York: Monthly Review Press.

Rubin, Nissan. 1989. "On Drawing Down the Prepuce and Incision of the Foreskin (Periah)." *Zion* 54 (1): 105–17.

Rubinkiewicz, R. 1983. "Apocalypse of Abraham: A Translation with Introduction." In *The Old Testament Pseudepigrapha*, ed. James H. Charlesworth, 1:681–706. Garden City, N.Y.: Doubleday.

Ruether, Rosemary. 1983. *Sexism and God-Talk: Toward a Feminist Theology*. Boston: Beacon.

Safrai, Shmuel. 1987. "Oral Torah." In *The Literature of the Sages*, part 1. Philadelphia: Fortress.

Sandars, N. K., trans. 1972. *The Epic of Gilgamesh*. London: Penguin Books.

Sanday, Peggy Reeves. 1981. *Female Power and Male Dominance*. Cambridge: Cambridge University Press.

Sapp, Stephen. 1977. *Sexuality, the Bible, and Science*. Philadelphia: Fortress.

Sarna, Nahum. 1970. *Understanding Genesis*. New York: Schocken.

———. 1986. *Exploring Exodus*. New York: Schocken.

———. 1989. *Genesis*. Philadelphia: Jewish Publication Society.

———. 1991. *Exodus*. Philadelphia: Jewish Publication Society.

Saslow, James. 1986. *Ganymede in the Renaissance*. New Haven: Yale University Press.

Sasson, Jack. 1968. "Bovine Symbolism and the Exodus Narrative." *Vetus Testamentum* 18:380–87.

Saussure, Ferdinand de. 1966. *Course in General Linguistics*. New York: McGraw-Hill.

Sawyer, John F. A. 1974. "The Meaning of 'In the Image of God' in Genesis I–XI." *Journal of Theological Studies*, n.s. 25:418–26.

Schaberg, Jane. 1987. *The Illegitimacy of Jesus*. San Francisco: Harper and Row.

Schäfer, Peter. 1984. "New Testament and Hekhalot Literature: The Journey into Heaven in Paul and in Merkavah Mysticism." *Journal of Jewish Studies* 35 (1): 19–35.

Schatzman, M. 1973. *Soul Murder: Persecution in the Family*. New York: Random House.

Schwartz, Regina. 1991. "Rethinking Voyeurism and Patriarchy: The Case of Paradise Lost." *Representations* 34:85–103.

Schechter, Solomon. 1887. *Aboth de Rabbi Nathan*. Vienna.

Scholem, Gershom G. 1946. *Major Trends in Jewish Mysticism*. New York: Schocken.

———. 1960. *Jewish Gnosticism, Merkabah Mysticism, and Talmudic Tradition*. New York: Jewish Theological Seminary of America.

———. 1991. *On the Mystical Shape of the Godhead*. New York: Schocken.

Schor, Naomi. 1987. "Dreaming Dissymetry: Barthe, Foucault, and Sexual Difference." In *Men in Feminism*, ed. Alice Jardine and Paul Smith, 98–110. New York: Methuen.

Schreber, Daniel Paul. 1955. *Memoirs of My Nervous Illness*. Translated by Ida Macalpine and Richard A. Hunter. London: Dawson.

Sedgwick, Eve Kosofsky. 1985. *Between Men: English Literature and Male Homosocial Desire*. New York: Columbia University Press.

Setel, T. Drorah. 1985. "Prophets and Pornography: Female Sexual Imagery in Hosea." In *Feminist Interpretation of the Bible*, ed. Letty M. Russell. Philadelphia: Westminster.

Shengold, Leonard. 1972. "A Parapraxis of Freud in Relation to Karl Abraham." *American Imago* 29 (2): 123–59.

Shutt, R. J. H. 1985. "Letter of Aristeas." In *The Old Testament Pseudepigrapha*, ed. James H. Charlesworth, 2:7–34. Garden City, N.Y.: Doubleday.

Smith, J. Z. 1982. *Imagining Religion*. Chicago: University of Chicago Press.

Smith, Mark S. 1990. *The Early History of God*. San Francisco: Harper and Row.

Smith, S. H. 1990. " 'Heel' and 'Thigh': The Concept of Sexuality in the Jacob-Esau Narratives." *Vetus Testamentum* 40 (4): 464–73.

Soler, Jean. 1979. "The Dietary Prohibitions of the Hebrews." Translated by Elborg Forster. *New York Review of Books* 26, no. 10 (June 14): 24–30.

Speiser, E. A. 1964. *Genesis*. The Anchor Bible. Garden City, N.Y.: Doubleday.

Spelman, Elizabeth V. 1988. *Inessential Woman: Problems of Exclusion in Feminist Thought*. Boston: Beacon.

Sperber, Alexander. 1962. *The Bible in Aramaic: Targum Jonathan*. Vol. 3. Leiden: Brill.

Spinoza, Benedict de. 1951. *A Theologico-Political Treatise*. Translated by R. H. M. Elwes. New York: Dover.

Stacey, Jackie. 1988. "Desperately Seeking Difference." In *The Female Gaze: Women as Viewers of Popular Culture*, ed. Lorraine Gamman and Margaret Marshment, 112–29. London: Women's Press.

Stahl, Nanette. 1993. "The Flawed Liminal Moment: Between Law and Narrative in the Bible." Ph.D. diss., University of California, Berkeley, California.

Starhawk. 1979. *The Spiral Dance*. San Francisco: Harper and Row.

Steinberg, Leo. 1983. *The Sexuality of Christ in Renaissance Art and in Modern Oblivion*. New York: Pantheon.

Stern, David. 1991. *Parables in Midrash*. Cambridge: Harvard University Press.

Stern, Menahem. 1974. *Greek and Latin Authors on Jews and Judaism*. 3 vols. Jerusalem: Israel Academy of Sciences and Humanities.

Strack, Hermann Leberecht, and Paul Billerbeck. 1965. *Kommentar zum Neuen Testament aus Talmud und Midrasch*. Vol. 1. München: Beck.

Strachey, James, ed. and trans. 1953–1974. *The Standard Edition of the Complete Psychological Works of Sigmund Freud*. 24 vols. London: Hogarth Press and the Institute of Psycho-Analysis.

Terrien, Samuel. 1978. *The Elusive Presence*. San Francisco: Harper and Row.

Teubal, Savina. 1984. *Sarah the Priestess*. Athens, Ga.: Swallow.

Theodor, Julius, and Chanoch Albeck, eds. 1965. *Midrash Bereshit Rabbah: Critical Edition with Notes and Commentary*. 3 vols. Jerusalem: Wahrmann.

Tigay, Jeffrey H. 1986. *You Shall Have No Other Gods: Israelite Religion in the Light of Hebrew Inscriptions*. Atlanta: Scholars.

Tobin, Thomas H. 1983. *The Creation of Man: Philo and the History of Interpretation*. Washington, D.C.: Catholic Biblical Association of America.

Torrey, C. C. 1989. "The Prophet Malachi." *Journal of Biblical Literature* 17:1–15.

Trible, Phyllis. 1983. *God and the Rhetoric of Sexuality*. Philadelphia: Fortress.

Turner, Victor. 1967. *The Forest of Symbols: Aspects of Ndembu Ritual*. Ithaca: Cornell University Press.

Tyler, Carole-Anne. 1991. "Boys Will Be Girls: The Politics of Gay Drag." In *Inside/Out: Lesbian, Gay Theories*, ed. Diana Fuss. New York: Routledge.

Urbach, Ephraim. 1967. "Traditions about Esoteric Doctrine in the Tannaitic Period" [Hebrew]. In *Studies in Mysticism and Religion Presented to Gershom G. Scholem*, 1–28. Jerusalem: Magnes.

———. 1971. "The Homiletical Interpretations of the Sages and the Expositions of Origen on Canticles, and the Jewish-Christian Disputation." *Scripta Hieroslymitana* 22:247–75.

————. 1987. *The Sages: Their Concepts and Beliefs.* Cambridge: Harvard University Press.

Umansky, Ellen. 1984. "Creating Jewish Feminist Theology: Possibilities and Problems." *Anima* 10:133–34.

Van Herik, Judith. 1982. *Freud on Femininity and Faith.* Berkeley: University of California Press.

Vasari, G. [1568] 1967. *The Lives of the Artists.* 2 vols. Translated by J. Foster. New York: Hermitage.

Veyne, Paul, ed. 1987. *A History of Private Life: From Pagan Rome to Byzantium.* Cambridge: Harvard University Press, Belknap Press.

Von Rad, Gerhard. 1962. *Old Testament Theology.* Translated by D. M. G. Stalker. New York: Harper and Row.

————. 1966. *Deuteronomy.* Philadelphia: Westminster.

————. 1976. *Genesis.* Translated by John H. Marks. Philadelphia: Westminster.

Vriezen, Th. C. 1970. *An Outline of Old Testament Theology.* Oxford: Blackwell.

————. 1972. "The Exegesis of Exodus XXIV 9–11." *The Witness of Tradition,* ed. M. A. Beek et al., 100–133. Leiden: Brill.

Walters, Margaret. 1978. *The Nude Male.* New York: Paddington.

Wegner, Judith Romney. 1988. *Chattel or Person? The Status of Women in the Mishnah.* New York: Oxford University Press.

Weinfeld, Moshe. 1972. *Deuteronomy and the Deuteronomic School.* Oxford: Clarendon.

Weininger, Otto. [1903]. *Sex and Character.* Translated from the sixth German edition. New York: Putnam's.

Wenham, G. J. 1979. *The Book of Leviticus.* The New International Commentary on the Old Testament. Grand Rapids: Eerdmans.

Westermann, Claus. 1984. *Genesis.* 3 vols. Translated by John J. Scullion. Minneapolis: Augsburg.

Wevers, John Williams, ed. 1969. *Ezekiel.* The Century Bible. New Series. London: Nelson.

————. 1990. *Notes on the Greek Text of Exodus.* Atlanta: Scholars.

Wilden, Anthony. 1968. *The Language of the Self.* Baltimore: Johns Hopkins University Press.

————. 1972. "Critique of Phallocentrism: Daniel Paul Schreber on Women's Liberation." In *System and Structure: Essay in Communication and Exchange.* London: Tavistock.

Williams, Michael. 1986. "Uses of Gender Imagery in Ancient Gnostic

Texts." In *Gender and Religion*, ed. Caroline Walker Bynum, Stevan Harrell, and Paula Richman, 196–230. Boston: Beacon.

Williams, Walter. 1986. *The Spirit and the Flesh: Sexual Diversity in American Indian Culture*. Boston: Beacon.

Williamson, Ronald. 1989. *Jews in the Hellenistic World: Philo*. Cambridge: Cambridge University Press.

Wimbush, Vincent, ed. 1990. *Ascetic Behavior in Greco-Roman Antiquity*. Philadelphia: Fortress.

Wintermute, O. S. 1985. "Jubilees: A New Translation and Introduction." In *The Old Testament Pseudepigrapha*, ed. James H. Charlesworth, 2:35–142. Garden City, N.Y.: Doubleday.

Wittig, Monique. 1980. "The Straight Mind." *Feminist Issues* 1 (1): 103–11.

Wolf, Naomi. 1991. *The Beauty Myth: How Images of Beauty Are Used against Women*. New York: Morrow.

Wolff, Hans Walter. 1974. *Hosea*. Philadelphia: Fortress.

Wolfson, Elliot. 1987. "Circumcision, Vision of God, and Textual Interpretation: From Midrashic Trope to Mystical Symbol." *History of Religions* 27 (2): 189–215.

———. 1992. "Images of God's Feet: Some Observations on the Divine Body in Judaism." In *People of the Body: Jews and Judaism from an Embodied Perspective*, ed. Howard Eilberg-Schwartz, 143–83. Albany: SUNY Press.

———. 1994. *Through a Speculum that Shines: Vision and Imagination in Medieval Jewish Mysticism*. Princeton: Princeton University Press.

———. N.d. "Weeping, Death and Spiritual Ascent in Sixteenth-Century Jewish Mysticism." Manuscript.

Yanagisako, Sylvia J., and Jane F. Collier. 1990. "The Mode of Reproduction in Anthropology." In *Theoretical Perspectives on Sexual Difference*, ed. Deborah L. Rhode. New Haven: Yale University Press.

Yerushalmi, Yosef Hayim. 1991. *Freud's Moses*. New Haven: Yale University Press.

Zimmerli, Walther. 1979. *Ezekiel*. Translated by Ronald E. Clements. Philadelphia: Fortress.